D0082825

U.S. EDUCATIONAL POLICY
INTEREST GROUPS

**Greenwood Reference Volumes on
American Public Policy Formation**

These reference books deal with the development of U.S. policy in various ''single-issue'' areas. Most policy areas are to be represented by three types of sourcebooks: (1) Institutional Profiles of Leading Organizations, (2) Collection of Documents and Policy Proposals, and (3) Bibliography.

Public Interest Law Groups: Institutional Profiles
Karen O'Connor and Lee Epstein

U.S. National Security Policy and Strategy: Documents and Policy Proposals
Sam C. Sarkesian with Robert A. Vitas

U.S. National Security Policy Groups: Institutional Profiles
Cynthia Watson

U.S. Agricultural Groups: Institutional Profiles
William P. Browne and Allan J. Cigler, editors

Military and Strategic Policy: An Annotated Bibliography
Benjamin R. Beede, compiler

U.S. Energy and Environmental Interest Groups: Institutional Profiles
Lettie McSpadden Wenner

Contemporary U.S. Foreign Policy: Documents and Commentary
Elmer Plischke

U.S. Aging Policy Interest Groups: Institutional Profiles
David D. Van Tassel and Jimmy Meyer, editors

U.S. Criminal Justice Interest Groups: Institutional Profiles
Michael A. Hallett and Dennis J. Palumbo

U.S. EDUCATIONAL POLICY INTEREST GROUPS

Institutional Profiles

Gregory S. Butler and James D. Slack

GREENWOOD PRESS
WESTPORT, CONNECTICUT • LONDON

Library of Congress Cataloging-in-Publication Data

Butler, Gregory S.
    U.S. educational policy interest groups : institutional profiles /
Gregory S. Butler and James D. Slack.
      p. cm.
    Includes bibliographical references and index.
    ISBN 0–313–27292–1 (alk. paper)
    1. Education—United States—Societies, etc.—Directories.
I. Slack, James D. II. Title.
L901.B88   1994
370'.2573—dc20   93–44516

British Library Cataloguing in Publication Data is available.

Library of Congress Catalog Card Number: 93–44516
ISBN: 0–313–27292–1

First published in 1994

Greenwood Press, 88 Post Road West, Westport, CT 06881
An imprint of Greenwood Publishing Group, Inc.

Printed in the United States of America

The paper used in this book complies with the
Permanent Paper Standard issued by the National
Information Standards Organization (Z39.48–1984).

10 9 8 7 6 5 4 3 2 1

For our families
Lauren and Emily Butler
Janis, Sarah, and Samuel Slack

CONTENTS

—————————— / ——————————

PREFACE   ix

INTRODUCTION   xiii

U.S. EDUCATIONAL POLICY INTEREST GROUPS   1

APPENDIX A: QUESTIONNAIRE   207

APPENDIX B: ORGANIZATIONS PARTICIPATING IN
              THE STUDY   209

APPENDIX C: PRIMARY GOVERNMENT PARTICIPANTS IN
              EDUCATION POLICY   215

APPENDIX D: U.S. LEGISLATIVE HEARINGS IN EDUCATION,
              1987–1992   217

SELECTED BIBLIOGRAPHY   219

INDEX   221

30894

PREFACE

—————————————— / ——————————————

This book is a reference guide to 182 associations in the United States that are concerned with the subject of education, broadly defined, and have an opportunity to help shape public policy. These groups are in a position to provide leadership in the educational community. Their ultimate task is to represent the views, respond to the needs, and protect the interests of the diverse and complex constituencies of students, parents, teachers, administrators, and institutions. The manner in which they perform a leadership function, from the perspective of both internal concerns and public policy, is the focus of the introduction.

We obtained information for this book in three ways. First, a questionnaire (see Appendix A) was constructed, pretested, and sent to associations listed as "educational groups" in the *Encyclopedia of Associations* (Detroit: Gale Research Inc., 1993), the *Washington Information Directory* (Washington, D.C.: Congressional Quarterly, Inc., 1991), and the *Washington Representative* (Washington, D.C.: Columbia Books, 1991). The questionnaire was sent in four separate mailings in 1992 and 1993.

A total of 178 organizations (see Appendix B) completed and returned usable questionnaires. These groups include associations broad in scope, such as the National Education Association, the American Federation of Teachers, and the National Association of State Universities and Land-Grant Colleges. It also includes single-issue groups, such as the Society for Health and Human Values, the National Association of Schools of Public Affairs and Administration, and U.S. English.

Second, information was obtained from annual reports and other association literature, when available. These provided additional insight into the workings of some groups, as well as association activities within the educational policy arena. Finally, information was obtained through phone calls to various organizations that did not respond to our mailings or were not listed in any of the three directories.

From the beginning of this project, our goal has been to provide the reader with a comprehensive and representative view of education groups in the United States. Special efforts have been made to include as many religious and ethnic associations as possible. While some groups chose not to respond to our many inquiries, we feel that the finished product accomplishes our tasks of comprehensiveness and representativeness.

The organizational profiles are arranged alphabetically. All entries follow a similar format. Addresses, phone numbers, and fax numbers (if available) are followed by a statement of the organization's general purpose. Following this is a review of the group's origin and development. The structure and budget of the organization are then examined. Policy concerns and tactics are discussed next, underscoring the degree to which each organization has developed national educational policy concerns as well as internal membership concerns. This section is followed by a discussion of the extent to which each organization engages in any significant political activity. Political activity is defined as direct interaction between association personnel and federal government officials regarding specific pieces of legislation or particular candidates for office. This would include congressional testimony, *amicus curiae* briefs, political action committee campaign contributions, and regulatory agency hearing participation. Our definition of political activity does not include monitoring governmental or legislative activity, nor does it include communication or information transfers between associations and government officials, except where such transfers occur in the formal setting of a congressional or regulatory agency hearing. Finally, the profiles include additional sources of information on each individual group. In constructing our profiles in all categories we have made every attempt to remain as faithful as possible to the self-interpretation of the associations themselves, except when such interpretations involve the use of boosterism or other prejudicial language. Asterisks denote organizations profiled elsewhere in the volume.

The completion of this project rested on the shoulders of several individuals. We are particularly indebted to three young scholars. Jack Medley, a graduate assistant at Cleveland State University, helped by acquiring the list of groups, and mailing and tracking the questionnaires. Valerie Elliott, a graduate assistant at New Mexico State University, researched the congressional hearings on education and provided much insight into the actual influence of each organization on legislation between 1987 and 1992. Finally, Mariah Davis, an undergraduate student at New Mexico State University, assisted with bibliographic research on the National Education Association. We also thank the Department of Government at New Mexico State University, especially secretaries Stella Ramos and Ella Chavez, who assisted in preparing and proofreading this manuscript.

Most important, we thank our family members. There were many times during the past year when this book had to take priority over much more important family activities. We could not have completed this project without their support, understanding, and love.

Naturally, we alone bear full responsibility for all factual and analytical errors found in this book.

INTRODUCTION

—————————— / ——————————

No other policies are as critical to the human and national condition as those that affect education. Policies in this area give both direction and substance to disseminating primary cultural values, such as patriotism, democracy, capitalism, and compassion. They have a tremendous bearing on the manner and extent to which the importance of individual initiative and competition are underscored, as well as the need for working cooperatively, caringly, and effectively with others. Furthermore, educational policies determine whether or not children are given opportunities to acquire fundamental skills that enable them to make meaningful contributions to the human condition.

As in other policy areas (Browne, 1988), the key actors involved in creating national educational policies and programs are the federal bureaucracy and committees in both houses of Congress (see Appendix C). Our focus here, however, is on external organizations as the third group of actors in this so-called "iron triangle" (Adams, 1981). During this century, external interest groups have become critical components in making public policy in the United States (Lowi, 1979). This introduction provides a short analysis of organized groups that have an opportunity to influence federal policies in education. Although the various states and localities are constitutionally more involved in the daily processes of education, the federal government can potentially play a large role in shaping the quality of education for all citizens. It is important, therefore, to gain a more thorough understanding of national educational interest groups so that we might better prepare for the challenges of educating people in the twenty-first century. The forthcoming analysis is based on information contained within the institutional profiles, located in the "U.S. Educational Interest Groups" section. The methodology used in acquiring that information is explained in the preface of this book.

EDUCATIONAL INTEREST GROUPS: A PROFILE IN DIVERSITY

As is the case with groups in other domestic public policy areas (Van Tassel and Meyer, 1992), one characteristic of U.S. educational interest groups is that they are both numerous and diverse. There are over 250 national-level groups interested in some aspect of educational policy. While almost all of these are classified as nonprofit, tax-exempt groups, and their organizational structures are often similar, they vary a great deal with respect to organizational age, budget size, membership and clientele base, and organizational purpose.

In terms of organizational age, some groups have been well established since the turn of the century (such as the National Education Association [NEA], National Rural Education Association, and School Science and Mathematics Association), while others are much younger and are still in a developmental stage (such as The Business–Higher Education Forum, The Advocacy Institute, and American Association for Adult and Continuing Education). Like groups in other policy areas (Berry, 1989:18–19), many educational interest groups are relatively new, with about 42 percent having been established since 1960.

Educational interest groups also vary significantly in terms of operating budgets and membership. Approximately one-quarter of these groups have operating budgets under $1 million, while almost 15 percent spend more than $10 million yearly. The NEA has one of the larger annual budgets at $150 million, and at under $55,000 the American Conference of Academic Deans and the Association for the Education of Teachers in Science are among the smallest. About 70 percent of the organizations have fewer than 10,000 members, yet 1 in 5 has more than twice that number. The National Parents-Teachers Association has a membership of over 7 million people. Membership in the National Association of State Directors of Special Education (NASDSE), on the other hand, is limited by the number of states in the nation. Other groups do not have a membership base and operate through user fees, as The Experiment in International Living, or function as a public service, like the National Women's Law Center.

Educational interest groups are also quite varied in terms of organizational purpose. While some groups concern themselves with a wide range of issues in education, the majority in this study have very specialized interests. The United Negro College Fund, for instance, is primarily concerned with financing historically African-American institutions of higher education and providing scholarships for students attending those colleges. U.S. English is singularly interested in keeping English as the official language in the American classroom. Even the more ''umbrella'' organizations that attempt to include a number of interests and a variety of constituencies tend to be rather selective in the issues they address. For example, the NEA is attentive to issues affecting elementary and secondary schools but is much less concerned with policies affecting higher or adult education. The American Association for Higher Education, on the other hand, focuses primarily on issues pertaining to colleges and universities and shows little interest in issues affecting younger students.

Scholars in the field of interest group research have often remarked that the variety we see among educational interest groups is a sign of political health, insofar as a plurality of groups ensures that a full range of issues has a chance to gain visibility (Berry, 1989:12–14, 230–231). Moreover, it is likely that almost anyone in the educational community can find an association that best represents his or her special and most directly felt interests. Hence, a high degree of participatory democracy is potentially possible as a result of the nature of these organizations.

EDUCATIONAL GROUPS AND NATIONAL POLITICS

Although organizational diversity tends to be the norm among educational interest groups, there does emerge a surprising pattern of consistency with respect to the national policy concerns of those same groups: Very few are engaged in a significant amount of direct political activity. Out of 178 organizations, only 4—the NEA, the National Alliance of Black School Educators, the American Federation of Teachers (AFT), and the Project on Equal Education Rights (PEER)—endorsed candidates for the presidency in 1992. Furthermore, the NEA and AFT are the only groups that endorse political candidates in state-level elections, and together with the Career College Association, are the only groups that contributed money to campaigns in 1992 through a political action committee.

In addition, there appears to be an aversion toward direct involvement in the educational policy arena. The vast majority of groups do not like to think of themselves as "pressure groups," seeking to gain congressional favors or benefits for their constituencies. The National Art Education Association, for example, reflects the attitude of most organizations when it characterizes itself as being "more of a professional association than a lobbying group." The extent to which most organizations try to shape public policy is simply to provide information to members about pending legislation and, to a much lesser extent, to provide information to Congress about their positions on bills.

This attitude is also illustrated by the extent to which groups appear at congressional hearings. The majority of educational interest groups in this study did not provide testimony at hearings on the 35 education bills (see Appendix D) that were before Congress during the period of 1987 through 1992. When looking at all 250 groups in the educational community, the pattern remains the same; approximately 70 percent of educational interest groups choose not to participate in the making of educational policy.

Table 1.1 lists all educational interest groups that provided congressional testimony on Capitol Hill during this six-year period. The table underscores the primary reality behind interest group activity and educational policy, namely that such activity (where it exists at all) is dominated by narrowly focused,

Table 1.1
Educational Interest Groups Testifying at Congressional Hearings on Bills Affecting Education, 1987–1992

Interest Group	Number of Bills
American Association for Adult and Continuing Education	1
American Association of Colleges for Teacher Education	1
American Association of Colleges of Nursing	1
American Association of Colleges of Pharmacy	1
American Association of Community Colleges	8
American Association of School Administrators	5
American Association of State Colleges and Universities	5
American Association of the Deaf-Blind	2
American Association of University Professors	1
American Education Association	9
American Federation of Teachers	9
American Foundation for the Blind	1
American Vocation Association	1
Association for the Advancement of Health Education	1
Association of Academic Health Centers	1
Association of Accredited Cosmetology Schools	1
Association of American Medical Colleges	2
Association of American Universities	2
Association of American Veterinary Medical Colleges	1
Association of Community College Trustees	5
Association of Jesuit Colleges and Universities	1
Association of Minority Health Professional Schools	1
Association of Schools of Public Health	1
Association of Teacher Educators	1
Association of University Programs in Health Administration	1
Association of Urban Universities	2
Center for Law and Education	1
College Board	1
Council for Basic Education	1
Council of Exceptional Children	2
Council of the Great City Schools	3
Council on Post-Secondary Accreditation	1
Experiment in International Living	1
Joint National Committee for Languages	1
National Association for the Advancement of Colored People (NAACP) Legal Defense and Education Fund	2
National Association of College and University Business Officers	3
National Association of Elementary School Principals	2
National Association of Equal Opportunities in Higher Education	3
National Association of Independent Colleges and Universities	5
National Association of Private Schools for Exceptional Children	1
National Association of School Psychologists	4

Table 1.1 (continued)

National Association of Secondary School Principals	1
National Association of State Boards of Education	1
National Association of State Directors of Special Education	1
National Association of State Directors of Vocational Education	2
National Association of State Universities and Land-Grant Colleges	2
National Association of Student Financial Aid Administrators	3
National Association of Trade and Technical Schools	4
National Coalition of the Deaf-Blind	1
National Council of La Raza	2
National Council of State Directors of Adult Education	1
National Council of Teachers of Mathematics	1
National Education Association	12
National Head Start Association	2
National Home Study Council	1
National Indian Education Association	1
National School Boards Association	7
National School Health Education Coalition	1
Overseas Education Association	1
Reading Is Fundamental	1
United Negro College Fund	3
United States Student Association	5
Very Special Arts	1

Source: *Congressional Record.*

special interest groups at the expense of generalist or umbrella organizations. No single group attempted to exert influence on all thirty-five bills. As one of the rare umbrella organizations, the NEA demonstrated interest in more areas than any other group; yet, the NEA testified at only 35 percent of the hearings. Its chief competitor for members and status in the educational community, the AFT, testified at approximately one-quarter of the hearings. Out of the sixty-three groups testifying, 56 percent spoke at hearings for only one piece of legislation. Nearly three-quarters of these groups testified at hearings for no more than two bills from 1987 through the end of 1992.

These findings raise some interesting questions. In particular, what possible explanations could there be for the relative lack of direct political activity on the part of U.S. educational groups? And why is the activity that is present so often narrow and specialized?

The failure to engage in significant political advocacy at the federal level cannot be fully explained by the advocacy restrictions placed on nonprofit organizations as defined by section 501(c)(3) of the U.S. Code. It is true that, in order to maintain its tax-exempt status, a 501(c)(3) group must not "participate in, or intervene in, any political campaign on behalf of any candidate for public office" (Shaiko, 1991:117). However, providing information or research to Congress is allowable, provided that the information is also available to the public. Moreover, it is possible for any 501(c)(3) organization to engage in the most aggressive forms of political activity by creating a distinct "piggyback" group that falls into the 501(c)(4) category. The (c)(4) category means that the group may lobby, but members may not deduct contributions. The advantage of the "piggyback" arrangement is that it is possible for the tax-exempt sector of the enterprise to channel a wide range of operating costs into the lobbying sector, thereby keeping it afloat financially (Shaiko, 1991).

Therefore, it is certainly possible for educational groups with 501(c)(3) tax status to exert a considerable amount of political influence within the bounds of the law. Given that the overwhelming majority of educational interest groups (95 percent) already have offices in the Washington, D.C., area, it would seem that political influence is primarily a function of organizational will. Indeed, Congress may be more accessible to educational interest group pressure than many organizations realize. William P. Browne (1988:243) notes that legislators tend to regard interest groups as "de facto lobbyists," regardless of how these organizations define themselves. Furthermore, legislators are quite willing to accord them a "special legitimacy" (Browne, 1988:39) in developing substantive legislation that affects their membership (Lowi, 1979:51). The overwhelming majority of educational interest groups simply do not take advantage of their special standing as "lobbyists" in the eyes of congressional committees. The result is that interest groups in other policy areas, such as agriculture (Browne and Cigler, 1990), are much more serious than their counterparts in education about the responsibility of shaping public policy.

From the perspective of interest group leaders, however, the prospect of becoming major political players is not quite so simple. As in other policy areas, educational groups are forced to operate in a competitive environment that depends heavily on the principles of the marketplace (Berry, 1989:56–57). The leadership of professional organizations must make every effort to address and satisfy the most immediate and specific needs of their membership or constituency. Doing so is absolutely imperative in the battle to protect their proportion of the total pool of potential members in the educational community.

This basic fact of life for educational groups might help to explain why internal issues tend to take precedence over any national political aspirations. Leaders are cautious about activities that may offend, distract, or alienate members and potential members. Leaders tend to venture into the political arena only in those rare instances when federal officials are dealing with a topic of direct and immediate interest to the concerns of the membership; they cannot afford to become idealistic, abstract, or ideological. This is because members must believe it is worthwhile to pay membership dues, and so a great deal of time, energy, and money is directed toward providing members with the concrete benefits associated with professional development opportunities (Berry, 1989: 50–57). Indeed, most of the organizations in our study sponsor workshops, annual meetings, and other programs designed to assist members in advancing their individual careers. Introspective behavior, therefore, helps to explain their rather narrow and specialized activity within the policy arena, when political activity occurs at all.

CONCLUSION

While virtually all issues are reflected in the missions of various groups, no single group embraces all the interests and constituencies within the educational community. Further, the memberships and clientele of educational groups insist that their leaders look inward, not outward, and this necessarily limits their ability to exert influence in both the political and policy arenas. Group leaders are not often in a position to expend the organization's scarce resources on politics and, consequently, the organization cannot take full advantage of opportunities to influence events that have direct bearing on the future of education. If we ask why other federal policy areas may be given higher fiscal and substantive priority, perhaps part of the answer lies in the nature, behavior, and direction of those interest groups that bear significant responsibility for helping to shape the future of education in America.

U.S. EDUCATIONAL POLICY INTEREST GROUPS

A

/

ACADEMIC COLLECTIVE BARGAINING INFORMATION SERVICE
Labor Studies Center
University of the District of Columbia
1321 H Street, N.W., Suite 212
Washington, D.C. 20005
(202) 727-2326

The Academic Collective Bargaining Information Service (ACBIS) is a university-based organization that disseminates information about labor relations, including court rulings and pertinent legislation, to unions at institutions of higher education.

ORIGIN AND DEVELOPMENT

ACBIS was founded in 1970, at a time when an increasing number of university faculties were organizing into collective bargaining units. ACBIS was created as an outreach arm of the Labor Studies Center at the University of the District of Columbia.

ORGANIZATION AND FUNDING

Isadore Goldberg has been the director of ACBIS since 1989. There are two staff members, one of whom is full-time. ACBIS relies on several student interns from the Law School at the University of District of Columbia.

While governed by the university, ACBIS does have an advisory council, which includes the following organizations: American Association of Community Colleges,* American Association of State Colleges and Universities,* American Association of University Professors,* American Council on Education, American Federation of Teachers,* The Association of American Colleges,* Association of Governing Boards of Universities and Colleges, College and University Personnel Association,* The Education Commission of the States,* National Association of College and University Attorneys,* National Association of State Universities and Land-Grant Colleges,* and National Education Association.*

Operations are based on an annual subscription rate of $125.

POLICY CONCERNS AND TACTICS

ACBIS is concerned with protecting wages, benefits, and jobs of university-based union members. It does so by providing its subscribers with a monthly newsletter, "Fact Sheet," that includes news about a variety of union issues: contract negotiation strategies, new contract clauses, strikes and job actions, interest arbitration, faculty supply, demand and employment trends, workplace legislation, court decisions, and information about workload and working conditions at various universities.

POLITICAL ACTIVITY

None

FURTHER INFORMATION

No information available.

THE ADVOCACY INSTITUTE
1730 Rhode Island Avenue, N.W., Suite 600
Washington, D.C. 20036-3188
(202) 659-8475   fax: (202) 659-8484

The Advocacy Institute (AI) provides education, leadership training, and technical counseling to individual advocates and organizations to increase their effectiveness in placing issues onto the public policy agenda.

ORIGIN AND DEVELOPMENT

AI was founded in 1984 by David Cohen, former president of Common Cause, and Michael Pertschuk, former chair of the Federal Trade Commission. It was created to protect and empower nonprofit organizations, including educational groups, to succeed in the policy arena. In doing so, it assists nonprofit organizations in attracting and retaining bright and dedicated young employees, especially those from minority groups.

ORGANIZATION AND FUNDING

AI has three co-directors, Michael Pertschuk, David Cohen, and Kathleen Sheeky. Pertschuk and Cohen have been co-directors since 1984, while Sheeky joined in 1992. There is a seventeen-person board of directors, which includes the three co-directors. AI has twenty-five full-time staff members and relies heavily on volunteers and about twelve student interns each year.

AI is funded through several sources. In recent years, its total budget has averaged about $1.5 million. The majority of funding (approximately 60 percent in 1992) has been acquired through workshop and seminar fees. In addition, nineteen foundations typically contribute about $500,000 to its operating budget, and individual contributions tend to total around $30,000 annually.

POLICY CONCERNS AND TACTICS

AI is concerned with a variety of issues. Its primary concern is one-on-one counseling. In fiscal year 1992, AI counseled over 160 organizations. The issues included improving educational opportunities, reforming campaign finance, increasing efficient use of energy, children's issues, and leadership development. The purpose is to increase the effectiveness of other organizations in bringing these issues to the forefront of the policy arena.

POLITICAL ACTIVITY

None.

FURTHER INFORMATION

Annual report; "Change for the Better: Building New Dimensions in Public Interest Leadership" (pamphlet); "The Elements of a Successful Public Interest Advocacy Campaign" (pamphlet); "The Advocate's Guide to Preemption" (conference report); "Bridging Washington and the Grassroots" (workshop transcript); and "The Advocate's Advocate" (monthly newsletter).

AEROSPACE EDUCATION FOUNDATION
1501 Lee Highway
Arlington, Virginia 22209-1198
(703) 247-5839   fax: (703) 247-5853

The Aerospace Education Foundation (AEF) is a nonprofit organization that seeks to communicate knowledge, develop skills, and shape attitudes and opinions about aerospace and the effect that related air and space technologies and systems have on society. AEF assists the Air Force Association by administering educational outreach programs.

ORIGIN AND DEVELOPMENT

AEF was established in 1956 during the Cold War. Its chief concern is to maintain America's competitiveness in the world. After the death of test pilot Mil Apt in 1957, the Milburn Apt Scholarship was established for the education of his daughters. The fund was retired in 1978 after $39,000 was expended and both daughters had received master's degrees.

Through educational and monetary donations, AEF established the Theodore von Karman collection of scientific and technical books at the U.S. Air Force

(USAF) Academy in 1964. From 1967 to 1972, AEF reviewed USAF technical courses to determine the feasibility of their use within public school systems. From 1972 to 1984, AEF distributed 58 different USAF courses to junior and community colleges, as well as business and industry. From 1968 to the present, AEF has conducted numerous workshops and symposia throughout the United States. There are over 1,000 members of AEF, and over 200,000 members of the Air Force Association often play a supportive role in AEF. AEF has 350 chapters throughout the United States and the world.

ORGANIZATION AND FUNDING

The full-time staff of AEF consists of three members. It is assisted by a staff of ninety employees who work for the Air Force Association. Since 1989 Gerald V. Hasler has been the president of AEF. The executive director of the Air Force Association since 1990, Monroe Hatch, Jr., serves as the executive director of AEF. AEF is governed by a board of directors, 51 percent of whom must be members of the Air Force Association's board of directors.

AEF's annual budget is over $1 million. Revenue is generated through chapter contributions and donations from more than thirty-five corporations and thousands of individuals. No funding is allocated to administrative overhead, which is taken care of by the Air Force Association. Funding is earmarked for the publication and dissemination of material, as well as for scholarships and outreach projects.

POLICY CONCERNS AND TACTICS

AEF is concerned primarily with advancing both aerospace studies and aerospace industries. In doing so, its goal is to support the efforts of the U.S. Air Force. It offers scholarships, such as the Christa McAuliffe Memorial Award, which is an annual award designed to recognize an outstanding science or math teacher who brings about a heightened awareness of aerospace activities to students. It also offers numerous workshops and publications, covering such topics as ''America's Next Crisis—The Shortfall in Technical Manpower'' and ''Lifeline in Danger—An Assessment of the U.S. Defense Industrial Base.''

POLITICAL ACTIVITY

None.

FURTHER INFORMATION

The Aerospace Education Foundation *Newsletter.*

ALEXANDER GRAHAM BELL ASSOCIATION FOR THE DEAF, INC.

3417 Volta Place, N.W.
Washington, D.C. 20007-2778
(202) 337-5220

The Alexander Graham Bell Association for the Deaf (AGB) is a nonprofit membership organization that exists to improve the condition of hearing-impaired people. The association:

—encourages hearing-impaired people to communicate by developing maximal use of residual hearing, speech reading, and speech and language skills;

—promotes better public understanding of hearing loss in children and adults;

—promotes early detection of hearing loss;

—provides in-service training for teachers of hearing-impaired children;

—provides scholarships to hearing-impaired students; and

—gathers and disseminates information on hearing impairment including its causes and options for remedial treatment.

ORIGIN AND DEVELOPMENT

AGB was founded in 1890 by Alexander Graham Bell and currently has members in over 35 countries. AGB has over 5,000 members.

ORGANIZATION AND FUNDING

Since 1991 Dr. William Castle has been president, and, since 1985, Dr. Donna Dickman has been the executive director. AGB has a full-time staff of twelve and utilizes eight student interns per year. AGB is administered by a board of directors that consists of eighteen voting members, including representatives from three sections: the Parents Section, the International Organization for the Education of the Hearing Impaired, and the Oral Hearing-Impaired Section.

AGB has an annual budget budget of $1,376,370, the greatest share of which is derived from private contributions, endowment earnings, and membership fees. Its funds are directed toward membership services, publications, and lobbying activities.

POLICY CONCERNS AND TACTICS

The primary concern is the dissemination of information about the hearing-impaired. The Volta Bureau Library, a research library, is maintained, which contains historical collections of publications, documents, and information on deafness. AGB also provides scholarships to the hearing-impaired.

POLITICAL ACTIVITY

AGB lobbies to enact legislation that protects the rights of the hearing-impaired. It was particularly effective in its support for the Education of All Handicapped Children Act (PL 94–142).

FURTHER INFORMATION

No information available.

AMERICAN ACADEMY OF TEACHERS OF SINGING
William Gephart, Secretary
75 Bank Street
New York, New York 10014
(212) 242-1836

The American Academy of Teachers of Singing (AATS) is dedicated to the improvement of the profession from the standpoints of both teaching and ethics.

ORIGIN AND DEVELOPMENT

AATS was founded in 1922 by a group of fifteen men, all professional teachers of singing. The founders were motivated by a desire to make contributions toward improving the profession, particularly contributions that could not be made individually or as a part of the activities of an overly large association. Membership in the academy is by invitation only and is constitutionally limited to forty members of the profession (current membership is 32). AATS maintains a close relationship with the National Association of Teachers of Singing.

ORGANIZATION AND FUNDING

Officers include chairman (Donald Read since 1990), vice-chairman (Shirlee Emmons), secretary/executive director (William Gephart since 1972), treasurer (Robert C. White), and publications officer (Robert Grooters). The academy employs no staff. Funding is entirely dependent upon membership fees, and all funds are allocated to publications and necessary small expenses.

POLICY CONCERNS AND TACTICS

AATS is concerned with supporting and advancing the profession as a whole and is particularly interested in maintaining ethical and professional standards. Although several political and legal battles are part of its history, AATS accomplishes its goals today primarily through member activities and publications.

POLITICAL ACTIVITY

AATS does no lobbying and has no current political agenda. Early in its history, however, the academy was involved in a number of local disputes: (1) In 1922 the academy organized and led a successful movement to prevent the licensing of teachers of singing by the city of New York; (2) from 1927 to 1930 the academy assisted the Federal Trade Commission with advice and information in the conduct of the commission's unfair competition case against a Chicago voice institute; and (3) in 1930 the academy brought about by intervention in the New York City Zoning Law Case its appeal to the New York Court of Appeals, whose decision affirmed the status of music teachers as professional people and thereby assured them the right to practice their profession unhindered by the provisions of the Zoning Law.

FURTHER INFORMATION

Various publications of interest to members; information brochure.

AMERICAN ASSOCIATION FOR ADULT AND CONTINUING EDUCATION

2101 Wilson Boulevard, Suite 925
Arlington, Virginia 22201
(703) 522-2234

The American Association for Adult and Continuing Education (AAACE) is a nonprofit organization that is concerned with promoting adult learning and development in the United States. The AAACE seeks to provide leadership in unifying individual adult education practitioners; foster the development and sharing of information, theory, research, and best practices; promote professional identity and growth; and advocate policy initiatives.

ORIGIN AND DEVELOPMENT

AAACE was founded in 1982. At that time, two adult education organizations merged: the Adult Education Association and the National Association of Programs and Schools to Educate Adults. AAACE has over 6,000 members.

ORGANIZATION AND FUNDING

AAACE is governed by a fifteen-member board of directors and a five-member executive committee. Since 1992, Dr. W. Franklin Spikes has been the president of AAACE and Dr. Drew Allbritten has been the executive director. AAACE employs twelve full-time staff members, as well as five student interns.

The annual operating budget is approximately $850,000; 40 percent is derived from membership fees, 30 percent comes from conference fees, and 25 percent is acquired from subscriptions to publications. More than 65 percent of funding is spent on membership services and conferences, with 20 percent being earmarked for administration.

POLICY CONCERNS AND TACTICS

AAACE is involved with several issues affecting adult education and literacy. It is concerned with the *America 2000* report, and notes a need for a more prepared workforce.

POLITICAL ACTIVITY

AAACE testifies on Capitol Hill in support of measures that will increase the amount of funding available for adult education. Recently, it testified in support of the Adult Literacy and Employability Act. There it argued for the creation of an Assistant Secretary for Adult Education in the Department of Education. AAACE also lobbies for legislation through the Coalition for Adult Education Organizations. The association does not support or endorse political candidates.

It does try to affect public policy through publications to its membership as well as involvement with congressional committees.

FURTHER INFORMATION

No information available.

AMERICAN ASSOCIATION FOR HIGHER EDUCATION
One Dupont Circle, Suite 600
Washington, D.C. 20036-1110
(202) 293-6440   fax: (202) 293-0073

The American Association for Higher Education (AAHE) is a nonprofit organization that strives to improve the quality of higher education.

ORIGIN AND DEVELOPMENT

Historically AAHE was a division, the Association for Higher Education, within the National Education Association.* In 1969 members felt that policies and programs of higher education were sufficiently separate from those of elementary and secondary education and, therefore, formed a separate nonprofit organization. Since then, AAHE has developed into a wide-ranging organization, with subgroups or caucuses that reflect a diverse membership and outlook. Caucuses exist for American Indians/Native Alaskans, Asian/Pacific Islanders, African-Americans, Hispanics, Lesbians/gays, students, and women. There are approximately 8,000 members in AAHE.

ORGANIZATION AND FUNDING

AAHE is governed by a nineteen-member board of directors and an appointed president. The current chair of the board is Blenda Wilson. Russell Edgerton has been president since 1975. There are forty-two full-time staff members. AAHE accepts two student interns annually.

The 1992 operating budget was for $2.4 million, 49 percent of which came from private foundations and 24 percent from membership fees. The remainder was acquired from government and corporations. About 80 percent of the budget is allocated to membership services and grant activities.

POLICY CONCERNS AND TACTICS

AAHE's concern with educational issues is general and diffuse. Its 1992 national conference reflected a number of diverse issues, ranging from increasing diversity within the ranks of higher education to regaining the trust of the public at large. AAHE attempts to affect public policy through its publications and by attracting high-ranking public officials to its conference. However, AAHE does not advocate policy changes except in very broad terms.

POLITICAL ACTIVITY

None.

FURTHER INFORMATION

AAHE's bimonthly magazine, *Change*, and a monthly newsletter, the *AAHE Bulletin*.

AMERICAN ASSOCIATION OF CHRISTIAN SCHOOLS
P.O. Box 2189
Independence, Missouri 64044
(816) 795-7709   fax: (816) 795-7709

The American Association of Christian Schools (AACS) seeks to promote, establish, advance, and develop Christian schools and Christian education in the United States.

ORIGIN AND DEVELOPMENT

AACS was founded in 1972 in order to provide leadership, protection, and service for the large number of church-related schools established in the late 1960s and early 1970s. Today AACS is an association of state organizations, with a membership of 38 state associations, 1,100 schools, and 170,000 students.

ORGANIZATION AND FUNDING

AACS is governed by a board of state representatives consisting of the executive officers (presidents, vice-presidents, and executive directors) of the state associations. A board of directors appoints the president of the association and makes recommendations to the board of representatives. The president from 1992 to 1993 was Dr. Carl Herbster, the educational director was Dr. Charles Walker, and the legislative director was Reverend Duane Motley. AACS employs a full-time staff of five.

AACS is a 501(c)(3) organization with an annual budget of approximately $287,500; 52 percent of funding is derived from membership fees, 43 percent from user fees, and 5 percent from individual contributions. A total of 70 percent of the budget is allocated to administration, 15 percent to membership services, 10 percent to lobbying activities, and 5 percent to publications and the dissemination of information.

POLICY CONCERNS AND TACTICS

The main concern of AACS is to improve the quality of education. The association offers several programs to help member schools improve academic programs including school accreditation, teacher certification, and achievement testing, conventions, and conferences, as well as other educational and school services. AACS would also like to increase the number of member institutions.

Current public policy concerns include: school choice and tax burden issues, the Educate America Act (Goals 2000), religious liberty issues in both legislative and judicial contexts, and family value issues.

POLITICAL ACTIVITY

According to association literature, AACS began as a national lobbying coalition for Christian schools and churches, and it continues its legislative efforts today. AACS maintains an office in Washington, D.C., to monitor the legislative issues that affect Christian schools. Regular contact is made with congressional offices, government officials, and conservative groups. AACS meets regularly with educational leaders at the U.S. Department of Education and keeps in contact with other private school leaders. Regional legislative directors and the grass-roots "Minuteman Alert Team" coordinate activity in their respective regions, and AACS state organizations have organized efforts to promote Christian education at the state level. AACS also holds an annual conference in Washington that deals primarily with national legislative concerns.

FURTHER INFORMATION

Capital Comments (newsletter that keeps members informed about national legislation); *The Parent Update, Teacher Placement Service*, and a directory.

AMERICAN ASSOCIATION OF COLLEGES FOR TEACHER EDUCATION

One Dupont Circle, Suite 610
Washington, D.C. 20036-1186
(202) 293-2450   fax: (202) 457-8095

The American Association of Colleges for Teacher Education (AACTE) is a nonprofit organization primarily interested in improving the quality of schools, colleges, and departments of education. AACTE seeks to renew interest in the administration and management of education units at universities and to develop "good practices" in the field of teacher education. AACTE is also involved in developing an agenda for teacher education policy at the state and federal levels.

ORIGIN AND DEVELOPMENT

AACTE was founded in 1948, but its roots go back to the 1840s when its predecessor, the American Association of Normal Schools, was founded in New England. Membership of AACTE is comprised of 710 departments, schools, and colleges of education in the United States.

ORGANIZATION AND FUNDING

AACTE has a twenty-four-person board of directors. In 1992 Marilyn J. Guy was elected president. David G. Imig has been the executive director since 1980. AACTE has a full-time staff of sixty-two employees and hires two student interns each year.

The operating budget in 1992 was approximately $2 million plus $750,000 in restricted funds. Most (65 percent) of the revenues come from membership fees, but 28 percent are derived from private foundations. Only 20 percent of funding goes toward administration. The remainder is invested in membership services, including publications and lobbying activities.

POLICY CONCERNS AND TACTICS

AACTE is concerned primarily with accreditation standards, professional development, and teacher preparation. To secure its goals, the association represents the needs and concerns of members at the state and federal levels, before governmental and nongovernmental agencies, and in the media and the education community. It is seeking to increase federal funding for teacher preparation.

Using data generated by its State Issues Clearinghouse, AACTE also publishes issue analysis papers on early childhood education, clinical schools, and school administrator licensure requirements.

POLITICAL ACTIVITY

During 1991 AACTE developed a legislative proposal to reauthorize Title V of the Higher Education Act. AACTE also monitored federal testing initiatives and participated in the Committee for Education Funding.

The Association also testified at hearings for the Education Excellence Act and the Equity and Excellence in Education Implementation Act. At these hearings, AACTE offered support for Title I (Loan Incentives for Teaching) and two parts of Title III, providing financial assistance for institutions that recruit and retain individuals seeking careers in teaching and establishing professional development academies. It also supported the Teacher Recognition Program, but cautioned Congress about the need to recognize teacher preparation programs. It spoke in opposition to allocating federal grants to states to create alternative teacher certification programs.

AACTE does not endorse or officially support political candidates.

FURTHER INFORMATION

No information available.

AMERICAN ASSOCIATION OF COLLEGES OF OSTEOPATHIC MEDICINE

818 Connecticut Avenue, N.W., Suite 1030
Washington, D.C. 20006
(301) 468-0990

The American Association of Colleges of Osteopathic Medicine (AACOM) is a nonprofit organization concerned with advancing osteopathic medicine and science, as well as lending support and assistance to the nation's osteopathic medical schools.

ORIGIN AND DEVELOPMENT

AACOM was founded in 1897 by colleges of osteopathic medicine. AACOM works closely with the American Osteopathic Association and the American

Osteopathic Hospital Association. AACOM has three sections: the Council of Deans, the Section of Student Affairs Officers, and the Council of Student Council Presidents. There are fifteen colleges of osteopathic medicine in the United States that comprise the membership of AACOM.

ORGANIZATION AND FUNDING

A board of governors is comprised of the dean of each institution. Philip Pumerantz is currently president. Since 1985, Sherry R. Arnstein has been executive director. AACOM has a full-time staff of sixteen employees.

In 1992 its annual operating budget was $1.4 million. Approximately $40,000 of the revenue is derived from private contributions, with the rest coming from institutional members. About one-quarter of the revenue is invested in administration. The remainder is spent on statistical studies, membership services, and governmental relations.

POLICY CONCERNS AND TACTICS

In 1992 AACOM was interested in financial aid issues, among others, and appeared before Congress to argue its position. AACOM also tries to affect public policy through news releases and publications.

POLITICAL ACTIVITY

In 1992 AACOM provided congressional testimony in favor of reauthorizing the extension of the Higher Education Act and the Health Professions Educational Assistance Act, both of which provide financial assistance to students.

FURTHER INFORMATION

Annual Statistical Report plus numerous booklets and papers.

AMERICAN ASSOCIATION OF COLLEGIATE REGISTRARS AND ADMISSIONS OFFICERS

One Dupont Circle, N.W., Suite 330
Washington, D.C. 20036-1171
(202) 293-9161   fax: (202) 872-8857

The American Association of Collegiate Registrars and Admissions Officers (AACRAO) is a professional education association of degree-granting postsecondary institutions, government agencies, private educational organizations, and education-oriented businesses in the United States and abroad. Its goal is to promote higher education and further the professional development of members working in admissions, enrollment management, financial aid, institutional research, records, and registration.

ORIGIN AND DEVELOPMENT

AACRAO was founded in 1910 when administrators at North Dakota Agricultural College called a meeting of registrars and accountants from other schools in order to discuss subjects and problems of common interest. Today AACRAO has a membership of 8,400.

ORGANIZATION AND FUNDING

The association is governed by a nine-member board of directors elected by the membership. The 1993 president was Jeffrey M. Tanner, and the executive director since 1989 has been Wayne E. Becraft. AACRAO maintains a staff of seventeen full-time employees (four clerical), one part-time employee, and up to three student interns per year.

The association is a 501(c)(3) organization and had a 1991-1992 annual operating budget of $2 million. Approximately 48 percent of the funding came from membership fees, 26 percent from user fees, 14 percent from government contracts, 6 percent from corporate sponsorship, 4 percent from endowment earnings, and 2 percent from miscellaneous sources. Approximately 50 percent of the budget was allocated to administrative expenses; 37 percent to membership services, such as the annual meeting, publications, professional development, and committee activities; and 13 percent to grants, contracts, and miscellaneous expenses.

POLICY CONCERNS AND TACTICS

In 1991-1992 AACRAO: (1) assisted the Department of Education in developing enforcement guidelines for federal legislation; (2) supported the continuing recognition of the Middle States Association of Colleges and Schools as an accrediting body with the Department of Education; (3) supported efforts to control personnel credentials fraud; (4) worked to address abuses in athletic recruiting and problems with student athlete academic standards and retention rates; (5) drafted standards for registrars; (6) promoted education in the international community; and (7) supported a variety of efforts designed to advance minority concerns.

In addition, the association is active in meeting the professional development needs of its members. The association hosts meetings and workshops, participates in government- and privately sponsored projects, offers internship and grant opportunities, and is planning a series of innovative projects for the future. Currently the association is involved in implementing an Electronic Data Interchange and other forms of technology to assist members, and it continues to work on standards and outcomes assessment issues.

The association attempts to meet its goals through member committees and task forces, annual meetings, publications, and by taking formal positions on certain political issues.

POLITICAL ACTIVITY

AACRAO occasionally attempts to influence legislation, usually by joining forces with related organizations and writing letters to members of Congress. The association has called for an end to the military's ban on homosexuals in the military and has endorsed positions supporting the awarding of minority scholarships. In addition, AACRAO has cooperated with the executive branch of the federal government on the Student Right to Know and Campus Security Act and maintains an interest in the Higher Education Act.

FURTHER INFORMATION

Annual report and various field-related publications.

AMERICAN ASSOCIATION OF COMMUNITY COLLEGES
One Dupont Circle, N.W., Suite 410
Washington, D.C. 20036-1176
(202) 728-2000　　fax: (202) 833-2467

The American Association of Community Colleges (AACC) works with other higher education associations, the federal government, Congress, and other national associations that represent the public and private sectors to promote the goals of community colleges and higher education.

ORIGIN AND DEVELOPMENT

In 1920 the U.S. Commissioner of Education called a group of 34 educators together in St. Louis, Missouri, to organize over 200 junior colleges in the United States. The meeting resulted in the creation of the American Association of Junior Colleges, later changed to the AACC. The association today has over 1,000 members.

ORGANIZATION AND FUNDING

AACC is governed by a board of directors consisting of thirty-two officers elected by the membership at large. Dr. David R. Pierce has been the president and executive director since 1991. The association employs a full-time staff of thirty-four.

AACC is a 501(c)(3) organization with an annual budget of approximately $3.6 million; 45 percent of revenues are generated through membership fees, 53 percent from convention and publication revenues, and 2 percent from user fees. A total of 61 percent of the budget is allocated to administration, 17 percent to publications, 20 percent to membership services, and 2 percent to lobbying activities.

POLICY CONCERNS AND TACTICS

Major policy concerns include direct lending issues, accreditation standards, enhanced state oversight, academic and occupational standards, and workforce preparation. AACC attempts to meet its goals through a program of national leadership and advocacy, by providing members with extensive information resources, and by a system of formal member networking.

POLITICAL ACTIVITY

AACC's lobbying activities are designed to provide members with a link to key committees of Congress, members of the House and Senate, and relevant federal agencies. The association follows up lobbying activity by monitoring and supporting federal legislation and regulations that affect the interests of members.

FURTHER INFORMATION

Brochures, several publications including *Community College Times*, the *Community College Journal*, and various topical books and monographs.

AMERICAN ASSOCIATION OF RETIRED PERSONS
601 E Street, N.W.
Washington, D.C. 20049
(202) 434-2277   fax: (202) 434-6499

The American Association of Retired Persons (AARP) is a nonprofit organization that serves the interest of older Americans. AARP is of special interest to retired teachers. The retired teachers division is open to former members of the National Retired Teachers Association (NRTA) and teachers, administrators, and other education professionals who are near retirement.

ORIGIN AND DEVELOPMENT

AARP was founded in 1958 by the late Dr. Ethel Percy Andrus and has grown to become the largest organization for senior citizens in the United States. AARP has focused on four areas that affect the quality of life for older Americans: health care issues, women's issues, worker equity, and minority issues.

AARP has recently created an educational/research division, which includes a Research Information Center and departments devoted to survey design and analysis, forecasting and environmental scanning, and program evaluation. AARP boasts a membership of more than 32 million people.

ORGANIZATION AND FUNDING

The current president is Lovola West Burgess, and the executive director is Horace B. Deets. The AARP is governed by a 15-member board of directors. AARP has a full-time staff of 1,050 employees and accepts 10 student interns each year.

Its current operating budget amounts to $319 million, all of it coming from membership fees. Approximately 20 percent goes toward administration, with the remainder invested in membership services, publications, and lobbying activities.

POLICY CONCERNS AND TACTICS

AARP is concerned with a variety of issues, including education. One of AARP's major education initiatives, the AARP/VOTE program, strives to provide critical issue information to voters in more than thirty states. AARP's Andrus Foundation also supports university-level research projects on the issue of aging.

POLITICAL ACTIVITY

AARP is a nonpartisan organization. It does, however, provide its membership with substantial information about candidates' positions on relevant issues.

FURTHER INFORMATION

Numerous publications, including *Modern Maturity* and the National Retired Teachers Association's *NRTA News Bulletin*.

AMERICAN ASSOCIATION OF SCHOOL ADMINISTRATORS

1801 North Moore Street
Arlington, Virginia 22209
(703) 528-0700

The American Association of School Administrators (AASA) is a nonprofit organization dedicated to ensuring quality leadership within all school systems. It does so through ongoing professional development for its members and by being involved in the national educational agenda.

ORIGIN AND DEVELOPMENT

AASA was founded in 1868, and in 1992 had a membership of over 18,000.

ORGANIZATION AND FUNDING

The current president is Paul W. Jung, and the executive director is Richard D. Miller. AASA has an executive committee of eight members, plus four national officers. There is a full-time staff of ten employees.

AASA has an operating budget of close to $10 million, over 75 percent of which comes from the annual convention, membership dues, and workshops and seminars. The vast majority of expenses (70 percent) are in the area of membership services.

POLICY CONCERNS AND TACTICS

Recent major issues for AASA have been national standards, testing, student financial aid, recruitment of minority teachers, improvement of instruction, and disability issues. According to its 1991 annual report, both the Federal Policy and Legislation Committee and the Urban Schools Advisory Committee of AASA argued that standards are desirable, but the committee advised caution regarding testing. Both committees gave testimony on Capitol Hill.

POLITICAL ACTIVITY

At the hearings for the Twenty-First Century Teachers Act, AASA supported loan incentives and loan forgiveness, grants to help local districts recruit minority teachers, and grants to help districts conduct site-based or districtwide mentoring, teaming, and clinical review for all teachers. AASA also testified at the hearings for the reauthorization of Expiring Federal Elementary and Secondary Education Programs, Chapter 2 of the Education Consolidation and Improvement Act. Here AASA argued for full funding of Chapter 2, opposed vouchers, and supported inclusion of incentive grants and increases in funding for concentration grants, secondary school grants, dropout prevention, and "Even Start."

AASA has also supported the reauthorization of Part H of the Individuals with Disabilities Education Act. It testified on behalf of differential participation and funding by states in early intervention and preschool programs, as well as the strengthening role of the Federal Interstate Commerce Commission under Part H to facilitate interagency coordination. AASA also supported the Regulatory Impact on Student Excellence Act. It opposed the National Education Report Card Act, claiming that its underlying assumptions on how to achieve quality in education were wrong. At the hearings for the Education Excellence Act and the Equity and Excellence in Education Implementation Act, AASA gave supportive testimony for the creation of a Children's Trust Fund and for the duplication of magnet school programs in alternative curriculum schools.

FURTHER INFORMATION

No information available.

AMERICAN ASSOCIATION OF STATE COLLEGES AND UNIVERSITIES
One Dupont Circle, Suite 700
Washington, D.C. 20036-1192
(202) 293-7070   fax: (202) 296-5819

The American Association of State Colleges and Universities (AASCU) is a nonprofit organization that acts as a resource for the continued advancement and development of state colleges and universities. According to its annual report, current areas of special attention in AASCU activities include public higher education finance, teacher education, institutional autonomy, and cultural and ethnic diversity of campuses and curricula.

ORIGIN AND DEVELOPMENT

The origins of AASCU can be traced to the Association of Teacher Education Institutions (ATEI), founded in 1951. During the 1950s, teacher colleges became the fastest growing, four-year, degree-granting institutions in the United States. According to published material, most of the ATEI institutions felt that a more broadly based national organization was needed that recognized the development of comprehensive, multipurpose state colleges and universities as a part of the nation's system of higher education. In 1961, AASCU was founded to meet this need.

AASCU has four divisions or program areas: Academic Programs, Educational Resources, Governmental Relations, and International Programs. The Governmental Relations division analyzes and addresses national policy and legislative issues affecting public higher education.

AASCU is affiliated with the Teacher Education Council of State Colleges and Universities, the American Association of State Colleges of Agriculture and Renewable Resources, and the National Association of System Heads.

ORGANIZATION AND FUNDING

AASCU membership includes 375 public colleges and universities and nearly 40 state higher education systems across the United States, Puerto Rico, Guam, and the Virgin Islands. It has a 16-member board of directors, which includes Eugene M. Hughes (board chair) and James B. Appleberry (AASCU president). AASCU employees 120 full-time workers and accepts 2 interns each year.

Revenues for AASCU have amounted recently to more than $5.3 million, the majority of which come from membership dues and contracts and grants. More than half (54 percent) of the budget goes toward personnel costs. Operations, publications, and staff travel consume approximately $2 million.

POLICY CONCERNS AND TACTICS

AASCU is concerned with enhancing educational opportunity and achievement in higher education. According to its annual report, its tactics include: (1) providing policy analyses on student aid issues and promoting balanced financial support to encourage greater participation by disadvantaged students underrepresented in college enrollments; (2) opposing significant shifts in federal and state education funding allocations; and (3) supporting proposals to increase or reallocate funding that may benefit AASCU students and institutions.

AASCU attempts to affect public policy through organizing collective efforts and responses by its member institutions, programs, or divisions; organizing and facilitating workshops; and communicating its position to the media and policy makers.

POLITICAL ACTIVITY

AASCU has testified in support of the reauthorization of the Higher Education Act of 1965, the Stafford Loan Program, and Title III and Title VIII of the Higher Education Act. It also testified during hearings for the Twenty-First Century Teachers Act, in support of loan incentives for teachers, expanding loan forgiveness programs, financial assistance for institutional recruitment and retention of individuals preparing to enter the teaching profession, establishing professional development academies, and the need to recognize exemplary teaching preparation programs.

During the reauthorization hearings for the Carl D. Perkins Vocational Education Act, AASCU was in support of funding that is based on performance and merit, including language that incorporated colleges offering associate degree programs; articulation between postsecondary vocational schools and community and state colleges and universities; and funding for state colleges and universities that offer associate degrees for vocational school graduates.

FURTHER INFORMATION

Numerous publications and reports, including an annual report.

AMERICAN ASSOCIATION OF TEACHERS OF FRENCH
Fred M. Jenkins, Executive Director
University of Illinois
57 East Armory Avenue
Champaign, Illinois 61820
(217) 333-2842   fax: (217) 333-2842

The overall mission of the American Association of Teachers of French (AATF) is to represent the French language in North America and to encourage the dissemination, both in schools and in the general public, of knowledge concerning all aspects of the culture of France and the French-speaking world. The association supports projects designed to advance the French language and literature, and encourages reciprocal communication among all levels of the teaching of French in North America.

ORIGIN AND DEVELOPMENT

AATF was founded in 1927.

ORGANIZATION AND FUNDING

The 11,000-member AATF is governed by an 18-member executive council, which meets once per year. The president since 1991 has been Rebecca M. Valette, and the executive director for the past 14 years has been Fred M. Jenkins. The organization employs 2 full-time staff members and 3 part-time staff members, and it relies on volunteers to assist at the annual convention. There are 76 local chapters, and AATF maintains ties with the Joint National Committee for Languages* and the Federation Internationale des Professeurs de Français.

AATF is a federal tax-exempt organization with an annual operating budget in 1992 of $583,639. A total of 57 percent of funding was from membership fees, and the remainder was from endowment earnings and other sources. Just 10 percent of the budget was allocated to administration; 44 percent to publications, scholarships, commissions, awards, and prizes; and 2 percent to the Joint National Committee for Languages for lobbying activities.

POLICY CONCERNS AND TACTICS

According to AATF literature, the association is interested in maintaining standards for students and teachers of French, defining proficiency, utilizing electronic messaging, promoting the study of foreign language in the elementary schools, promoting the teaching of business French at all levels, and in general promoting the study of French wherever possible. AATF pursues these goals by means of publications, an electronic network, flyers promoting French in the schools, and promotional videos.

POLITICAL ACTIVITY

AATF does indirect legislative lobbying through contributions to the Joint National Committee for Languages. AATF does not support or endorse political candidates.

FURTHER INFORMATION

The French Review (scholarly journal).

AMERICAN ASSOCIATION OF TEACHERS OF GERMAN
112 Haddontowne Court #104
Cherry Hill, New Jersey 08034
(609) 795-5553   fax: (609) 795-9398

The American Association of Teachers of German (AATG) seeks to advance and improve the teaching of the language, literature, and culture of the German-speaking countries.

ORIGIN AND DEVELOPMENT

AATG was founded in 1926. It was modeled after the newly formed American Association of Teachers of French* and the American Association of Teachers of Spanish and Portuguese.* Current membership is 7,350.

ORGANIZATION AND FUNDING

AATG is governed by a 10-member executive council. Six of the members represent a geographical region made up of between 9 and 12 chapters each. Within the council are 10 internal committees, each charged with oversight of the association's programs, publications, and services. In addition, there are 15 external committees and task forces comprised of over 100 additional members involved in various projects. The current president is Elizabeth Hoffman (since 1992), and the executive director for the past 8 years has been Helene Zimmer-Loew. The association employs a staff of 8 (4 part-time), and relies on volunteers as chapter officers, committee members, and other jobs.

AATG is a 501(c)(3) organization with an annual operating budget of approximately $1 million. A total of 20 percent of funding is derived from membership fees, 54 percent from sales and advertising, 16 percent from the German government, 5 percent from endowment earnings, and 5 percent from private contributions; 39 percent of the budget is allocated to membership services, 35 percent to administration, 25 percent to publications, and 1 percent to lobbying activities.

POLICY CONCERNS AND TACTICS

Current policy concerns include student academic standards, teacher standards at all levels, and cultural/racial diversity in the profession and among students. According to association literature, the long range plan of AATG includes: (1) improving quality of instruction at all levels; (2) increasing German enrollments in American colleges and schools; (3) improving relations with organizations that have similar interests; (4) strengthening the association's financial status; (5) increasing the quality of member services and developing new member programs; (6) improving the internal structure of the association in order to facilitate better communication; and (7) promoting research into the German language, literature, and culture. The association seeks to meet its goals by holding annual meetings, utilizing committee and task force work, providing consulting services, providing classroom materials at reasonable cost, conducting awards programs, publishing standards guidelines, promoting international professional development and research programs via satellite, publishing newsletters and other informational materials, promoting a variety of other adjunct programs, and supporting the Joint National Committee for Languages* lobbying group.

POLITICAL ACTIVITY

AATG contributes to and supports the lobbying activities of the Joint National Committee for Languages.

FURTHER INFORMATION

Newsletters, journals, letters, and special bulletins.

AMERICAN ASSOCIATION OF TEACHERS OF SPANISH AND PORTUGUESE

Lynn A. Sandstedt, Executive Director
University of Northern Colorado
Greely, Colorado 80639
(303) 351-1090   fax: (303) 351-1095

The American Association of Teachers of Spanish and Portuguese (AATSP) seeks to promote, develop, and advance the study and teaching of Hispanic, Luso-Brazilian, and related languages, literatures, and cultures in the United States and other countries.

ORIGIN AND DEVELOPMENT

AATSP was founded in 1917 and incorporated as a nonprofit organization in 1967. The association has a membership of 13,500.

ORGANIZATION AND FUNDING

The association is governed by a board of directors, called the executive council. The council consists of the vice-president and six members elected by the association membership. In addition, the council consists of eight *ex officio* members: the president, the executive director (who also serves as secretary and treasurer), the editor of *Hispania*, the last three past presidents, the retiring executive director, and the retiring editor of *Hispania*. The 1992 president was Don Bleznick, and the 1993 executive director was Lynn A. Sandstedt. AATSP employs a full-time staff of four and a part-time staff of two. All funding is derived from membership fees. Operating budget figures are unavailable.

POLICY CONCERNS AND TACTICS

According to association literature, the major concern of AATSP is to provide opportunities for members to increase their knowledge of the Hispanic and Luso-Brazilian languages and teaching practices and to increase their professional capabilities in these fields. The association seeks to accomplish these goals through research, discussion, exchange of information, and other activities. More specifically, the association: (1) conducts annual meetings; (2) publishes and distributes journals and other publications; (3) unites through membership persons interested in its purposes; (4) provides relevant educational services to its members; (5) disseminates results of member research; (6) seeks to enhance public awareness of its goals and purposes; (7) furnishes an institutional framework within which Hispanic and Luso-Brazilian language personnel may cooperate in the pursuit of common goals; and (8) seeks to cooperate with business, industry, government agencies, and other organizations and individuals in promotion of its purposes.

Immediate policy issues facing the organization include the setting of national standards for language students and teachers, encouraging the study of foreign language at the elementary level, and developing curricula for native Spanish speakers.

POLITICAL ACTIVITY

AATSP attempts to affect legislation indirectly through its support of the Joint National Committee for Languages.* The association does not support or endorse political candidates.

FURTHER INFORMATION

Newsletter (*Enlace*), ERIC/CLL News Bulletin, quarterly academic journal (*Hispania*), and brochure.

AMERICAN ASSOCIATION OF UNIVERSITY AFFILIATED PROGRAMS FOR PERSONS WITH DEVELOPMENTAL DISABILITIES

8630 Fenton Street, Suite 410
Silver Spring, Maryland 20910
(301) 588-8252   fax: (301) 588-2842

The American Association of University Affiliated Programs for Persons with Developmental Disabilities (AAUAP) is a nonprofit organization dedicated to supporting the independence, productivity, and integration into the community of all citizens who are developmentally disabled.

ORIGIN AND DEVELOPMENT

AAUAP was founded in 1967 as the national organization representing University Affiliated Programs (UAP) for the Developmentally Disabled. AAUAP represents fifty-five UAP programs and their consumers throughout the United States. AAUAP has a membership of seventy institutions.

ORGANIZATION AND FUNDING

A board of directors drawn from UAP programs appoints an executive director. Deborah Spitalnik was the 1992 president. Since 1985, William E. Jones has been the executive director. There is a full-time staff of twelve employees.

The 1992 operating budget was $1 million, derived from membership and user fees. Over 50 percent of the budget goes toward membership services, and 20 percent goes toward administrative costs and publications. The remainder goes toward the National UAP Data Collection System and the Training/Technical Assistance to Members program.

POLICY CONCERNS AND TACTICS

AAUAP is concerned with four issues: (1) increasing interdisciplinary training; (2) creating exemplary service programs; (3) providing technical assistance for information sharing at local, state, and national levels; and (4) encouraging applied research in prevention, treatment, management, and remediation of developmental disabilities. AAUAP addresses these issues through dissemination of information to members.

POLITICAL ACTIVITY

None.

FURTHER INFORMATION

No information available.

AMERICAN ASSOCIATION OF UNIVERSITY PROFESSORS

1021 14th Street, N.W., Suite 500
Washington, D.C. 20005
(202) 737-5900   fax: (202) 737-5526

The American Association of University Professors (AAUP) is a nonprofit organization that represents faculty members at universities and colleges throughout the United States. AAUP promotes the principles of academic freedom and shared governance. AAUP develops and implements standard governing personnel policies, professional ethics, and academic due process.

ORIGIN AND DEVELOPMENT

In 1915 a group of professors banded together to promote academic freedom and tenure and to establish sound procedures pertaining to academic governance. Three subsections have emerged in AAUP: Committee "A," on academic freedom and tenure; Committee "W," on the status of women in the academic profession; and Committee "Z," on the academic status of the profession. There are 42,000 members in AAUP.

ORGANIZATION AND FUNDING

AAUP has an elected president, first vice-president, second vice-president, and secretary/treasurer. An executive committee acts as a steering committee, and an elected council serves as a legislative body. Since 1990, Barbara R. Bergmann has been president, and Ernst Benjamin has been executive director since 1984. AAUP employs a staff of fifty-two and accepts two interns annually.

The 1992 annual budget totaled $3,177,000; 90 percent of revenues comes from membership fees and 10 percent comes from business contributions. About 25 percent of the budget goes toward administration; the remainder goes to membership development, publications, lobbying activities, and litigation.

POLICY CONCERNS AND TACTICS

AAUP is concerned with a variety of academic-workplace issues, including confidentiality of personnel files, speech codes, equity issues, and part-time and nontenure track appointments. It is also involved with monitoring abuses in intercollegiate athletics. These issues are addressed through the three committees, which develop and disseminate policy positions. The association also tries to affect public policy through litigation, press releases, and publication of journal articles.

POLITICAL ACTIVITY

AAUP maintains a government relations office that lobbies on higher education issues. It testified during the reauthorization hearings of the Higher Education Act of 1965, in support of placing financial operations of athletic departments under direct control of universities' central administration, full disclosure of athletic departments' budgets and long-term plans, and approval of budgets and long-term plans under regular government procedures.

FURTHER INFORMATION

AAUP *Journal* and other publications.

AMERICAN ASSOCIATION OF UNIVERSITY WOMEN
1111 16th Street, N.W.
Washington, D.C. 20036-4873
(202) 785-7761   fax: (202) 872-1425

The American Association of University Women (AAUW) is a nonprofit organization that works to facilitate educational opportunities and equity for women.

ORIGIN AND DEVELOPMENT

In 1881 AAUW was established by 17 women who had baccalaureate degrees and who shared a commitment to working to increase educational opportunities for other women. Two subsections have been established: the AAUW Education Foundation (1958) and the AAUW Legal Advocacy Fund (1981). There are 135,000 members in AAUW.

ORGANIZATION AND FUNDING

The 22-member AAUW and 15-member Education Foundation boards are elected by delegates to the annual convention. The 7-member Legal Advocacy Fund board of directors includes both convention-elected members of the AAUW board and non-AAUW board members elected by the Legal Advocacy Fund board members. Since 1989, Sharon Schuster has been president of AAUW, and Anne L. Bryant has been executive director since 1986. AAUW has a full-time staff of 145 and employs 3 interns annually.

Recent budgets have totaled over $4 million in revenues, most of it coming from membership dues. The majority of expenditures have been for communications, membership services, and policy development.

POLICY CONCERNS AND TACTICS

In addition to a variety of internal concerns, AAUW is interested in educational equity, pay equity, reproductive rights, and family and medical leave. The association pursues its goals through its programs and publications and through congressional testimony.

POLITICAL ACTIVITY

AAUW provided supportive testimony at the hearings for the Equal Remedies Act. The group supports the enforcement of Title IX and the Higher Education Act.

FURTHER INFORMATION

Magazine, *Outlook*, which includes annual report.

AMERICAN ASSOCIATION OF WOMEN IN COMMUNITY COLLEGES

Yosemite Community College District
P.O. Box 4065
Modesto, California 95352
(209) 575-6508   fax: (209) 575-6565

The American Association of Women in Community Colleges (AAWCC) seeks to advance educational equity and excellence for women in community colleges.

ORIGIN AND DEVELOPMENT

AAWCC was founded in 1973, and today it is divided into ten regions, state sections, and local chapters.

ORGANIZATION AND FUNDING

A national board of directors meets semiannually. An annual business meeting for members is scheduled in conjunction with the American Association of Community Colleges'* convention each spring. The president since July 1993 has been Dr. Pamila Fisher. The entire operating budget is funded through membership fees.

POLICY CONCERNS AND TACTICS

Current policy concerns include access for women, worker preparation (particularly in nontraditional fields), upward mobility for community college women, diversity in the workplace, sexual harassment issues, and program funding issues related to the needs of women and minorities in community colleges. AAWCC attempts to meet its goals by means of national political advocacy; coalition building with similar organizations; leadership training and professional development at national, regional, and local levels; and various local programs and projects.

POLITICAL ACTIVITY

AAWCC cooperates with the joint legislative council and advocacy efforts of the American Association of Community Colleges and the Association of Community College Trustees.

FURTHER INFORMATION

No information available.

AMERICAN COLLEGE HEALTH ASSOCIATION
15879 Crabbs Branch Way
Rockville, Maryland 20855
(410) 859-1500   fax: (410) 859-1510

The American College Health Association (ACHA) is a nonprofit organization concerned with improving and extending health care services to college and university students.

ORIGIN AND DEVELOPMENT

Since 1920 ACHA has attempted to provide its institutional and individual members information needed to be effective administrators and health care providers. ACHA has developed a variety of programs and publications designed to serve its members in 3 general areas: management and administration, continuing professional growth, and client services. ACHA has 3,000 individual and 900 institutional members.

ORGANIZATION AND FUNDING

ACHA is governed by a nineteen-member board of directors, including a six-person executive committee. David P. Kraft was elected president in 1992. Charles H. Hartman has been executive director since 1990. ACHA has a staff of twenty-seven full-time employees and also hires student interns.

The 1992 annual operating budget was $2.1 million, with only 30 percent derived from membership fees. The remainder came from user fees and government grants and contracts. Over 80 percent of the budget goes toward membership services and publications.

POLICY CONCERNS AND TACTICS

ACHA is concerned with minimizing health care–related finances at universities. It attempts to assist members by providing information on this subject.

POLITICAL ACTIVITY

None.

FURTHER INFORMATION

A newsletter, Action; occasional papers; and an annual report.

AMERICAN COLLEGE TESTING PROGRAM
P.O. Box 168
Iowa City, Iowa 52243
(319) 337-1000

The American College Testing Program (ACT) is a nonprofit organization that seeks to provide numerous educational services to students, parents, high schools, colleges, professional associations, and government agencies.

ORIGIN AND DEVELOPMENT

ACT was founded in 1959 and is perhaps best known for its standardized college admissions testing program. According to its annual report, ACT also offers a variety of programs and services in the areas of college admissions and advising, career and educational planning, student aid, continuing education, and professional certification.

ORGANIZATION AND FUNDING

There are three levels within ACT's governance: the state councils, the corporation, and the board of trustees. The state councils are established by action of the institutions participating in ACT in states or regions that qualify for membership in the ACT corporation and are approved by the board of trustees.

Their membership consists of representatives of the sixty-two institutions that use ACT's programs and services. The ACT corporation is composed of the elected representatives of the thirty-one states and regions that participate in ACT as members. The elected members of the corporation serve three-year terms and can succeed themselves. The corporation meets annually. The board of trustees is composed of fifteen members. ACT's president, since 1988 Richard Ferguson, serves as an *ex officio* member; eight of the members are also members of the corporation; seven members are appointed at-large. The board normally meets four times a year. The members of the board are appointed for three-year terms and are eligible to succeed themselves. ACT employs a full-time staff of 900 people.

The 1992 annual operating budget was $60 million, all of it coming from user fees. Approximately 40 percent of expenditures went toward services, and the remainder was invested into personnel costs.

POLICY CONCERNS AND TACTICS

ACT is concerned with providing services, primarily student assessment, to clients. It typically does not become involved with policy issues. It does not attempt to affect legislation or public attitudes.

POLITICAL ACTIVITY

None.

FURTHER INFORMATION

Publications include a *Fact Sheet* and an annual report.

AMERICAN CONFERENCE OF ACADEMIC DEANS
1818 R Street, N.W.
Washington, D.C. 20009
(202) 387-3760

The American Conference of Academic Deans (ACAD) is a nonprofit organization that provides forums for discussion of varied issues affecting liberal arts deans and academic administrators.

ORIGIN AND DEVELOPMENT

ACAD was founded in 1943 and is affiliated with The Association of American Colleges.* The group has approximately 550 members.

ORGANIZATION AND FUNDING

ACAD is governed by an elected board of directors. Tamar March has been the board chair since 1991. Maria-Helena Price has been the executive director since 1989. ACAD has two full-time staff members.

Its current annual operating budget is $40,000, which comes from membership fees and user fees. Only 15 percent of the budget is expended on administration; the remainder goes toward membership services.

POLICY CONCERNS AND TACTICS

ACAD does not take policy positions, except generally in support of liberal arts education. It does not try to affect legislation.

POLITICAL ACTIVITY

None.

FURTHER INFORMATION

Proceedings from conferences.

AMERICAN COUNCIL FOR DRUG EDUCATION
204 Monroe Street, Suite 110
Rockville, Maryland 20850
(800) 488-DRUG

The American Council for Drug Education (ACDE) is a nonprofit organization that provides information, programs, and guidance to the public as well as to leaders in government, education, and private and nonprofit sectors.

ORIGIN AND DEVELOPMENT

Founded in 1977, ACDE is aided by a voluntary scientific advisory board that assists in translating scientific research on drug abuse into lay language.

ORGANIZATION AND FUNDING

ACDE has a seventeen-member board of directors. M.G.H. Gilliam is chair of the board. Since 1981 the executive director of ACDE has been Lee I. Dogoloff, a former presidential drug policy advisor. ACDE receives funding from numerous foundations and corporations, including IBM, Kellogg, American Express, and Bristol-Myers.

POLICY CONCERNS AND TACTICS

According to its brochure, ACDE concentrates on three areas:

—eliminating illegal drug use by shaping individual and societal attitudes and developing non-drug-use behaviors;

—ensuring that an independent, nonpartisan perspective influences public policy in drug abuse prevention; and

—responding to the public's need for factual information about drugs and effective programs to curb drug abuse.

ACDE addresses these concerns through the dissemination of information to members and lawmakers.

POLITICAL ACTIVITY

None.

FURTHER INFORMATION

No information available.

AMERICAN COUNCIL OF THE BLIND
1155 15th Street, N.W.
Washington, D.C. 20005
(202) 467-5081   fax: (202) 424-8666

The American Council of the Blind (ACB) is a nonprofit organization that serves the interests of blind and visually impaired people. According to association material, ACB attempts to meet the needs of blind and visually impaired people in part by facilitating public education programs designed to enhance greater awareness and understanding of the capabilities of blind people. It also offers scholarships to blind students in postsecondary educational and training programs.

ORIGIN AND DEVELOPMENT

ACB was founded in 1961 and incorporated in the District of Columbia. It has fifty-two state and regional affiliates and twenty-one national special interest and professional affiliates.

ORGANIZATION AND FUNDING

ACB's membership is over 25,000. Membership is not limited to blind or visually impaired individuals. With the exception of the secretary and treasurer positions, legal blindness is a requirement to serve on the elected 19-member board of directors. LeRoy Saunders is chair of the board, and Oral O. Miller heads the national office. There are 3 full-time, nonclerical staff members at the national office.

Latest available budget information suggests that ACB's operating budget averages over $500,000, the majority of which comes from thrift store operations. Expenses center on publications and public education.

POLICY CONCERNS AND TACTICS

ACB is interested in several current issues that affect its clientele, including the Americans with Disabilities Act. It has been an advocate of training airline personnel on how to serve blind passengers and encouraging the production and use of reading materials in accessible media including braille, recording, and large print. The group actively lobbies Congress and disseminates information to secure its goals and to affect public opinion.

POLITICAL ACTIVITY

ACB has testified on Capitol Hill in support of the enactment of the Americans with Disabilities Act and the reauthorization of the Education of the Handicapped Act.

FURTHER INFORMATION

Numerous publications including a monthly magazine, *The Braille Forum*, and an annual report.

AMERICAN EDUCATION FINANCE ASSOCIATION
5249 Cape Leyte Drive
Sarasota, Florida 34242
(813) 349-7580

The mission of the American Education Finance Association (AEFA) is to integrate research, policy, information, and discussion relating to issues in education finance. AEFA serves as a forum and information network for the exchange of ideas concerning education finance issues among academic researchers, program administrators, and policy makers in the United States, Canada, and other jurisdictions.

ORIGIN AND DEVELOPMENT

AEFA was organized in 1976 as an outgrowth of the University of Florida's National Education Finance Project (1972-1975).

ORGANIZATION AND FUNDING

AEFA is governed by a board of directors and an executive committee composed of the president, president-elect, executive director, and immediate past president. The 1992 president was Dr. C. Philip Kearny, and the executive director for 15 years has been George R. Babigian. The organization employs one part-time staffer and relies on volunteers for assisting the board, auditing, editing the newsletter, and writing for the yearbook.

AEFA is a nonprofit organization with an annual operating budget of approximately $40,000. A full 97 percent of budget funding is from membership fees, and the remainder is from private contributions; 55 percent of the budget is allocated to membership services, 25 percent to administration, and 20 percent to publications and the dissemination of information.

POLICY CONCERNS AND TACTICS

According to association literature, AEFA is concerned with all matters relating to school finance, including traditional school finance concepts, issues of public policy that have an impact on the field, and the review and debate of emerging issues. AEFA promotes research, development, experimentation, and reform in order to make the field of education finance responsive to emerging needs.

Toward this end, AEFA facilitates communication among the various groups and individuals involved through annual meetings, newsletters, and yearbooks. Through its various media AEFA encourages its members to raise issues and to debate them in order that all members and others in policy positions may improve their knowledge of education finance. According to association literature, AEFA supports as the fundamental purposes of education finance systems: (1) the provisions of resources adequate to accomplish educational goals; (2) the distribution of resources with the highest possible degree of equity for students and patrons of education; and (3) the efficient use of resources by all agencies providing education services.

POLITICAL ACTIVITY

AEFA does not attempt to influence legislation, does not support political candidates, and does not try to affect public opinion at large.

FURTHER INFORMATION

Newsletter and yearbook.

AMERICAN FEDERATION OF TEACHERS
555 New Jersey Avenue, N.W.
Washington, D.C. 20001
(202) 879-4400

The American Federation of Teachers (AFT) is a nonprofit organization that is concerned with improving working conditions for its members, as well as improving the quality of education for all students. As a union, it is affiliated with the American Federation of Labor–Congress of Industrial Organizations (AFL-CIO).

ORIGIN AND DEVELOPMENT

AFT was founded in 1916. Eight local teacher unions throughout the United States met at the City Club in Chicago to form the union. The charter was signed by Samuel Gompers. It has been closely aligned with organized labor since its inception and has supported unions outside of education and outside of the United States. There are currently several subsections in AFT: the Federation of Nurses and Health Professionals; the Federation of State Employees, Paraprofessionals and School-Related Personnel; and the Higher Education Steering Committee. There are 790,000 members of AFT.

ORGANIZATION AND FUNDING

The highest policy making body of AFT is the National Convention, where local delegates meet to vote on resolutions and elect the 38-member executive council. Albert Shanker has been the president since 1974. AFT has a full- time staff of 220 and does employ interns each year.

Annual operating budgets tend to surpass $54 million, over $50 million of it coming from membership dues with the remainder from interest and subscriptions. Expenses total over $56 million, with approximately half spent on membership services and a quarter going toward administrative and personnel costs.

POLICY CONCERNS AND TACTICS

AFT is concerned with all policies affecting education and is currently interested in the issues of school choice and vouchers, safety at schools, and collective bargaining rights of AFT members. The AFT legislation department lobbies in Congress and at the state and local levels. Information and policies are disseminated to local school districts. AFT also assists local chapters with contract negotiations.

POLITICAL ACTIVITY

AFT testified in opposition to the voucher program in the America 2000 Excellence in Education Act. During the hearings for the Twenty-First Century Teachers Act, it testified in support of funding for teacher education for individuals who already work in schools, tracking results of institutional support, targeting funds to individuals and not institutions, reversing authorization ceilings on Title I and Title II, redefining eligibility requirements for individual teachers for professional development academies, and making school restructuring the highest priority activity for Title III activities. At congressional hearings on the Education Excellence Act and the Equity and Excellence in Education Implementation Act, AFT argued that the Merit Schools Program be redirected toward locally based education reform activities and opposed the proposal that allocated $25 million to states to change their laws regarding certification. It also opposed the development of new magnet schools and advised Congress that funding for the Drug Free School program as well as scholarships in math and science were insufficient.

AFT presented a strong voice at the congressional hearings for the reauthorization of Title V of the Higher Education Act of 1965. In addition to advocating increases in the Pell Grant program and including aid to part-time students, it supported the establishment of a Professional Practice Schools program and grants for professional development. It argued that colleges and universities should set admission standards that are comparable to those found in other industrialized nations. It opposed the adoption of a singular model for professional development activities.

At the congressional hearings for the Prekindergarten Early Dropout Intervention Act of 1988, it questioned the strength of the bill's comprehensive initiative in early childhood education and the use of standardized testing. It also expressed concerns about the relationship between the bill's programs and those of Head Start and other existing programs focusing on early childhood development.

AFT was also active in providing supportive testimony during the reauthorization hearings for the Expiring Federal Elementary and Secondary Education Programs, Chapter 2 of the Education Consolidation and Improvement Act, and the Carl D. Perkins Vocational Education Act; Smart Start: The Community Collaborative for Early Childhood Development Act; and the National Demonstration Program for Educational Performance Agreements for School Restructuring.

According to Federal Election Commission data, the AFT-PAC (Committee on Political Education) contributed during the 1992 calendar year a total of $1,077,400 to 246 Democratic candidates, $23,850 to 14 Republican candidates, and $10,000 to 1 unaffiliated candidate. The group also endorsed Bill Clinton for the presidency in 1992.

FURTHER INFORMATION

Numerous publications including a biannual report. See also the following books about or relating to the AFT:

Berube, Maurice. *Teacher Politics: The Influence of Unions.* Westport, CT: Greenwood Press, 1988.

Braun, Robert J. *Teachers and Power: The Story of the American Federation of Teachers.* New York: Simon and Schuster, 1972.

Cresswell, Anthony, et al. *Teacher's Unions and Collective Bargaining in Public Education.* Berkeley, CA: McCutchan Publishing Corporation, 1980.

Eaton, William E. *The American Federation of Teachers 1916–1961: A History.* Edwardsville: Southern Illinois Press, 1975.

Eberts, Randall and Joe Stone. *Unions and Public Schools.* Lexington, MA: Lexington Books, 1984.

Johnson, Susan. *Teacher's Unions in Schools.* Philadelphia: Temple UP, 1984.

Murphy, Marjorie. *Blackboard Unions: The AFT and the NEA.* New York: Cornell UP, 1990.

Selden, David. *The Teacher's Rebellion.* Washington, DC: Howard UP, 1985.

Urban, Wayne. *Why Teachers Organized.* Detroit: Wayne State UP, 1982.

AMERICAN HOME ECONOMICS ASSOCIATION
1201 16th Street, N.W.
Washington, D.C. 20036
(703) 706-4600   fax: (703) 706-4663

The American Home Economics Association (AHEA) is a nonprofit educational and scientific organization dedicated to improving the quality of individual and family life through education, research, cooperative programs, and public information.

ORIGIN AND DEVELOPMENT

Home economics professionals held conferences at Lake Placid, New York, from 1898 to 1908. Discussions about the field of home economics culminated in the founding of AHEA in Washington, D.C., in 1909. Since then, AHEA has developed numerous sections: subject group sections, professional sections, 53 state affiliates, a Council of Accreditation, and a Council of Certification. There are 23,000 members of AHEA.

ORGANIZATION AND FUNDING

AHEA is governed by an assembly elected and convened at annual conferences. Virginia Caples was president for 1991–1992. Karl Weddle has been interim executive director since 1990. AHEA employs thirty-five full-time staff members, as well as several student interns each year.

AHEA's 1992 operating budget amounted to $2.3 million. The income was split rather evenly between membership fees and conference fees. Over half (52.8 percent) of funding is expended on administrative costs, and approximately 20 percent goes toward marketing. The remaining funds are directed toward membership services.

POLICY CONCERNS AND TACTICS

AHEA has a broad range of interests, including the funding of home economic programs in schools and universities as well as in cooperative extension programs. AHEA is particularly supportive of funding for consumer and home-making education programs under the Carl D. Perkins Vocational Education Act. In pursuing its interests, AHEA provides information to its members and to members of Congress.

POLITICAL ACTIVITY

None.

FURTHER INFORMATION

Journal of Home Economics, a refereed professional journal, was established in 1909 and is published quarterly. *Home Economics Research Journal*, a refereed professional research journal, was established in 1972 and is also published quarterly. *AHEA ACTION*, a newspaper reporting AHEA business and news items of interest to members, was established in 1974 and is published five times a year.

AMERICAN POLITICAL SCIENCE ASSOCIATION

1527 New Hampshire Avenue, N.W.
Washington, D.C. 20036
(202) 483-2512   fax: (202) 483-2657

The American Political Science Association (APSA) is a nonprofit organization that strives to facilitate and enhance research and education in political science, public policy, and government.

ORIGIN AND DEVELOPMENT

APSA was founded in 1903 to represent college faculty in political science and to separate political science departments from those in history and law. It cooperates with other social sciences and humanities societies in seeking support for National Science Foundation and National Endowment for the Humanities funding. Since 1976, APSA has participated in joint projects on the Constitution with the American History Association.

APSA has developed a number of subsections based on subject interest and social outlook. Subject areas include subfields in American politics, comparative analysis, and international relations. Sections based on political outlook include the New Caucus for Political Science, the Gay and Lesbian Caucus, and the Women's Caucus. There are more than 14,000 members in APSA.

ORGANIZATION AND FUNDING

Governance centers on elected national officers and council. The 1992 president was James Q. Wilson. Catherine E. Rudder has been the executive director since 1987. APSA has a full-time staff of twenty and hires five to eight student interns each year.

APSA's annual operating budgets tend to approximate $3 million. Over $1 million typically comes from membership dues and over $800,000 comes from grants. The remainder is derived from sales, conference fees, and dividends and interest. APSA spends approximately $2.9 million annually. More than $850,000 is earmarked for administration, and over $400,000 is spent on publications. The remainder is spent on special programs, marketing, and other membership services.

POLICY CONCERNS AND TACTICS

APSA does not take positions on public policies. The one exception was the Equal Rights Amendment, when APSA refused to hold national conferences in states that did not pass the amendment. Otherwise, it is concerned with the plight of minorities and women within the profession of political science, as well as the recognition of professional rights and collegiality for all political scientists. APSA staff does testify on Capitol Hill when research funding is at issue. APSA does not try to affect public policy.

POLITICAL ACTIVITY

None.

FURTHER INFORMATION

A refereed journal, *The American Political Science Review*, published quarterly; a journal, *PS*, focusing on news within the profession; and an annual financial statement.

AMERICAN SCHOOL COUNSELOR ASSOCIATION

5999 Stevenson Avenue
Alexandria, Virginia 22304
(703) 823-9800   fax: (703) 823-0252

The American School Counselor Association (ASCA) is a nonprofit organization that promotes excellence in professional school counseling.

ORIGIN AND DEVELOPMENT

ASCA was founded in 1952. A group of school counselors banded together to form a professional association to develop standards and ethical guidelines for school counseling. In 1953, ASCA became a charter member of the American Personnel and Guidance Association (now the American Counseling Association). Today there are 50 chartered state divisions and one in the District of Columbia. There are more than 13,000 members in ASCA.

ORGANIZATION AND FUNDING

A thirteen-member governing board is elected by membership and meets three times annually. An executive committee from that board carries on business in the interim. The president of ASCA, also on the governing board, takes a year's leave of absence from his or her employer to serve full-time. ASCA pays his or her salary to the employer. The current president is Nancy S. Perry. Since 1985 Carol Neiman has been the director of administrative services. ASCA has four full-time employees.

ASCA's operating budget for 1992 was approximately $700,000. One-half of the funding comes from membership fees, and the other half is derived from sales of publications, subscriptions, and conference fees. More than 40 percent of the revenues are spent on administration, and nearly the same proportion is spent on membership services. The remaining funds are targeted for publications.

POLICY CONCERNS AND TACTICS

ASCA is concerned with several issues affecting the profession of school counseling: (1) the use of noncredentialed personnel in counseling programs; (2) the fragmentation of school counseling programs due to budget constraints; (3) lack of understanding and support for comprehensive school counseling programs; and (4) lack of school counseling programs in elementary schools. ASCA addresses these issues through disseminating information to members and local school district officials.

POLITICAL ACTIVITY

ASCA tries to affect legislation about these issues through lobbying and the dissemination of information to state and federal elected officials.

FURTHER INFORMATION

Several publications including *The ASCA Counselor, Elementary School Guidance and Counseling,* and *The School Counselor.*

AMERICAN SOCIETY FOR TRAINING AND DEVELOPMENT

1640 King Street
Box 1443
Alexandria, Virginia 22313-2043
(703) 683-8100   fax: (703) 683-8103

The American Society for Training and Development (ASTD) is a nonprofit organization that provides employer-based training for the workforce.

ORIGIN AND DEVELOPMENT

ASTD was founded in 1944 when World War II caused a shortage of trained employees. The group was created to help in training a new workforce. There are more than 55,000 members of ASTD.

ORGANIZATION AND FUNDING

ASTD has an elected board of governors, which meets once a year. In the interim, a board of directors implements policies and programs. Stephen K. Merman was president in 1992, and Curtis E. Plott has been executive vice-president since 1980. ASTD has 120 full-time employees and accepts three to five student interns annually.

ASTD's 1992 operating budget was $15 million, mostly derived from three sources: membership fees, foundations, and user fees. More than 50 percent goes toward personnel and administration, 30 percent is spent on publications, 7 percent on membership services, and the remainder on marketing.

POLICY CONCERNS AND TACTICS

ASTD is interested in a variety of human resource development issues. Recently the group has attempted to place work-based training issues on the national agenda and lobbies for that purpose.

POLITICAL ACTIVITY

ASTD lobbies the Senate Labor and Human Resources Committee and the House Education and Labor Committee for legislation on education, training, and other human resource development issues. It also consults with the Senate Commerce, Science and Transportation Committee and House Science, Space and Technology Committee on developing high performance, competitive workplaces, technical assistance to American business, and the effects of technology implementation on the workforce and organization of the workplace. ASTD also advises the House Ways and Means Committee and Senate Finance Committee on issues pertaining to competitiveness and taxation of human resources.

FURTHER INFORMATION

Forty-eight-page publications catalog and a quarterly newsletter.

AMERICAN STUDIES CENTER
499 South Capitol Street, S.W., Suite 417
Washington, D.C. 20003
(202) 488-7122

The American Studies Center (ASC) is a nonprofit organization whose mission is to inform the public about the major policy issues that affect the general welfare of the United States. Its purpose is also to "reawaken" an understanding of and appreciation for American history, culture, and institutions.

ORIGIN AND DEVELOPMENT

ASC was founded in 1978.

ORGANIZATION AND FUNDING

ASC is governed by a board of trustees. Since 1978, James C. Roberts has been president, and Marc Lipsitz has been executive director. ASC has a full-time staff of eight employees and accepts three student interns each year. Annual operating budget is unavailable.

POLICY CONCERNS AND TACTICS

ASC's current focus is on the issue of "political correctness" at universities.

POLITICAL ACTIVITY

None.

FURTHER INFORMATION

No information available.

AMERICANS UNITED FOR SEPARATION OF CHURCH AND STATE
8120 Fenton Street
Silver Spring, Maryland 20910
(301) 589-3707

The Americans United for Separation of Church and State (AU) is a nonprofit organization that seeks to provide information about the U.S. Constitution's guarantee of religious freedoms. According to its annual report, AU believes that the principle of church-state separation is crucial both to good government and to the vitality and integrity of religious faith.

ORIGIN AND DEVELOPMENT

AU was founded in 1947 by a group of political, religious, and educational leaders.

ORGANIZATION AND FUNDING

AU is governed by a 15-member board of trustees and a 125-member National Advisory Council (NAC). The board of trustees, elected from among the NAC, meets periodically through the year to make decisions about organizational governance and policy. Trustees serve for a 3-year period and are eligible for reelection for two additional terms. The NAC meets once a year (during the national conference) to approve the organization's budget, select officers and trustees, and address other policy concerns. NAC members serve for a 3-year period and are also eligible for reelection for 2 additional terms. Foy Valentine is president, and Robert L. Maddox is executive director. AU has a full-time staff of sixteen employees.

AU's 1991 revenues amounted to over $2.3 million; the overwhelming majority came from general contributions. Total expenses surpassed $1.5 million. Approximately $800,000 went toward administrative and personnel costs, with the remainder going to educational programs, a national conference, and membership marketing.

POLICY CONCERNS AND TACTICS

AU has two major educational initiatives: (1) an annual national conference on ''Church and State''; and (2) an annual Madison/Jefferson Student Seminar for law and theology students, which is designed to help students understand how religious freedom developed in the United States. AU tries to affect policy and opinion through radio and television programs, as well as the dissemination of literature.

POLITICAL ACTIVITY

AU speaks on Capitol Hill on a variety of educational issues relating to ''church and state.'' AU testified in support of the Bush administration's America 2000 education package.

FURTHER INFORMATION

Monthly magazine, *Church & State*, and an annual report.

ASSOCIATED COLLEGES OF THE MIDWEST
18 South Michigan Avenue, Suite 1010
Chicago, Illinois 60603
(312) 263-5000   fax: (312) 263-5879

The Associated Colleges of the Midwest (ACM) represents fourteen independent liberal arts colleges located in Illinois, Iowa, Minnesota, Wisconsin, and Colorado. According to association literature, the chief purpose of ACM is to enrich the curricula of its member institutions in ways they could not accomplish alone.

ORIGIN AND DEVELOPMENT

ACM was founded in 1958 as schools of the Mid-west Athletic Conference saw fit to collaborate in academic areas.

ORGANIZATION AND FUNDING

ACM is governed by a board of directors comprised of the presidents of each member institution. An advisory board of deans, comprised of the chief academic officer of each member institution, assists with program oversight. The chair of the board is David Marker, and the current president is Elizabeth R. Hayford. She has held this position since 1984. The association employs a staff of eleven, all full-time.

ACM is a 501(c)(3) organization with an annual operating budget of $5 million. A full 90 percent of funding comes from academic program tuition, and 10 percent from membership fees; 90 percent of the budget is allocated to membership services (academic programs, faculty workshops) and 10 percent to administrative expenses.

POLICY CONCERNS AND TACTICS

ACM is devoted primarily to academic concerns, especially curriculum development. Toward this end, ACM works closely with faculty and administrators, offering a variety of member benefits: off-campus study programs, faculty development programs, information exchange services, and a variety of student services and resources.

ACM is also interested in federal policy on higher education, particularly financial aid programs. Since 1966, ACM has operated an office in Washington, D.C., to assist member colleges in obtaining government and foundation grants and to keep the colleges informed about federal legislation and policies affecting higher education.

POLITICAL ACTIVITY

ACM has no active legislative or political agenda; the association seeks merely to keep members abreast of relevant policy developments.

FURTHER INFORMATION

No information available.

ASSOCIATION FOR CHILDHOOD EDUCATION INTERNATIONAL
11141 Georgia Avenue, Suite 200
Wheaton, Maryland 20902
(301) 572-4852   fax: (301) 942-3012

The Association for Childhood Education International (ACEI) is a nonprofit organization that promotes the inherent rights of the child in the home, school, and community and facilitates the professional development of the professionals who care for them.

ORIGIN AND DEVELOPMENT

ACEI was founded in 1892. A group of kindergarten teachers met in Saratoga Springs, New York, to organize a movement to professionalize kindergarten teachers, known at that time as the International Kindergarten Union. Founders were members of the National Education Association.* Today ACEI has several subsections: infancy, early childhood, and later childhood/early adolescence. The group has 14,000 members.

ORGANIZATION AND FUNDING

ACEI is governed by an executive board of elected members. Glen Dixon was president in 1992. Gerald Odland has been executive director since 1991. There are nine full-time staff members.

ACEI's 1992 annual budget was $90,000, with 63 percent from membership fees and the remaining from conferences and publications. Approximately 60 percent of the budget is allocated for administration and personnel and the remaining portion going toward membership services, conferences, and publications.

POLICY CONCERNS AND TACTICS

ACEI is concerned about four issues: (1) school restructuring and standards; (2) cultural rights and diversity; (3) children of families at risk; and (4) assessment and testing. It tries to affect policy through publications and position papers.

POLITICAL ACTIVITY

None.

FURTHER INFORMATION

No information available.

ASSOCIATION FOR COMMUNITY-BASED EDUCATION
1806 Vernon Street, N.W.
Washington, D.C. 20009
(202) 462-6333   fax: (202) 232-8044

The Association for Community-Based Education (ACBE) is a nonprofit organization dedicated to advancing education that is derived from the resources of communities.

ORIGIN AND DEVELOPMENT

ACBE was founded in 1976 and today has 200 members.

ORGANIZATION AND FUNDING

ACBE is governed by an eleven-member board of directors. John Zippert was the president in 1992. Chris Zachariadis has been executive director since 1976. ACBE has a full-time staff of six employees.

ACBE's 1992 operating budget was $750,000. Much of the funding is derived from foundations and corporations. Expenditures consist of administration costs (20 percent) and membership services (80 percent).

POLICY CONCERNS AND TACTICS

ACBE is concerned with four issues: literacy, community economic development, community-based colleges, and increasing leadership opportunities among youth. ACBE affects policy and public opinion through publications and brochures.

POLITICAL ACTIVITY

None.

FURTHER INFORMATION

No information available.

ASSOCIATION FOR GERONTOLOGY IN HIGHER EDUCATION
600 Maryland Avenue, N.W., Wing 204
Washington, D.C. 20024
(202) 429-9277   fax: (202) 429-6097
The Association for Gerontology in Higher Education (AGHE) is a nonprofit organization that seeks to advance gerontology as a field of study in institutions of higher learning.

ORIGIN AND DEVELOPMENT

AGHE was founded in 1974. Members of the Gerontological Society of America, a membership association of researchers in the field of gerontology, decided that there needed to be a national organization solely devoted to strengthening educational programs in gerontology and advocating for their development and growth. There are about 330 institutional members in AGHE.

ORGANIZATION AND FUNDING

AGHE is governed by a nine-member board of directors elected by the membership. The nine elected officers and additional appointed committee chairs constitute the executive committee. J. Richard Connelly was the president for

1992. Elizabeth B. Douglas has been the executive director since 1980. AGHE has a full-time staff of two people. It accepts one or two student interns annually.

The 1992 operating budget was approximately $450,000, 38 percent from membership fees, 31 percent from conference fees, 18 percent from grants, and the remainder from publications, investments, and sales. Administrative costs take 40 percent of the budget, and membership services account for nearly 60 percent.

POLICY CONCERNS AND TACTICS

AGHE is concerned with aging-related research, education, and training. It has supported the reauthorization of the Older Americans Act and the implementation of the 1992 White House Conference on Aging. It addresses these issues through publications, advocacy, research, and informing its membership on critical issues.

POLITICAL ACTIVITY

AGHE works with the House and Senate staff of appropriations and authorization committees and by testifying when appropriate before congressional committees.

FURTHER INFORMATION

No information available.

ASSOCIATION FOR THE ADVANCEMENT OF HEALTH EDUCATION
1900 Association Drive
Reston, Virginia 22091
(703) 476-3400

The Association for the Advancement of Health Education (AAHE) is a professional membership organization dedicated to advancing the field of health education.

ORIGIN AND DEVELOPMENT

Founded in 1937, AAHE is 1 of 6 associations that make up the American Alliance for Health, Physical Education, Recreation and Dance (AAHPERD). AAHE has over 10,000 members.

ORGANIZATION AND FUNDING

AAHE is governed by a board of directors and a board of governors of AAHPERD. Thomas O'Rourke has been president since 1988, and Beck Smith has been executive director since 1986. AAHE employs six full-time staff members. Annual budget is unavailable.

POLICY CONCERNS AND TACTICS

AAHE is concerned with all health education issues. The group testifies on Capitol Hill and keeps its members informed on legislative developments through a computer network called the Health Education Action Link (HEAL Network).

POLITICAL ACTIVITY

AAHE testified at the hearings for the Jacob K. Javits Gifted and Talented Children and Youth Education Act and the Office of Comprehensive School Health Education Act. At both hearings, AAHE advocated giving schools grants to enhance quality health education programs. Further, it argued that the Department of Education should: (1) develop support staff with expertise in health education to assist in internal policy and program development; and (2) assist state and local agencies in finding technical assistance located in other federal departments.

FURTHER INFORMATION

A monthly newspaper, *Update*; a bimonthly publication, *Journal of Health Education*; and a bimonthly newsletter, *HE-XTRA*.

ASSOCIATION FOR THE BEHAVIORAL SCIENCES AND MEDICAL EDUCATION
6728 Old McLean Village Drive
McLean, Virginia 22101
(703) 556-9222

The Association for the Behavioral Sciences and Medical Education (AB-SAME) is a nonprofit organization that seeks to integrate the knowledge, skills, and perspectives of the social and behavior sciences into medical education.

ORIGIN AND DEVELOPMENT

ABSAME was founded in 1975 after several years of discussions between physicians and behavioral scientists. Initially these discussions were facilitated through a program funded by the National Institute of Child Health and Human Development. ABSAME has a membership of 120.

ORGANIZATION AND FUNDING

ABSAME is governed by a twelve-member board of directors elected by the membership. Margaret Moore-West was the president for 1992. Carol Ann Kiner has been the executive director since 1989. There are no full-time staff members. Information about annual revenues is not available.

POLICY CONCERNS AND TACTICS

ABSAME's primary concern is to integrate behavioral science content into the curriculum of medical schools. This is done through publications and conferences.

POLITICAL ACTIVITY

None.

FURTHER INFORMATION

Newsletter.

ASSOCIATION FOR THE EDUCATION OF TEACHERS IN SCIENCE

5040 Haley Center
Auburn University
Auburn, Alabama 36849-5212
(205) 844-6799   fax: (205) 844-5785

The Association for the Education of Teachers in Science (AETS) seeks to foster the educational improvement of science teachers.

ORIGIN AND DEVELOPMENT

AETS was founded in 1930, and 1993 members totaled 737.

ORGANIZATION AND FUNDING

The association is governed by a board of directors. The 1992-1993 president was Peter Rubba, and the executive secretary since 1988 has been William E. Baird. AETS does not have any paid staff and relies on volunteers for its entire operation. AETS is a tax-exempt organization. Its 1993 operating budget was $54,000. Approximately 52 percent of funding was derived from journal publications, 27 percent from the annual meeting, 13 percent from annual dues, and 8 percent from miscellaneous sources. The 1993 budget allocated approximately 54 percent to publications, 27 percent to the annual meeting, and 19 percent to administrative and other miscellaneous expenses.

POLICY CONCERNS AND TACTICS

The sole concern of AETS is the educational development of its members. This is accomplished through annual conferences, publications, and the conferring of four teaching awards each year.

POLITICAL ACTIVITY

None.

FURTHER INFORMATION

Journal of Science Teacher Education, Science Education, newsletter, and yearbooks.

ASSOCIATION OF ACADEMIC HEALTH CENTERS
1400 16th Street, N.W., Suite 410
Washington, D.C. 20036
(202) 265-9600   fax: (202) 265-7514

The Association of Academic Health Centers (AHC) is a national, nonprofit organization dedicated to improving the health of the people through leadership and cooperative action with others. AHC seeks to influence public dialogue on significant health and science policy issues, to advance education for health professionals, to promote biomedical and health services research, and to enhance patient care.

ORIGIN AND DEVELOPMENT

AHC was founded in 1969. A group of senior health administrators began meeting to discuss mutual health center problems. Membership is on an institutional basis. Since 1969 AHC has emphasized cooperation with other educational and health-related organizations, including the Association of American Medical Colleges,* the American Association of Colleges of Nursing, American Association of Colleges of Pharmacy, the Association of Schools of Public Health,* and the Association of Schools of Allied Health Professions. AHC has developed several task forces to deal with critical issues: health care delivery, health promotion and disease prevention, human resources for health, leadership and institutional values, and science policy. There are 103 members in AHC.

ORGANIZATION AND FUNDING

A nine-member board of directors is elected. The president is a full-time position, held by Roger J. Bulger since 1987. AHC has a full-time staff of eight people and accepts one student intern per year.

The 1992 operating budget was $1 million, with 90 percent from membership fees and 10 percent from foundations. The majority (80 percent) goes toward membership services, and the remainder goes toward administration and personnel (15 percent) and publications (5 percent).

POLICY CONCERNS AND TACTICS

AHC supports a program of activities that seeks to: (1) provide a forum for the exchange of information on a broad range of issues related to the education and training of health professionals, biomedical and health services research, and the organization and delivery of health care services; (2) enhance the involvement of the association and its members in the national dialogue on health and science policy issues; (3) increase liaison activities with local and state officials, members of Congress, and officials in the executive branch of the federal government; (4) increase liaison with appropriate education and health-related associations and professional groups; (5) explore and study issues that are related to the collective interests of its member institutions; (6) increase coordination of health-related schools programs both within and among institutions, and interdisciplinary and interprofessional concerns; and (7) disseminate issues and ideas through association publications to the members, lawmakers, media, and other interested parties.

POLITICAL ACTIVITY

AHC provided supportive testimony at the hearings to amend Part D (Provide for Income Dependent Education Assistance) of Title IV of the (reauthorized) Higher Education Act of 1965.

FURTHER INFORMATION

Numerous publications and an annual report.

THE ASSOCIATION OF AMERICAN COLLEGES
1818 R Street, N.W.
Washington, D.C. 20009
(202) 387-3760   fax: (202) 265-9532

The Association of American Colleges (AAC) is a nonprofit organization dedicated to advancing liberal arts education. Its mission is to strengthen undergraduate curriculum, improve teaching and learning, increase opportunities for access and achievement, and develop institutional and academic leadership.

ORIGIN AND DEVELOPMENT

AAC was founded in 1914. According to *AAC at Seventy-Five,* AAC was created to address the problem of many institutions calling themselves "liberal arts colleges" yet having little college-level curriculum and standards. A total of 150 college presidents met at the invitation of the Council of Church Boards of Education. To be eligible for membership in AAC, the group decided that a college had to require 14 Carnegie units for admission into the freshman class and the completion of 120 semester hours of course work for graduation.

ORGANIZATION AND FUNDING

Membership in AAC includes 636 private and public 2- and 4-year colleges and universities. It is governed by a 19-member board of directors, elected by membership. Linda Koch Lorimer has been elected as board chair for a one-year term, and Paula P. Brownlee has been president since 1990. AAC has a full-time staff of thirty employees.

Recent budgets have totaled approximately $2 million, of which approximately $1.3 million comes from membership dues, conference fees, administrative fees and service charges, and publications. Over 90 percent of expenditures go toward programs and membership services.

POLICY CONCERNS AND TACTICS

According to its annual report, AAC is concerned with four issues: strengthening undergraduate curriculum, improving teaching and learning, increasing opportunities for women for access and achievement, and developing institutional and academic leadership. According to its annual report, AAC addresses these issues through a number of projects, including the Project on Liberal Learning, Study-in-Depth, and the Arts and Sciences Major; Engaging Cultural Legacies; the Asheville Institute on General Education; Program on Studying Philanthropy; Curriculum Assessment Service; The International Dimension in U.S. Higher Education; Planning for Campus Leadership; AAC/Vassar Project on Community College Transfer; and General Education.

AAC does not try to affect legislation. Through dissemination of publications, AAC attempts to educate the public about the importance of liberal education.

POLITICAL ACTIVITY

None.

FURTHER INFORMATION

AAC at Seventy-Five (Washington, D.C.: Association of American Colleges, 1988); and several additional publications, including an annual report.

ASSOCIATION OF AMERICAN LAW SCHOOLS
1201 Connecticut Avenue, N.W., Suite 800
Washington, D.C. 20036
(202) 296-8851   fax: (202) 296-8869

The Association of American Law Schools (AALS) seeks to improve the legal profession through legal education. It is an association of law schools and serves as the law teachers' learned society.

ORIGIN AND DEVELOPMENT

The AALS was founded in 1900 during a meeting held at Saratoga Springs, New York; 32 law schools became charter members of the Association. Professor Michael H. Cardozo of Cornell University became the association's first executive director in 1963 and established the association's national office. AALS was incorporated as a nonprofit organization in 1971. Of the 176 American Bar Association (ABA)–approved law schools, 158 are members of AALS.

ORGANIZATION AND FUNDING

The governing body of the association is called the House of Representatives, composed of one representative from each member school. The House of Representatives elects an executive committee, which has the responsibility of conducting the affairs of the association in the interim between the annual meetings of the House. The president (since 1993, Curtis Berger), president-elect, immediate past president, and six committee members constitute the executive committee. Standing and special committees are established by the executive committee. The AALS has a full-time staff of approximately twenty and utilizes volunteers as committee members, section chairs, speakers, and site evaluators. The executive director since 1992 has been Carl Monk.

AALS is a 501(c)(3) organization. Approximately 50 percent of the association's income is from membership dues. Fees support certain services and functions, such as the annual meeting, professional development programs, and faculty recruitment services.

POLICY CONCERNS AND TACTICS

AALS is concerned solely with the professional advancement and development of its member institutions and their faculty. Toward this end, the association maintains a variety of standing committees, holds an annual meeting and conference, provides a variety of faculty recruitment services, sponsors a variety of professional development programs, and publishes a range of materials of interest to the legal profession. The association also monitors public policy activity that might be of interest to members through a governmental relations committee.

POLITICAL ACTIVITY

None.

FURTHER INFORMATION

Journal of Legal Education, annual meeting proceedings, directory, newsletter, handbook, and survey information from law faculty and deans.

ASSOCIATION OF AMERICAN MEDICAL COLLEGES
2450 N Street, N.W.
Washington, D.C. 20037-1126
(202) 828-0400

The Association of American Medical Colleges (AAMC) is a nonprofit organization dedicated to improving the nation's health through the advancement of academic medicine. AAMC works with its members to set a national agenda for medical education, biomedical research, and health care. It also assists its members by providing services at the national level that facilitate the accomplishment of their missions.

ORIGIN AND DEVELOPMENT

AAMC was founded in 1876. Representatives of 22 medical colleges met for the purpose of reforming medical education by raising the standards that medical schools required of their graduates. At that meeting it was recommended that medical schools offer 3 courses of lectures and that all candidates for graduation be examined in all branches of medicine. AAMC works closely with several organizations: the Liaison Committee on Medical Education, the American Medical Association, the national Board of Medical Examiners, and the Accreditation Council for Graduate Medical Education. There are 787 institutional members in AAMC.

ORGANIZATION AND FUNDING

Governance is diffused: AAMC Executive Council; AAMC Assembly; the Council of Deans; the Council of Teaching Hospitals; the Council of Academic Societies; Organization of Student Representatives; and the Organization of Resident Representatives. AAMC Assembly determines policy, and the AAMC Executive Council implements policy. J. Robert Buchanan was the 1992 president. Since 1986, Robert G. Petersdorf has been executive director. AAMC has a full-time staff of 214 employees.

AAMC's 1992 operating budget was $20.1 million; 43 percent came from member programs, 37 percent from dues, and the remainder from publications and investments. Expenses equaled income, with approximately 78 percent going toward administrative and personnel costs and the remainder going toward membership services.

POLICY CONCERNS AND TACTICS

AAMC is concerned with several issues: support for biomedical research, financing of medical education, support for the use of animals in research and education, scientific misconduct and fraud in research, and participation of and support for minorities in medicine. AAMC tries to address these issues through studies and legislative testimony.

POLITICAL ACTIVITY

AAMC was involved in the reauthorization hearings for the Stafford Loan Program of the Higher Education Act of 1965. It supported increasing the number of Patricia Roberts Harris graduate fellowships, lengthening Title IV student loans deferment to at least three years, and increasing loan limits. It also testified in support of allowing graduate and professional students to participate in the Perkins loan program, and increasing funding for Title III and other programs for disadvantaged and underrepresented minorities.

FURTHER INFORMATION

Annual report.

ASSOCIATION OF AMERICAN MILITARY COLLEGES AND SCHOOLS OF THE U.S.

See Council for American Private Education.

ASSOCIATION OF AMERICAN VETERINARY MEDICAL COLLEGES

1023 15th Street, N.W.
Washington, D.C. 20005-2602
(202) 371-9195   fax: (202) 842-4360

The Association of American Veterinary Medical Colleges (AAVMC) is a nonprofit organization representing the scientific and educational concerns of veterinary medical schools and colleges.

ORIGIN AND DEVELOPMENT

AAVMC was founded in 1968. Veterinary medical deans desired an organization to speak to their collective interests in research and education. AAVMC has developed close relations with the American Veterinary Medical Association and with the Federated Associations of Schools of the Health Professions. There are thirty-nine institutional members in AAVMC.

ORGANIZATION AND FUNDING

AAVMC is governed by an executive committee of six voting members. Ed Andrews was president in 1992. Billy E. Hooper has been executive director since 1986. AAVMC has a full-time staff of two employees.

AAVMC had a 1992 operating budget of $265,000, with 81 percent from membership fees and the remainder from conference fees and interest on reserves. Expenditures matched income, with 20 percent going towards administrative costs, 62 percent to membership services, and the remainder going towards publications and lobbying activities.

POLICY CONCERNS AND TACTICS

AAVMC is concerned with several issues: outcome assessment in higher education, student financial aid, federal funding of research, animal welfare, and legal control of veterinary medicine. AAVMC has been active in supporting the reauthorization of the Higher Education Act and the Public Health Service Act. It has an ongoing National Minority Recruitment Project.

AAVMC addresses these issues through research and publication, as well as extensive liaison with legislators and other professional organizations.

POLITICAL ACTIVITY

None.

FURTHER INFORMATION

Annual report.

ASSOCIATION OF COLLEGIATE SCHOOLS OF ARCHITECTURE

1735 New York Avenue, N.W.
Washington, D.C. 20006
(202) 785-2324

The Association of Collegiate Schools of Architecture (ACSA) is a nonprofit organization that seeks to advance the quality of architectural education.

It provides a major forum for ideas on the leading edge of architectural thought.

ORIGIN AND DEVELOPMENT

ACSA was founded in 1912.

ORGANIZATION AND FUNDING

ACSA has over 150 schools in several membership categories. These include full membership for all accredited programs in the United States and government-sanctioned schools in Canada; candidate membership for schools seeking accreditation; and affiliate membership for 2-year, foreign, and other nonaccredited programs. In addition, there are approximately 750 supporting members composed of architecture firms, product associations, and individuals. It is governed by a 13-member board of directors, elected by the full membership category schools. John Meunier is the current president, and Richard E. McCommons is the executive director. ACSA has a full-time staff of 7 employees.

Annual revenues have averaged over $1 million over the past several years. Most of the revenues are derived from membership, program fees, contracts, and grants. About 20 percent of expenses goes toward administrative costs, with the remainder divided relatively equally among scholarships, publications, conferences, and programs.

POLICY CONCERNS AND TACTICS

In very general terms, ACSA is concerned with advancing architectural education. It does so through publications.

POLITICAL ACTIVITY

None.

FURTHER INFORMATION

Journal of Architectural Education, a refereed journal that is published quarterly; *ACSA News*, a monthly newsletter; a survey guide to architecture schools in North America; *ACSA Annual Meeting Proceedings*; and an annual report.

ASSOCIATION OF EPISCOPAL COLLEGES

815 Second Avenue
New York, New York 10017-4594
(212) 986-0989   fax: (212) 986-5039

The mission of the Association of Episcopal Colleges (AEC) is to foster international and intercultural education and volunteer service as a part of undergraduate education.

ORIGIN AND DEVELOPMENT

AEC was founded in 1962 to raise funds on behalf of all Episcopal colleges but with a special emphasis on support for the historically black colleges. The association works closely with the Partnership for Service Learning and with the newly formed Colleges and Universities of the Anglican Communion.

ORGANIZATION AND FUNDING

The president of the association is responsible for the general operation of the organization, while a board of trustees determines policy issues. According to current by-laws, the president of one of the twelve-member Episcopal colleges or universities shall serve as chair of the board of trustees. The president of the association (since 1985) is Linda A. Chisholm, and the current chair of the board of trustees is Prezell Robinson (since 1986). The association employs four full-time staff members (one clerical) and occasionally relies on the advice of outside financial managers.

Although annual budget figures are unavailable, approximately 25 percent of the association's funding comes from membership fees, 20 percent from endowment earnings, 20 percent from private contributions, 20 percent from the Partnership for Service Learning, 10 percent from foundation support, and 5 percent from user fees. Approximately 30 percent of the budget is allocated to administration, 50 percent to student programs, and 20 percent to publicity and admissions materials.

POLICY CONCERNS AND TACTICS

The AEC is interested in expanding its "Learning Through Service" programs to include more student volunteers and more service agencies that might sponsor learning experiences for affiliated students. The association is also interested in the creation of a national youth service program and federal grant programs related to international and intercultural education. The AEC works closely with member colleges to place students in meaningful volunteer service assignments and works closely with parishes and service agencies to facilitate service opportunities and programs.

POLITICAL ACTIVITY

The association has joined forces with the Partnership in Service Learning in an effort to influence national youth service legislation, especially in terms of developing service criteria. The AEC does not endorse or support political candidates and does not otherwise attempt to influence public opinion.

FURTHER INFORMATION

No information available.

ASSOCIATION OF HIGHER EDUCATION FACILITIES OFFICERS

1446 Duke Street
Alexandria, Virginia 22314-3492
(703) 684-1446   fax: (703) 549-2772

The Association of Higher Education Facilities Officers (AHEFO) seeks to preserve and enhance the quality of the facilities required to meet the needs of higher education.

ORIGIN AND DEVELOPMENT

AHEFO was founded in 1914 and developed as an extension of the "big ten" group of supporters of buildings and grounds. AHEFO maintains close ties with the Council of Higher Education Management Associations and with the Washington Higher Education Secretariat. AHEFO maintains a membership of 1,600 institutions and 4,150 individuals.

ORGANIZATION AND FUNDING

The organization is governed by a twenty-one-person board of directors, including an executive committee of six officers elected by the membership as a whole, fourteen delegates representing seven regions, and one at-large appointee. The president for 1992-1993 was Donald L. Mackel, and the executive director since 1985 has been Walter Schaw. AHEFO employs sixteen full-time staff members (eight nonclerical), and relies on volunteers to do writing, lecturing, long-term committee work, short-term task force work, and evaluations. AHEFO also relies on a variety of outside professionals to develop programs requiring special expertise. AHEFO maintains a special subsection, the Australia International Region.

AHEFO is a 501(c)(3) organization with an annual budget of $2.3 million. Between 65 and 67 percent of funding comes from user fees, 30 percent from membership fees, between 2 and 4 percent from foundation support, and approximately 1 percent from endowment earnings. AHEFO allocates between 22 and 23 percent of its budget to administration, 26 percent to publications and publicity, 24 percent to educational seminars, 20 percent to an annual meeting and exhibition, between 5 and 6 percent to membership services (directory), and 2 percent to lobbying efforts (regulatory monitoring and liaison services).

POLICY CONCERNS AND TACTICS

AHEFO's immediate concern is with short-term decision making that has long-term adverse consequences. Specifically, the members are concerned with the "downsizing" of facilities, especially insofar as such downsizing accelerates the extent of long-term deferred maintenance. Their goals are: (1) to update the status of deferred maintenance backlogs (currently around $100 billion); (2) to define and promote leadership for facility administrators in middle management, as well as define the consequences of such training; and (3) to expand concepts and standards of space management as a critical need in the body of field knowledge.

Toward such ends, AHEFO seeks to foster communication between facilities officers and business officers and to enhance such communication with more comprehensive data acquisition. In turn, AHEFO wishes to increase communication between presidents, trustees, and other decision makers with policy implications involving the data. AHEFO also seeks to continue the process of identifying facilities as capital assets and to continue to develop and promulgate the financial theory required to preserve such assets. Such efforts involve influencing public opinion by documenting and reporting on the condition of facilities.

POLITICAL ACTIVITY

AHEFO offers nonpartisan testimony on the impact of proposed legislation, especially in terms of cost effectiveness. AHEFO does not endorse or support any political candidates.

FURTHER INFORMATION

Annual report; directory; and *The Decaying American Campus* and *Custodial Staffing Guidelines for Educational Facilities* research reports.

ASSOCIATION OF JESUIT COLLEGES AND UNIVERSITIES
1424 16th Street, N.W., Suite 504
Washington, D.C. 20036
(202) 667-3889

The Association of Jesuit Colleges and Universities (AJCU) did not respond to our inquiries. According to the 1993 edition of the *Encyclopedia of Associations*, AJCU was founded in 1970 and has twenty-eight members. Its president is the Reverend Paul S. Tipton. AJCU has a staff of six and an annual budget of approximately $200,000. Its primary purpose is to assist, by providing workshops and statistical information, institutions of higher education that are operated by the Jesuits. AJCU has several publications, including the *Annual Directory of Jesuit High Schools, Colleges and Universities* and a monthly report called the *Association of Jesuit Colleges and Universities—Higher Education Report*.

ASSOCIATION OF MERCY COLLEGES
c/o Dr. William P. Garvey
Mercyhurst College
501 E. 38th Street Boulevard
Erie, Pennsylvania 16501
(814) 825-0269

The Association of Mercy Colleges (AMC) did not respond to our inquiries. According to the 1993 edition of the *Encyclopedia of Associations*, AMC was founded in 1982 and has eighteen members consisting of colleges operated by the Religious Sisters of Mercy. Its president is Dr. William P. Garvey. The primary purpose of AMC is to facilitate better cooperation and communication among Mercy colleges. Three times a year, it publishes the *Association of Mercy Colleges—Newsletter.*

ASSOCIATION OF PRESBYTERIAN COLLEGES AND UNIVERSITIES
100 Witherspoon Street
Louisville, Kentucky 40202-1396
(502) 569-5606   fax: (502) 569-5018

The mission of the Association of Presbyterian Colleges and Universities (APCU) is to recognize the common heritage of its member institutions and their mission to serve the church by providing their students a quality education grounded in the values of the Reformed tradition.

ORIGIN AND DEVELOPMENT

The APCU was founded in 1983 as a result of the merger of the Association of Presbyterian Colleges and the Presbyterian College Union. The organization today maintains a membership of sixty-eight colleges and universities.

ORGANIZATION AND FUNDING

The APCU is governed by the membership at large during the annual meeting, with the executive committee handling between-meeting business. The 1992-1993 president was John Griffith, and the executive director since 1990 has been Duncan Ferguson. The association maintains a staff of three (two full-time).

The APCU operates on an annual budget of approximately $40,000. Funding for the operating budget is derived from membership fees and support from the Presbyterian Church (U.S.A.) Office of Higher Education. Budget allocation figures are unavailable.

POLICY CONCERNS AND TACTICS

The major concern of APCU is to promote and strengthen its member institutions. In collaboration with the Presbyterian Church (U.S.A.)'s Committee on Higher Education, APCU offers a range of services, including consulting, advocacy, organization, fund raising, publications, and chaplain support.

In addition, APCU disseminates major policy papers related to studies conducted by the Presbyterian Church (U.S.A.) to be used in curriculum development. Recent policy topics include peace studies, environmentalism, and the relationship of Presbyterianism to science and technology issues. The association is also interested in developing global awareness and international programs.

POLITICAL ACTIVITY

APCU engages in an indirect form of political activity through the dissemination of policy papers on a variety of current issues. More direct political activity is largely limited to advocacy for public policy issues that impact higher education through the National Association of Independent Colleges and Universities.* The association does not support or endorse political candidates and does no lobbying.

FURTHER INFORMATION

Services brochure, COHERE (newsletter of Committee on Higher Education), occasional papers on the church's mission in higher education, and policy papers.

ASSOCIATION OF SCHOOL BUSINESS OFFICIALS INTERNATIONAL
11401 North Shore Drive
Reston, Virginia 22090
(703) 478-0405   fax: (703) 478-0205

The Association of School Business Officials International (ASBOI) is a nonprofit organization dedicated to enhancing the professionalism of school business management executives through professional development.

ORIGIN AND DEVELOPMENT

Founded in 1910, ASBOI was originally known as the National Association of School Accounting Officers. In 1922 ASBOI absorbed the National Association of School Building Officials. Since then, it has developed 58 state and Canadian province affiliates. ASBOI has 6,400 members.

ORGANIZATION AND FUNDING

ASBOI is governed by a six-member elected executive committee. Jack Morris was the 1992 president. Don I. Tharpe has been the executive director since 1989. ASBOI has a full-time staff of eighteen employees.

ASBOI had a 1992 operating budget of $2 million. Approximately one-third comes from each of these categories: membership fees, annual meeting fees, and publications. About one-third of the budget goes toward administrative and personnel costs with the remainder going toward membership services and publications.

POLICY CONCERNS AND TACTICS

ASBOI is concerned about increasing more international membership and generating more nondues revenue. It also wishes to provide awards for school districts. It does not attempt to affect legislation or public opinion, except indirectly through promotional pieces.

POLITICAL ACTIVITY

None.

FURTHER INFORMATION

No information available.

ASSOCIATION OF SCHOOLS OF PUBLIC HEALTH
1015 15th Street, N.W., Suite 404
Washington, D.C. 20005
(202) 842-4668   fax: (202) 289-8274

The Association of Schools of Public Health (ASPH) is a nonprofit organization representing the interests of deans, faculty, and students of schools of public health.

ORIGIN AND DEVELOPMENT

ASPH was established in 1953 to facilitate communication among the leadership of public health schools. 24 institutions are members of ASPH.

ORGANIZATION AND FUNDING

ASPH is governed by members at an annual meeting. Since 1988, Gilbert Omenn has been president. Michael K. Gemmell has been executive director since 1978. ASPH employs a full-time staff of six people. Budget information is unavailable.

POLICY CONCERNS AND TACTICS

ASPH is generally concerned with enhancing academic public health programs. It also assists member schools in developing and responding to national health policies. ASPH works with various health and education agencies in Washington, D.C.

POLITICAL ACTIVITY

ASPH testified in support of reauthorization of the Federal Direct Student Loan Program of Part D of Title IV of the Higher Education Act of 1965.

FURTHER INFORMATION

Brochures and operations manual.

ASSOCIATION OF TEACHER EDUCATORS
1900 Association Drive, Suite ATE
Reston, Virginia 22091-1599
(703) 620-3110   fax: (703) 620-9530

The Association of Teacher Educators (ATE) seeks to promote the improvement of teacher education and to serve as a national voice for education development and reform.

ORIGIN AND DEVELOPMENT

ATE originated in 1920 as the Association for Student Teaching. The name was changed in 1970. Current membership is 4,000.

ORGANIZATION AND FUNDING

The association is governed by a board of directors, a delegate assembly, and seven standing committees. The organization contains twenty-two special interest groups, ten commissions, and task forces addressing current issues in education. The current president is Leonard Kaplan, and the executive director is Gloria Chernay. ATE employs four staff members (one part-time), and uses volunteers as meeting planners, journal and newsletter editors, and government relations personnel.

ATE is a 501(c)(3) organization with an annual operating budget of approximately $400,000; 33 percent of budget funding comes from membership fees, 33 percent from meetings, 33 percent from publications, and 1 percent from individual/private contributions. As for allocations, 33 percent of the budget goes toward administration, 33 percent to professional development programs, 33 percent to publications (journal, newsletter, books, tapes), and a minimal percentage to governmental "advocacy" specialists.

POLICY CONCERNS AND TACTICS

ATE's educational concerns involve interprofessional teacher preparation, outcomes assessment, diversity/multicultural/global education, quality assessment and accreditation, and certification/licensure issues. ATE is also concerned with pending legislation on the reauthorization of the Elementary and Secondary Education Act, particularly research and development implications, technology education implications, and the impact of national education goals.

ATE seeks to accomplish its goals by means of study commissions, position statements, publications, workshops, seminars, speeches, and what is referred to in association literature as governmental "advocacy."

POLITICAL ACTIVITY

Governmental "advocacy" includes providing information to divisions within the U.S. Department of Education and to the Secretary of Education on education initiatives and reform. The association also provides testimony and issues position statements to public policy personnel. ATE does not support or endorse political candidates.

FURTHER INFORMATION

Journal and newsletter.

ASSOCIATION OF TEACHERS OF JAPANESE
Hillcrest 9
Middlebury College
Middlebury, Vermont 05753-6119
(802) 388-3711, extension 5915   fax: (802) 388-4329

The Association of Teachers of Japanese (ATJ) is an international organization dedicated to teaching and scholarship in the fields of Japanese language, literature, linguistics, film, and other aspects of Japanese culture.

ORIGIN AND DEVELOPMENT

ATJ was founded in 1963, and today has a membership of 1,250.

ORGANIZATION AND FUNDING

ATJ is governed by a board of directors and the officers of the association: president, secretary, and treasurer. The association is an affiliate of the Association for Asian Studies. The current president is Hiroshi Miyaji (since 1990). The group employs one part-time staff member. Membership fees support the association's budget, which is allocated primarily to the publication of a newsletter and a journal. No other budget information is available.

POLICY CONCERNS AND TACTICS

ATJ is concerned primarily with the exchange of relevant information about Japanese culture among teachers and other professionals in all levels of education, government, and business. The group pursues its goals by means of conferences, raising on endowment, establishing an archives, and disseminating information through a newsletter and a journal.

POLITICAL ACTIVITY

None.

FURTHER INFORMATION

Newsletter and journal.

ASSOCIATION OF TEACHERS OF TECHNICAL WRITING
Department of English
University of Central Florida
Orlando, Florida 32816
(407) 823-2212

The Association of Teachers of Technical Writing (ATTW) seeks to encourage dialogue among teachers of technical communication as an academic discipline.

ORIGIN AND DEVELOPMENT

ATTW was formed in 1973 and has over 1,000 members, including graduate and undergraduate students of technical communications and professional technical communicators in business and industry. ATTW is closely associated with the Modern Language Association.

ORGANIZATION AND FUNDING

ATTW is governed by an executive committee that meets annually prior to a conference general session. The president for the past two years has been Elizabeth Tebeaux, and the executive secretary/treasurer for the past four years has been Dan Jones. The nonprofit organization has an annual budget of approximately $60,000. Approximately 80 percent of the budget is funded through membership fees, 10 percent through user fees, and 10 percent through publications; 85 percent of the budget is allocated to publications (journal, newsletter, anthologies), 10 percent to administration, and 5 percent to the annual conference and awards.

POLICY CONCERNS AND TACTICS

ATTW is concerned with faculty promotion and tenure policies in higher education, pay equity issues, and certification and accreditation of technical writing teachers and programs. ATTW seeks to accomplish its goals by means of publications, meetings and workshops at the annual convention of the Modern Language Association and the Conference on College Composition and Communication, interchange among members, and a service and research awards program.

POLITICAL ACTIVITY

None.

FURTHER INFORMATION

Technical Communication Quarterly (journal), *ATTW Bulletin* (newsletter), membership directory, annual bibliography, anthologies, and other books on both teaching and practice of technical communication.

ASSOCIATION OF THEOLOGICAL SCHOOLS

10 Summitt Park Drive
Pittsburgh, Pennsylvania 15275-1103
(412) 788-6505   fax: (412) 788-6505

The Association of Theological Schools (ATS) seeks to strengthen and support theological education through accreditation and programs for member schools.

ORIGIN AND DEVELOPMENT

ATS was founded in 1918 in the form of a conference of theological schools that met biennially to confer on matters of mutual interest. Association status was achieved in 1936. Quality standards were established in 1936, and a list of accredited schools was established in 1938. Current membership is 222 theological schools.

ORGANIZATION AND FUNDING

ATS is governed by an executive committee elected by the member schools at each biennial meeting of the association. The current president is Robert E. Cooley, and the current executive director is James L. Waits. The association employs a staff of sixteen (fifteen full-time) and relies on the volunteer work of representatives from member schools.

ATS is a 501(c)(3) organization with an annual operating budget of $2,550,000. A total of 63 percent of funding comes from foundation support, 21 percent from membership fees, and 16 percent from investment earnings, subscriptions, and other unspecified income; 70 percent of the budget is allocated to membership services, 17 percent to administrative expenses, and 13 percent to the Commission on Accrediting.

POLICY CONCERNS AND TACTICS

The association is currently engaged in a four-year process of redeveloping accrediting standards. The process involves representatives from nearly all member schools. Other priorities include issues of organizational structure and governance, issues of technological change, issues of pluralism and globalization, institutional resource issues, and executive leadership issues. The association seeks to address these issues through programs of leadership development, research grants, data and information services, conferences and seminars, and other specialized programs.

In addition, ATS is concerned about how the regulations contained within the 1992 reauthorization of the Higher Education Act will affect the organization's structure and the concept of peer-based accreditation.

POLITICAL ACTIVITY

None.

FURTHER INFORMATION

Biennial bulletin containing official documents of the association.

ASSOCIATION OF UNIVERSITY PROGRAMS IN HEALTH ADMINISTRATION
1911 North Fort Myers Drive
Arlington, Virginia 22209
(703) 524-5500

The Association of University Programs in Health Administration (AUPHA) is a nonprofit organization that seeks to improve health services through education for health management.

ORIGIN AND DEVELOPMENT

AUPHA was founded as a consortium in 1966.

ORGANIZATION AND FUNDING

Membership in AUPHA includes 101 university programs, 495 individuals, 311 health care organizations, and 107 international institutions. It is governed by an 8-member, elected board of directors. The 1992 chair of the board was Deborah A. Freund. A 7-member professional staff is headed by President Gary L. Filerman.

Recent operating budgets have approximated $550,000, with most from membership dues, contributions, and annual meeting fees. Over half of the expenses incurred are for administrative and personnel costs.

POLICY CONCERNS AND TACTICS

AUPHA is primarily concerned with curriculum development, baccalaureate education standards, and graduate education accreditation criteria. It addresses these and other concerns through a variety of programs and publications, as well as congressional testimony.

POLITICAL ACTIVITY

AUPHA testified in congressional hearings in support of continuation of the Federal Direct Student Loan Program (Part D, Title IV) as part of the reauthorization of the Higher Education Act of 1965.

FURTHER INFORMATION

The Journal of Health Administration Education (in the United States) and *Health Services Management Research* (in Great Britain).

ASSOCIATION ON HIGHER EDUCATION AND DISABILITY
P.O. Box 21192
Columbus, Ohio 43221-0192
(614) 488-4972   fax: (614) 488-1174

The Association on Higher Education and Disability (AHEAD) is an international organization committed to full participation in higher education for persons with disabilities.

ORIGIN AND DEVELOPMENT

AHEAD was founded in 1978 to improve the quality of services available to disabled persons in higher education settings.

ORGANIZATION AND FUNDING

AHEAD is governed by a board of directors, which is assisted by elected officials and a full-time staff of four (one clerical position). The current president is Wayne Cocchi, and the executive director since 1979 has been Jane Jarrow. AHEAD is a nonprofit organization that derives 50 percent of its funding from user fees, 40 percent from membership fees, and approximately 10 percent from book sales. Budget allocation information is unavailable.

POLICY CONCERNS AND TACTICS

AHEAD's major concern is with member services, such as providing educational conferences, publications, employment information, and training workshops. the association has developed a communication network that addresses the needs of special interests within the organization. Special interest groups provide in-depth attention to current issues affecting that group. The special interest groups include: AIDS, Blindness/Visual Impairment, Canadian Programs, Career Placement, Community College, Computers, Deafness, Disability Studies, Head Injury, Historically Underrepresented Populations, Independent Colleges and Universities, Learning Disabilities, Psychological Disabilities, and Women and Disability.

POLITICAL ACTIVITY

None.

FURTHER INFORMATION

Journal of Postsecondary Education and Disability (a refereed publication that provides in-depth examination of research, issues, policies, and programs in higher education), ALERT (a bimonthly newsletter), and membership directory.

ATLANTIC COUNCIL OF THE UNITED STATES

1616 H Street, N.W.
Washington, D.C. 20006
(202) 347-9353   fax: (202) 737-5163

The Atlantic Council of the United States is a nonprofit policy center dedicated to nurturing Atlantic and Pacific alliances, which together form the cornerstone of U.S. foreign policy. The council identifies challenges and opportunities, illuminates choices, and fosters informed public debate about U.S. foreign, security, and international economic policies. It is also dedicated to the education of generations to succeed to America's international leadership.

ORIGIN AND DEVELOPMENT

The Atlantic Council was founded in 1961. Secretary of State Christian Herter, Dean Acheson, Will Clayton, William Foster, and a number of other distinguished Americans recommended the consolidation of the proliferating U.S. citizens' groups supporting the North Atlantic Treaty Organization (NATO). Since 1961 the Atlantic Council has remained fundamentally a bipartisan citizens' organization of private individuals who are convinced of the pivotal importance of trans-Atlantic—and, more recently, trans-Pacific—cooperation in promoting the strength and cohesion of the free world. The Atlantic Council has 1,000 members.

ORGANIZATION AND FUNDING

The council is governed by an elected board of directors. Since 1989, Ambassador Rozanne L. Ridgway has been president. Since 1984 Joseph W. Harned has been executive director. The Atlantic Council has a full-time staff of twenty-four employees and accepts about twenty student interns per year.

Recent operating budgets have surpassed $2.3 million. All but 6 percent of the budget comes from foundations, corporations, individuals, and government contributions. Administrative and personnel costs amount to 13 percent of the budget, and membership services account for 11 percent. The remaining portion of the budget goes toward program services.

POLICY CONCERNS AND TACTICS

The Atlantic Council is concerned with East-West relations, Atlantic-Pacific interrelations, international change, security and arms control, economics, energy and the environment, international and youth education, and policy education. It addresses these issues through policy studies and forums.

POLITICAL ACTIVITY

None.

FURTHER INFORMATION

Numerous publications on these issues.

AUGUSTINIAN SECONDARY EDUCATION ASSOCIATION
12096 Ventura Avenue
Ojai, California 93023
(805) 646-1464   fax: (805) 646-4330

The Augustinian Secondary Education Association (ASEA) seeks to foster unity, efficiency, and continued development within the Augustinian ministry to secondary education.

ORIGIN AND DEVELOPMENT

The ASEA was founded in 1986 as the successor to the Augustinian Educational Association. Current membership is 9 institutions.

ORGANIZATION AND FUNDING

The executive director for the past four years has been Rev. John Pejza, O.S.A. The association has no operating budget.

POLICY CONCERNS AND TACTICS

The association is intended to be a forum and vehicle for the sharing of resources, for the advancement of Augustinian ideals in education, for the promotion of secondary education as a vital and proper ministry for the Order, and for assuring authentic Augustinian identity for member schools. The association seeks to meet its goals through annual meetings, inservice day programs, and informal networking.

POLITICAL ACTIVITY

None.

FURTHER INFORMATION

No information available.

B

/

BOARD OF JEWISH EDUCATION
426 West 58th Street
New York, New York 10019
(212) 245-8200   fax: (212) 586-9579

The Board of Jewish Education (BJE) seeks to transmit the knowledge that helps assure Jewish continuity, and to support, strengthen, and spread Jewish education. As a training institution and curriculum resource center, BJE focuses on pedagogical skills and Judaic knowledge of educators at all levels of formal and informal Jewish educational practice.

ORIGIN AND DEVELOPMENT

BJE was founded in 1910. BJE is not a membership organization; it maintains 286 supplementary school affiliates and 203 Yeshivot/Day School affiliates, with a total clientele of 126,000 students.

ORGANIZATION AND FUNDING

BJE is governed by a fifty-four-member board of trustees. The current president is Stephen A. Kramer, and the current executive director is Dr. Don Well. The organization employs a staff of sixty-seven (twenty-one part-time) and utilizes volunteers as tutors in special education.

BJE is a 501(c)(3) organization with an annual operating budget of $3.6 million. A total of 67 percent of the budget is funded by the United Jewish Appeal Federation, 6 percent from foundation support, and 2 percent from private contributions. Additional funding information is not available. A full 76 percent of the budget is allocated to membership services (guidance, workshops, conferences, materials, media), 18 percent to administration, 4 percent to publications, and 2 percent to lobbying activities.

POLICY CONCERNS AND TACTICS

Current issues of concern include voucher issues, the provision of special and remedial educational services for students of nonpublic schools, and school food program issues. BJE employs a governmental liaison in order to represent the interests and concerns of constituents whenever possible, often working with other nonpublic school organizations.

POLITICAL ACTIVITY

BJE attempts to influence legislation by active participation in the following governmental forums: U.S. Department of Education, National Leadership Committee on Private Education, the New York State Commissioner's Advisory Committee on Nonpublic Schools, the New York State Commissioner's Advisory Panel on Special Education, and the New York City Committee of Nonpublic School Officials.

FURTHER INFORMATION

Brochures and other informational materials.

BROADCAST EDUCATION ASSOCIATION
1771 N Street, N.W.
Washington, D.C. 20036
(202) 429-5355

The Broadcast Education Association (BEA) is a nonprofit association of professors who teach broadcasting.

ORIGIN AND DEVELOPMENT

BEA was founded in 1955, and today has approximately 1,000 members.

ORGANIZATION AND FUNDING

BEA is governed by an elected board of directors and an executive committee. The 1992 chair of the board was J. William Poole. Since 1987, Louisa Nielsen has been executive director. BEA has a full-time staff of two employees. It accepts eight student interns each year. Budget information is unavailable.

POLICY CONCERNS AND TACTICS

BEA is primarily concerned with standards of teaching broadcast journalism. It addresses this issue at its annual conference.

POLITICAL ACTIVITY

None.

FURTHER INFORMATION

No information available.

THE BUSINESS–HIGHER EDUCATION FORUM
One Dupont Circle, Suite 800
Washington, D.C. 20036
(202) 833-4716

The Business–Higher Education Forum is a nonprofit organization dedicated to addressing issues of mutual concern to the corporate and higher education communities. It strives to build consensus on how the two sectors can collaborate more effectively for the benefit of all society.

ORIGIN AND DEVELOPMENT

The forum was founded in 1978 by the American Council on Education.

ORGANIZATION AND FUNDING

Membership consists of 100 academic and corporate chief executives. The forum is governed by an 11-member executive committee, with membership divided between corporation and academic members. Chairpersonship rotates between academic and corporate members every two years. The 1992–1994 chair is William H. Danforth. Don M. Blandin is the forum director. The organization is supported by membership dues and project grants from philanthropic foundations. Current budget information is unavailable.

POLICY CONCERNS AND TACTICS

According to published material, the forum is very selective in identifying issues for debate and action. Issues must be important to both sectors, as well as to the nation as a whole, and must also lend themselves to consensus. Issues primarily center on education and training of the workforce, the environment and the workplace, economic development and education, and health care.

POLITICAL ACTIVITY

None.

FURTHER INFORMATION

Forum papers and summaries from meetings.

C

/

THE CALIFORNIA ASSOCIATION FOR COUNSELING AND DEVELOPMENT
2555 E. Chapman Avenue, Suite 201
Fullerton, California 92631
(714) 871-6460

The California Association for Counseling and Development (CACD) is designed to promote the advancement of excellence in the counseling and development of people of all ages throughout the state. It serves its members to advance the field in the broad areas of mental health, career, and education.

ORIGIN AND DEVELOPMENT

CACD was incorporated in 1967, and today has a membership of 2,054.

ORGANIZATION AND FUNDING

CACD acts as the umbrella organization for fifteen divisions and affiliates within the profession. Its program is carried out at local levels through area chapters designed to respond to local needs and situations.

The association is governed by a board of directors. The 1993 president was Mary Honer, and the executive director for the past twenty years has been Richard Hoover. The association maintains a staff of three (one part-time) and relies on volunteers to do leadership, committee, and publication work.

CACD is a 501(c)(3) organization with an annual operating budget of $160,000. A full 80 percent of funding comes from membership fees, 10 percent from individual contributions, and 10 percent from conference publications; 45 percent of the budget is allocated to administration, 18 percent to membership services (including position referral listings, insurance programs, and consultation services), 15 percent to conferences and an annual convention, 11 percent to publications (journal, newsletters), and 11 percent to lobbying activities.

POLICY CONCERNS AND TACTICS

Recent public policy concerns of CACD involve mandatory school counseling, professional standards and definitions, increased taxpayer support for adult counseling services, and insurance company regulation. In-house concerns revolve around professional growth issues, especially keeping members abreast of current research, legislation, and trends within the profession, and financial security issues involving retirement plans and insurance for members. The association seeks to achieve its goals by means of an organized program of professional development, program advocacy, and an effective presence in the legislature.

POLITICAL ACTIVITY

According to association literature, CACD is "action oriented" at the state level insofar as it acts to support legislation to enhance the profession, strengthen the position of each individual counselor, and protect clients through consumer advocacy. The association is well-organized for contacting legislators and sponsors through a network of communication between CACD members and public officials. CACD does not support or endorse political candidates.

FURTHER INFORMATION

Brochures, "Compass" newsletter, affiliated groups' newsletters, and other periodicals.

CAREER COLLEGE ASSOCIATION
750 First Street, N.E., Suite 900
Washington, D.C. 20002-4242
(202) 336-6700   fax: (202) 336-6828

The Career College Association (CCA) is an educational membership association of private, postsecondary institutions offering career-specific educational programs in the United States and abroad.

ORIGIN AND DEVELOPMENT

CCA was formed in 1991 through the consolidation of the Association of Independent Colleges and Schools and National Association of Trade and Technical Schools. This consolidation made CCA the largest organization in the United States representing the private career college sector. According to association literature, the organization represents over 1,650 nondegree and degree-granting business, trade, and technical colleges and schools in the United States, Western Europe, the Caribbean, and the South Pacific. Combined, these institutions educate more than 1 million students annually.

ORGANIZATION AND FUNDING

The current president of the association is Stephen J. Blair. No other information is available.

POLICY CONCERNS AND TACTICS

According to CCA literature, the association is committed to helping member institutions achieve the highest possible standards of educational quality and service to their students and to improving the public accountability and integrity of all institutions in the postsecondary community. Toward these ends, CCA sponsors and supports two independent commissions to oversee private career schools and colleges: the CCA Accrediting Commission for Independent Colleges and Schools and the CCA Accrediting Commission for Trade and Technical Schools. In addition, the association encourages public policy debate on workforce and educational quality issues by publicizing relevant information and sponsoring conferences and workshops. The conference involve leading members of Congress, workforce preparedness experts, and other prominent policy makers. Lately, the association has paid particular attention to issues of educational finance, including problems with student loans and grants, and issues of fairness with respect to financial aid guidelines.

POLITICAL ACTIVITY

To help curtail the number of student loan defaults, CCA has worked closely with the U.S. Department of Education and with Congress to bring down default rates. CCA has recommended a number of legislative proposals including tightening requirements that institutions refund students' tuition if they drop out and barring loans to students at schools that have withdrawn from an accrediting agency or whose accreditation has been revoked. CCA has supported the argument that the U.S. Department of Education should be granted the power to suspend temporarily all financial aid to an institution if the department has reliable information that an institution is abusing federal funds or to prevent an institution from misusing federal funds.

CCA was the only higher education organization to support Representative Larry Smith's (D-Fla.) Student Loan Abuse Prevention Act, former U.S. Secretary of Education Lauro Cavazos's default reduction regulations, and legislation requiring all postsecondary institutions to disclose graduation rates and job placement rates.

The CCA's political action committee (The Association of Independent Colleges and Schools PAC) contributed during 1992 a total of $14,375 to fifteen Democratic candidates and $9,675 to thirteen Republican candidates (according to Federal Election Commission data).

FURTHER INFORMATION

''CCA Backgrounder'' (newsletter), news releases, and fact sheets.

THE CENTER FOR APPLIED LINGUISTICS
1118 22nd Street, N.W.
Washington, D.C. 20037
(202) 429-9292   fax: (202) 659-5641

The Center for Applied Linguistics (CAL) is a nonprofit organization that serves as a clearing house of individuals concerned with the application of linguistic science to practical problems.

ORIGIN AND DEVELOPMENT

CAL was established in 1959 by the Modern Language Association with an initial grant from the Ford Foundation. It still has close and cooperative ties with the Modern Language Association, as it does with the National Association of Foreign Student Advisors, the Teachers of English to Speakers of Other Languages, the National Association of Bilingual Education, the American Association for Applied Linguistics, the Joint National Committee for Languages,* the Linguistic Society of America, and the National Network for Early Language Learning.

ORGANIZATION AND FUNDING

CAL is governed by a fifteen-member board of trustees. Since January of 1990, Kenji Hakuta has been chair of the board. It has a full-time staff of seventy employees and accepts ten student interns each year. Recent revenues have surpassed $3.9 million, with over $3.4 million from grants and contracts. It spends a little over $3.6 million, almost all of which goes to program services.

POLICY CONCERNS AND TACTICS

CAL is concerned with the demands of English teaching abroad and the training of Americans in foreign languages. It addresses these issues by providing publications and producing adequate language-related materials.

POLITICAL ACTIVITY

None.

FURTHER INFORMATION

A variety of publications, including a bimonthly newsletter, *Forum*; *Focus*, a series of occasional papers; *Practitioner Information Guides*; the *ERIC/CLL News Bulletin*; *Language in Education*; professional reference books on linguistics and literacy; reports on various languages; and an annual report.

THE CHRISTIAN COLLEGE COALITION
329 8th Street, N.E.
Washington, D.C. 20002-6158
(202) 546-8713   fax: (202) 546-8913

The Christian College Coalition is a nonprofit organization committed to serving and strengthening Christian liberal arts colleges and universities across the United States.

ORIGIN AND DEVELOPMENT

The coalition was founded in 1976 as an information association of approximately thirty Christ-centered colleges. Coalition institutions meet eight criteria for membership: an institutional commitment to the centrality of Jesus Christ to all campus life, integration of biblical faith with academics and student life, hiring practices that require a personal Christian commitment from each full-time faculty member and administrator, accreditation and primary orientation as a four-year liberal arts college, fund-raising activities consistent with the standards set by the Evangelical Council for Financial Accountability, a commitment to participating in coalition programs, cooperation with and support of other coalition colleges, and responsible financial operation.

ORGANIZATION AND FUNDING

There are eighty-three colleges and universities in the coalition. The coalition is governed by a thirteen-member board of directors who are typically college presidents. Since 1989 Myron S. Augsburger has served as president. There are twenty-one full-time staff members.

The 1992 operating budget surpassed $1.5 million, with 75 percent from user fees. The remaining income was derived from foundation support, membership fees, corporations, government, and individual contributions. Approximately 85 percent of the budget is spent on membership services with the remainder going toward administration and personnel costs.

POLICY CONCERNS AND TACTICS

The coalition is primarily interested in maintaining what it calls confessional pluralism in higher education. It supports state regulation of accreditation as opposed to regional accreditation. It is also concerned with increasing the number of minority scholarships available at member institutions. The coalition addresses these issues through providing information to member institutions and potential funders.

POLITICAL ACTIVITY

The coalition tries to affect legislation through disseminating information through a governmental relations committee.

FURTHER INFORMATION

A monthly newsletter, an annual report, and *Consider a Christian College*, a biennial guide to coalition schools.

CITIZENS FOR EDUCATIONAL FREEDOM
927 South Walter Reed Drive, Suite 1
Arlington, Virginia 22204
(703) 486-8311

Citizens for Educational Freedom (CEF) is a nonprofit organization dedicated to protecting and preserving the human right of parents to choose the kind of education that shall be given to their own children.

ORIGIN AND DEVELOPMENT

CEF was founded in 1959 out of a concern about the future of private schools. At this time the first federal aid package was proposed that would have discriminated against children attending private schools. CEF has developed ties with the Educational Freedom Foundation, the Clearinghouse for Educational Choice, and Americans for Choice in Education. There are 20,000 members in CEF.

ORGANIZATION AND FUNDING

CEF is governed by a board of trustees and an executive board. Mae Duggan has been president since 1988. In 1986 Robert Marlowe was appointed executive director. CEF has a full-time staff of four employees. Funding information is unavailable.

POLICY CONCERNS AND TACTICS

CEF is concerned with the issue of parental choice in education and the provision of a voucher of education tax funds to make that choice a reality. It advocates a total reform of the U.S. educational system to allow greater choice among public, private, and home education. It addresses these issues by organizing chapters, lobbying, and using the media to affect public opinion.

POLITICAL ACTIVITY

Lobbying of state and federal lawmakers.

FURTHER INFORMATION

A newsletter.

THE COALITION FOR THE ADVANCEMENT OF JEWISH EDUCATION
261 West 35th Street, Floor 12A
New York, New York 10001
(212) 268-4210   fax: (212) 268-4214

The Coalition for the Advancement of Jewish Education (CAJE) is designed to bring together classroom teachers, rabbis, principals, cantors, youth workers, informal educators, academics, camp personnel, parents, students, and others for the purpose of transmitting the Jewish heritage in North America.

ORIGIN AND DEVELOPMENT

Founded in 1977, CAJE maintains a membership of approximately 4,000.

ORGANIZATION AND FUNDING

CAJE is governed by an eighteen-member board of directors, with eight directors appointed by the chairperson and ten elected positions. The president since 1990 has been Michael Weinberg; the executive director since 1981 has been Eliot G. Spack. The coalition employs a staff of nine (six full-time) and utilizes student interns (two to three per year) and volunteer services (primarily for committee work).

The Coalition is a 501(c)(3) organization with an annual operating budget of approximately $643,000, of which 40 percent is derived from conference revenues; 24 percent from membership fees; 15 percent from individual contributions; 11 percent from sales, advertising, and exhibits; and 10 percent from foundation support. A full 55 percent of the budget is allocated to program development, 20 percent to publications, 15 percent to administration, and 10 percent to miscellaneous membership services.

POLICY CONCERNS AND TACTICS

CAJE is interested in issues of Jewish heritage continuity, issues of Jewish communal fund allocation, increasing the financial base of the organization, recruiting and retaining new members, and personnel issues in Jewish education. The organization is presently forming a CAJE endowment campaign as a vehicle to raise money and build support and is developing a strategy to help "empower" today's Jewish educator. CAJE attempts to recruit members via telemarketing, direct mail, Mini-CAJEs, and other internal outreach programs. The coalition is also involved in a variety of member services, such as conferences, publications, a curriculum bank, formal information and research networks, and educator training programs.

POLITICAL ACTIVITY

None.

FURTHER INFORMATION

Brochures, pamphlets, press releases, *Bikurim* (CAJE Curriculum Bank publication), and *Jewish Education News* (quarterly magazine).

COLLEGE AND UNIVERSITY PERSONNEL ASSOCIATION
1233 20th Street, N.W., Suite 503
Washington, D.C. 20036
(202) 429-0311   fax: (202) 429-0149

The College and University Personnel Association (CUPA) seeks to provide leadership in the advancement of contemporary and effective human resource management in higher education.

ORIGIN AND DEVELOPMENT

CUPA was founded in 1946 when 28 institutions in the Midwest sent representatives to set up an organization of those interested in personnel work. CUPA is a member of the Secretariat of Washington Higher Education. It also has developed close ties with the Council of Higher Education Management Association and the Council of Human Resource Management Associations. CUPA maintains a membership of 1,600 institutions and 6,000 individuals.

ORGANIZATION AND FUNDING

The organization is governed by a board of directors, executive committee, and five regional boards. The 1993–1994 president was Charlotte Fugitt, and the executive director since 1985 has been Richard C. Creal. CUPA maintains a full-time staff of fifteen (two clerical) and relies on up to four student interns per year, as well as volunteers, to assist in planning and working conferences and doing book reviews.

CUPA is a 501(c)(3) organization with an annual operating budget of $2 million. Membership fees account for 49 percent of funding, publications 22 percent, professional development services 26 percent, investment income 1 percent, and miscellaneous 2 percent; 34 percent of the budget is allocated to administration, 26 percent to professional development, 18 percent to publications, 14 percent to membership services, and 9 percent to miscellaneous.

POLICY CONCERNS AND TACTICS

According to association literature, CUPA is concerned with developing educational programming that responds to the diverse human resource needs of members. A staff legislative coordinator monitors federal legislation that may have an impact on CUPA. Issues of concern include the Americans with Disabilities Act, possible health care reform measures, and diversity in the workplace. In conjunction with other associations in higher education, CUPA periodically offers information to Congress regarding important higher education issues.

POLITICAL ACTIVITY

None.

FURTHER INFORMATION

Numerous books, *CUPA News* (newsletter), *CUPA Journal* (quarterly), and an annual report.

THE COLLEGE BOARD

45 Columbus Avenue
New York, New York 10023-6992
(212) 713-8000   fax: (212) 713-8255

The College Board is a nonprofit organization dedicated to assisting students in the transition from high school to college. In doing so, it is committed to maintaining academic standards and broadening access to higher education.

ORIGIN AND DEVELOPMENT

The College Board was founded in 1900 as a forum for greater collaboration between secondary and higher education. Much of this is done in conjunction with the Educational Testing Service. There are 2,800 institutional members of the College Board.

ORGANIZATION AND FUNDING

Institutional members designate representatives who meet annually. Member representatives elect a 25-member board of trustees who govern the organization. In 1990 Alice C. Cox was elected chair of the board of trustees. In 1987 Donald M. Steward was appointed president of the College Board. There is a full-time staff of 318 employees.

The 1992 operating budget was $186 million, 97 percent of which was derived from user fees. The remaining portion came from foundation support and membership fees. Expenses totaled $178 million, of which 89 percent went toward programs and services. The remainder of funds went toward publications and general administration.

POLICY CONCERNS AND TACTICS

The College Board is concerned with two issues: financing higher education and educational standards and equity. It addresses these issues by informing lawmakers of the current underrepresentativeness of specific groups in society and by disseminating research findings and recommendations to the media and the general public. In 1991, the College Board initiated a new program called Equity. According to its annual report, the Equity project is intended to eliminate discrepancies between the proportion of minority students entering college and that of nonminority students.

POLITICAL ACTIVITY

The College Board testified at congressional hearings on the recent reauthorization of the Higher Education Act of 1965. At the hearings, it argued for simplification of the application form, removing veterans' benefits from the needs analysis formula, placing greater discretion in the judgment of aid administrators, repealing the Income Contingent Loan Program, and providing earlier outreach to at-risk students.

FURTHER INFORMATION

Annual report.

COLUMBIA UNIVERSITY TEACHER'S COLLEGE
See National Association for Women in Education.

COUNCIL FOR ADVANCEMENT AND SUPPORT OF EDUCATION
11 Dupont Circle, Suite 400
Washington, D.C. 20036-1261
(202) 328-5926   fax: (202) 387-4973

The Council for Advancement and Support of Education (CASE) is a nonprofit organization representing the interests of professionals in the field of institutional advancement. This field includes educational fund-raising, alumni administration, communications, government relations, student recruitment, and the management of these areas.

ORIGIN AND DEVELOPMENT

CASE was founded in 1974, with the merger of the American Alumni Council and the American College Public Relations Association. It has grown to include members in more than 3,000 colleges, universities, and independent elementary and secondary schools in the United States, Canada, Mexico, and 20 other countries. Today CASE has 14,200 members.

ORGANIZATION AND FUNDING

CASE is organized into eight geographic districts in North America. CASE is governed by a forty-member board of trustees. The Board employs the president who serves as the chief executive officer. Peter McE. Buchanan is the current president. The CASE full-time staff is composed of approximately seventy individuals. It accepts one student intern each year.

Recent operating revenues have been around $8.6 million. Approximately $8 million has come from membership dues, conference fees, and publications. Expenses have totaled about $8.1 million, of which over $5 million has gone toward personnel and administrative costs. The remainder has gone toward membership services.

POLICY CONCERNS AND TACTICS

CASE is primarily concerned with providing members with professional development opportunities. It addresses this issue through conferences, workshops, publications, and videos. CASE also informs lawmakers on pertinent issues. CASE alerts its members to call upon members of Congress to protect or restore full tax deductability for gifts. It also works to head off increases in nonprofit mail rates, or reductions in eligibility for those rates, that would affect the budgets of schools, colleges, universities, and alumni associations.

POLITICAL ACTIVITY

None.

FURTHER INFORMATION

Numerous books on professional development and an annual report.

COUNCIL FOR AMERICAN PRIVATE EDUCATION
1726 M Street, N.W., Suite 1102
Washington, D.C. 20036
(202 659-0016   fax: (202) 659-0018
The Council for American Private Education (CAPE) is a nonprofit organization representing diverse national educational associations of private elementary and secondary schools. CAPE seeks to keep its member organizations informed about key issues of concern and to work cooperatively with public sector educators and officials to improve the quality of education in general.

ORIGIN AND DEVELOPMENT

CAPE was founded in 1971.

ORGANIZATION AND FUNDING

There are fourteen associations that are members in CAPE: The American Montessori Society, the Association of American Military Colleges and Schools of the U.S., Christian Schools International, the Evangelical Lutheran Church in America, the Friends Council on Education, the Lutheran Church–Missouri Synod, the National Association of Episcopal Schools, the National Association of Independent Schools,* the National Association of Private Schools for Exceptional Children,* the National Catholic Educational Association,* the National Society for Hebrew Day Schools, the Seventh-day Adventist's Board of Education, the Solomon Schechter Day School Association, and the U.S. Catholic Conference. CAPE is governed by a board of directors. The 1992 president was Catherine McNamee, and since 1989 Joyce G. McCray has been executive director. CASE has a full-time staff of three employees. Funding information is unavailable.

POLICY CONCERNS AND TACTICS

CAPE is primarily concerned with advocating the role of private schools. It monitors legislation that might affect parents' right to "choice" in education and provides information about private schools to policy makers and the public.

POLITICAL ACTIVITY

None.

FURTHER INFORMATION

A monthly newsletter, *CAPE Outlook*.

THE COUNCIL FOR INTERNATIONAL EXCHANGE OF SCHOLARS

3400 International Drive, N.W., Suite M-500
Washington, D.C. 20008-3097
(202) 686-7870   fax: (202) 362-3442

The Council for International Exchange of Scholars (CIES) is a nonprofit organization that facilitates the exchange of scholars between the United States and foreign countries. It administrates the Fulbright Scholarship Program.

ORIGIN AND DEVELOPMENT

CIES was founded in 1947 after the passage of the Fulbright Act. The Conference Board of Associated Research Councils, a group composed of the American Council of Learned Societies, the National Academy of Sciences, the Social Science Research Council, and the American Council on Education, established CIES to cooperate with the U.S. government in the administration of the Fulbright Scholar Program.

ORGANIZATION AND FUNDING

CIES is not a membership organization. The CIES board consists of fourteen members appointed by the Conference Board of Associated Research Councils. The board appoints an executive director, which since 1981 has been Cassandra A. Pyle. CIES has a full-time staff of seventy-five individuals. It accepts two student interns each year.

The CIES 1992 operating budget was approximately $6 million for administration and $22 million in program funding.

POLICY CONCERNS AND TACTICS

CIES concerns are set by its mandate: to administer the grant competition for Fulbright awards for U.S. faculty and to provide services and affiliations for Fulbright Visiting Scholars to the United States.

POLITICAL ACTIVITY

None.

FURTHER INFORMATION

Annual report.

THE COUNCIL OF CHIEF STATE SCHOOL OFFICERS

One Massachusetts Avenue, N.W., Suite 700
Washington, D.C. 20001-1431
(202) 408-5505   fax: (202) 408-8072

The Council of Chief State School Officers (CCSSO) is a nonprofit organization that provides professional development opportunities for chief state school officers and their management teams. In addition CCSSO undertakes projects that address areas of concern at the state level and are designed to strengthen public education through each state education agency.

ORIGIN AND DEVELOPMENT

CCSSO was founded in 1927.

ORGANIZATION AND FUNDING

The chief state school officers from each state, plus the District of Columbia, Puerto Rico, and the Virgin Islands, are members. A nine-member executive committee is elected by membership. The 1992 president was Jeanne Knight, and the administrative manager was Tommie Williams. CCSSO has a full- time staff of seven employees.

Average annual revenues are about $4.5 million, with over $3.2 million coming from grants and contracts and $1.1 million from membership dues. The remaining funds come from investments. Over $4 million is spent on programs and $300,000 on administrative costs. The remainder is spent on fund-raising.

POLICY CONCERNS AND TACTICS

CCSSO is concerned with three issues: (1) increasing efforts to connect school districts with health and child care, housing, and juvenile justice; (2) bridging the gap between schools and employment; and (3) expanding programs of teacher assessment.

POLITICAL ACTIVITY

None.

FURTHER INFORMATION

Numerous electronic newsletters and bulletin boards, including *Hill Notes*, a weekly legislative briefing; numerous books and policy papers, such as "Learning Technologies Policy Statement" (pamphlet), *Learning Technologies Papers* (Washington, D.C.: CCSSO, 1992), and *Developing a 50-State System of Education Indicators* (Washington, D.C.: CCSSO, 1992).

COUNCIL OF COLLEGES OF ARTS AND SCIENCES
186 University Hall
230 North Oval Mall
Ohio State University
Columbus, Ohio 43210-1319
(614) 292-1882   fax: (614) 292-8666

The Council of Colleges of Arts and Sciences (CCAS) is a national association of baccalaureate degree–granting colleges and universities whose purpose is to sustain the arts and sciences as a leading influence in U.S. higher education. The council serves as a forum for the exchange of ideas and information among deans of arts and sciences representing the member institutions and as a representative of the liberal arts at the national policy-making level.

ORIGIN AND DEVELOPMENT

CCAS was founded in 1965. Currently, the membership includes more than 575 deans of colleges of arts and sciences at some 409 institutions. The council is made up of the majority of eligible public institutions in the United States. Private colleges and universities are eligible for membership.

ORGANIZATION AND FUNDING

Policy is affirmed by the CCAS officers and board of directors, who are elected each year during the CCAS annual meeting. The nine board members serve staggered three-year terms. Bill Wilkins was the 1992–1993 president, and the executive director since 1987 has been Richard J. Hopkins. The nonprofit organization operates on an annual budget of approximately $186,500, 52 percent of which is funded through user fees, 45 percent through membership fees, and 3 percent through interest earnings. A full 75 percent of the budget is allocated to the annual meeting and seminars, 14 percent to operating service fees, 10 percent to publications, and 1 percent to administration.

POLICY CONCERNS AND TACTICS

Current policy concerns include accreditation issues, faculty workload, fundraising problems, multicultural education, general education requirements, and international exchanges. CCAS seeks to meet its goals by means of a four-day annual meeting that deals with timely issues, deans' seminars, department chair seminars, and a variety of publications.

POLITICAL ACTIVITY

None.

FURTHER INFORMATION

CCAS Membership Directory, CCAS Newsletter, and a brochure.

COUNCIL OF GRADUATE SCHOOLS
One Dupont Circle, N.W.
Washington, D.C. 20036
(202) 223-3791   fax: (202) 331-7157

The Council of Graduate Schools (CGS) is a nonprofit organization dedicated to improving and advancing graduate education.

ORIGIN AND DEVELOPMENT

CGS was founded in 1960. Graduate deans perceived the need for a national organization based in Washington, D.C., to represent graduate education. There are 400 members in CGS.

ORGANIZATION AND FUNDING

Member graduate deans elect a board of directors. Since 1984, the president has been Jules B. Lapidus. CGS has a full-time staff of seven employees. It accepts two student interns each year.

The 1992 operating budget was $1 million, of which 65 percent came from membership fees and the remainder was split evenly between conference fees and publications.

POLICY CONCERNS AND TACTICS

CGS is concerned with increasing support for minority students, maintaining high standards of graduate education, and increasing funding for graduate research and teaching. It addresses these goals through publications, discussions at conferences, and informing lawmakers.

POLITICAL ACTIVITY

None.

FURTHER INFORMATION

No information available.

THE COUNCIL OF INDEPENDENT COLLEGES

One Dupont Circle, Suite 320
Washington, D.C. 20036
(202) 466-7230   fax: (202) 466-7238

The Council of Independent Colleges (CIC) is a nonprofit, international organization of independent liberal arts colleges. CIC seeks to improve educational programs, administrative and financial performance, and institutional visibility at member colleges.

ORIGIN AND DEVELOPMENT

CIC was founded in 1956 to help in two tasks: (1) to meet the need to educate the dramatically increasing number of people attending college; and (2) to maintain private institutions in the process of serving the expanding number of students. CIC was formerly called the Council for the Advancement of Small Colleges (1956–1981).

ORGANIZATION AND FUNDING

There are over 300 member colleges. CIC is governed by a board of directors consisting of college presidents and corporate and foundation executives. The board is elected by institutional members. Term of office for college presidents is 3 years; there is no term limit for corporate/lay directors. Allen P. Splete has been president since 1986. CIC has a full-time staff of 9 employees.

Recent operating budgets have been over $1.5 million. The revenues come from membership fees (31 percent), user fees (26 percent), foundations (27 percent), corporations (9 percent), government (5 percent), and interest (2 percent). Expenditures go toward administration and personnel (48 percent), membership services (47 percent), publications (2 percent), and the reserve fund (3 percent).

POLICY CONCERNS AND TACTICS

CIC is concerned with a variety of issues: improving higher education, promoting independent colleges, emphasizing the importance of teaching and research, integrating liberal arts traditions with practical and professional study, encouraging both a focus on individual students and a sense of community, ensuring the presence of values in education, capitalizing on the organizational flexibility of small size and independence, and fostering a spirit of institutional responsiveness and inventiveness.

CIC addresses these issues by conducting numerous professional development workshops, disseminating publications on these subjects, and monitoring congressional activity that pertains to these issues.

POLITICAL ACTIVITY

CIC testified at the hearings for reauthorizing the Stafford Loan Program of the Higher Education Act of 1965. It argued for requiring lenders to provide graduated repayment schedules and the consolidation of all deferments into one "understood" hardship deferment category. It also supported the elimination of the Income Contingent Loan Program and the removal of PLUS loan limits.

FURTHER INFORMATION

Numerous issue-publications; a newsletter, *The CIC Independent*; and an annual report.

THE COUNCIL OF THE GREAT CITY SCHOOLS
1413 K Street, N.W., Suite 400
Washington, D.C. 20005
(202) 371-0163   fax: (202) 371-1365
The Council of the Great City Schools (CGCS) is a nonprofit organization that promotes the cause of urban education and serves as an advocate of innercity schools before both policy-making bodies and the public.

ORIGIN AND DEVELOPMENT

CGCS was founded in 1961 in response to educators' concerns that no national organization was focused on issues affecting large urban school systems.

ORGANIZATION AND FUNDING

CGCS has forty-seven member institutions. It is governed by a board of trustees consisting of the superintendent and one board of education member from each district. An executive committee of twenty members governs affairs when the board is not in session. The 1992 president was Constance E. Clayton. Michael Casserly was appointed interim executive director in 1992. CGCS has a full-time staff of six employees.

The 1992 budget was $1.1 million, all of which came from membership fees. A little more than 20 percent went toward administration and personnel costs, 10 percent toward membership services, almost 13 percent toward publications, 20 percent toward lobbying, 5 percent toward litigation, and the remainder toward conferences and special projects.

POLICY CONCERNS AND TACTICS

CGCS is concerned with federal budget allocations to educational programs, school-based services to increase academic achievement, and vouchers and "choice" plans that would fund private schools. It addresses these issues through advocacy before Congress and state and local government officials. CGCS also disseminates information to member institutions and other national organizations and corporations.

POLITICAL ACTIVITY

CGCS testified on behalf of Smart Start: The Community Collaborative for Early Childhood Development Act, supporting a greater need for targeting in-state funding formulas. It also testified at the reauthorization hearings of Expiring Federal Elementary and Secondary Education Programs, Chapter 2 of the Education Consolidation and Improvement Act. At these hearings, CGCS argued for increasing the eligibility of schools and for the elimination of the restriction that only 35 percent of secondary school funds can be used for noninstructional services. It also argued for an increase in authorized spending for the preschool Even Start program.

CGCS also was involved in the Education Excellence Act and the Equity and Excellence in Education Implementation Act. In the joint hearings, it argued for a rewriting of merit school proposals to create locally based incentives for improvement in schools with high levels of need, restricting eligibility for incentives to Chapter 1 schools with low achievement and high need, deleting magnet schools of excellence, incorporating teacher recruitment provisions, and transferring more funds into urban drug programs, magnet schools, and urban education research.

FURTHER INFORMATION

No information available.

THE COUNCIL ON EDUCATION OF THE DEAF

Gallaudet University
800 Florida Avenue, N.E.
Washington, D.C. 20002-3695
(202) 651-5020   fax: (202) 651-5508

The Council on Education of the Deaf (CED) is a nonprofit organization that serves educators and professional personnel involved in the education of hearing-impaired children and youth in the United States and Canada. CED is responsible for setting certification standards and certifying those professionals who meet the certification requirements.

ORIGIN AND DEVELOPMENT

CED was founded in 1969.

ORGANIZATION AND FUNDING

CED has four member organizations: the Association of College Educators of the Hearing Impaired, the Alexander Graham Bell Association for the Deaf,* the Conference of Education Administrators Serving the Deaf, and the Convention of American Instructors of the Deaf. CED has a twelve-member executive board that consists of representatives from these four associations. Since 1990, Harold Meyer, Jr., has been president. There are no full-time staff members.

The 1992 operating budget was $30,000. The majority of revenues (78 percent) was derived from certification fees and accreditation fees. The remainder came from membership fees. Half (50 percent) of the budget is spent on administration, 20 percent on publications, and 30 percent on professional standards review.

POLICY CONCERNS AND TACTICS

CED is concerned with certification standards of professionals and certification of academic institutions offering programs for the professional preparation of teachers. It addresses these issues through dissemination of information and by evaluating both individual professionals and academic programs.

POLITICAL ACTIVITY

None.

FURTHER INFORMATION

Brochures and published guidelines.

THE COUNCIL ON GOVERNMENTAL RELATIONS
One Dupont Circle, N.W., Suite 670
Washington, D.C. 20036
(202) 861-2595

The Council on Governmental Relations (COGR) is a nonprofit organization that deals primarily with policies and technical issues involved in the administration of federally sponsored programs at universities. It keeps under continuing review the problems potentially inherent in the development of federal policies, regulations, and other federal initiatives. As part of this process, COGR provides advice and information to its membership.

ORIGIN AND DEVELOPMENT

COGR was established in 1948. According to association information, the Central Association of the College and University Business Officers passed a resolution that established COGR to represent the 5 regional associations of college and university business officers. There are 136 institutional members in COGR.

ORGANIZATION AND FUNDING

COGR is governed by a nineteen-member board of management, with each member serving a staggered term. Marvin E. Ebel is the chair of COGR. Staff size is unavailable. Recent operating budgets have surpassed $5.1 million. More than $2.2 million has come from membership dues and $1.6 million from workshop fees. COGR has spent over $4.7 million annually, approximately $3 million of which goes toward administrative and personnel items. The remainder goes toward membership services.

POLICY CONCERNS AND TACTICS

COGR is concerned with several issues: interpreting for federal officials the management and administrative practices that are characteristic of research universities; making recommendations with respect to policies and regulations that may affect the performance of sponsored research programs and instructional practices at universities; and studying problem areas in relation to federal policy or university practice and giving to the government or universities appropriate information or guidance on possible effects or changes. A major goal of COGR is to minimize the intrusion of the federal government in the activities of its member universities.

POLITICAL ACTIVITY

None.

FURTHER INFORMATION

An annual *Chairman's Report*.

E

_____ / _____

THE EDUCATIONAL EXCELLENCE NETWORK
1112 16th Street, N.W., Suite 500
Washington, D.C. 20036
(202) 785-2985   fax: (202) 785-3948

The Educational Excellence Network (EEN) is a nonprofit organization that functions as an information exchange and clearinghouse on education improvement and school reform, serving educators, policy makers, parents, and other interested individuals in the nonprofit and private sectors. While having a concern that spans the entire spectrum of education, EEN focuses primarily on the improvement of elementary and secondary education. Here it emphasizes improvements in the areas of literature, history, geography, and social studies.

ORIGIN AND DEVELOPMENT

EEN was founded in 1982 by Chester E. Finn and Diane S. Ravitch, then professors of history and education at Teachers College, Columbia University, to enhance the flow of information, research findings, current developments, and promising ideas among individuals who shared a strong concern for educational excellence. EEN has approximately 1,900 members.

ORGANIZATION AND FUNDING

EEN is governed by the Institute for Public Policy Studies at Vanderbilt University. A fifteen-member National Advisory Council is appointed by Vanderbilt University. Chester E. Finn has been director of EEN since 1982. EEN has a full-time staff of seven and accepts ten student interns each year.

The 1992 operating budget was $450,000, of which 85 percent came from foundations and individual contributions, 10 percent from membership fees, and

5 percent from government; 15 percent of the budget went toward administrative costs, 20 percent toward membership services, and the remainder toward publications and projects.

POLICY CONCERNS AND TACTICS

EEN is involved in a variety of projects and activities designed to enhance education. As a clearinghouse, EEN helps members obtain needed education information. It also provides technical assistance and briefs policy makers and leaders in education. Some current projects include: "Education: The Consumer's View," a series of op/ed pieces run in the *New York Times* that have argued for greater consumer responsiveness on the part of the schools; "Fairfax County Outcomes Project," which is assisting the school system in Fairfax County, Virginia, to determine what its graduates should know and be able to do; and "Better Education through Informed Legislation," which is an intensive institute for legislators from fifteen states to inform them about education policy issues.

POLITICAL ACTIVITY

None.

FURTHER INFORMATION

News & Views, a monthly compilation of journal articles about educational issues.

THE EDUCATION COMMISSION OF THE STATES
707 17th Street, Suite 2700
Denver, Colorado 80202-3427
(303) 299-3600   fax: (303) 296-8332

The Education Commission of the States (ECS) is a nonprofit organization that seeks to assist state leaders in improving the quality of education. ECS conducts policy research, surveys, and special studies; maintains an information clearinghouse; organizes state, regional, and national forums; provides technical assistance to states; helps states implement changes in education; and fosters nationwide leadership and cooperation in education.

ORIGIN AND DEVELOPMENT

ECS was created in 1965 as an interstate compact. Primary constituents include governors, legislative leaders and their senior policy aides, chief state school officers, state higher education executive officers and their senior policy associates, members of state education boards, and leaders of local schools.

ORGANIZATION AND FUNDING

Forty-nine states (all but Montana), the District of Columbia, Puerto Rico, American Samoa, and the Virgin Islands have passed legislation to join ECS.

Every jurisdiction pays an annual fee and is represented by seven commissioners, most often the governor, a member of the house, a member of the senate, and four others appointed by the governor. The 1992 chair of the board of commissions was John R. McKernan, Jr., governor of Maine. Frank Newman is the appointed president of ECS. There are fifty-two full-time staff members. ECS accepts one student intern per year.

Recent operating budgets have surpassed $3 million, with more than $2.4 million from state fees. ECS spends more than $2.9 million yearly, with almost $1 million toward administration and personnel costs. The remainder goes toward ECS projects.

POLICY CONCERNS AND TACTICS

The general concern of ECS is to inform policy makers and state agencies about the need for systems change—that is, comprehensive, long-term restructuring of the education system. According to published materials, ECS has three specific objectives: (1) help create a clearer, richer, more focused vision of the desired outcomes of education; (2) create a clearer, more focused understanding of the important strategies and steps requisite to fundamental, systematic change in education; and (3) contribute to developing a critical mass of women and people of color in leadership roles across the education system.

ECS addresses these concerns through a variety of activities and programs. The Advanced Legislative Program Services in Education (ALPS) Program provides periodic conferences, co-sponsored with the National Conference of State Legislatures, which enable state legislative leaders to share information and talk with experts about education issues. The State Education Policy Seminars (SEPS), co-sponsored with the Institute for Educational Leadership, involve a wide range of leaders in forty-two participating states. The Advisory Commission Network links national experts in education with ECS members.

POLITICAL ACTIVITY

None.

FURTHER INFORMATION

Periodic reports on elementary, secondary, and higher education finance, governance, and legal issues; a publications catalog of its various books and reports; and *State Education Leader*, a quarterly review of issues and happenings in education and politics.

THE ETHICS RESOURCE CENTER, INC.
1120 G Street, N.W., Suite 200
Washington, D.C. 20005
(202) 737-2258   fax: (202) 737-2227
    The Ethics Resource Center, Inc. (ERC) is a nonprofit organization dedicated

to restoring ethical foundations by fostering integrity, encouraging ethical conduct, and supporting basic values.

ORIGIN AND DEVELOPMENT

Founded in 1977, in the aftermath of the Watergate crisis, ERC's roots can be traced back to 1922 when its predecessor organization, American Viewpoint, Inc., began teaching principles of good citizenship to immigrants on Ellis Island.

ORGANIZATION AND FUNDING

ERC is a nonmembership organization. More than two-thirds of Fortune 100 firms have called upon ERC for advice, training products, and counsel in the area of business ethics. ERC has also aided major government agencies, including the Department of Defense, the U.S. Postal Service, the Internal Revenue Service, and two presidential commissions.

ERC is governed by a corporate board of directors under New York State Corporate Charter. Chairman of the board is C. J. Silas, chief executive officer of Phillips Petroleum. Since 1990, Gary Edwards has been president. ERC has a full-time staff of fifteen employees and accepts two student interns annually.

The 1992 operating budget was approximately $1.5 million, with one-third coming respectively from foundations and corporations, client fees, and video and publication sales.

POLICY CONCERNS AND TACTICS

ERC is focusing more and more on primary and secondary education. Its educational team addresses local and national audiences of business and educational leaders on the importance of ethics and character education in the schools. The university-level *Ethics at Work* video series is also being used by high schools to talk about ethical issues students will face in the workplace.

POLITICAL ACTIVITY

None.

FURTHER INFORMATION

Several videos, including *Ethics at Work, Ethics for Life*, and *Not for Sale: Ethics in the American Workplace*; a weekly radio show, "Ethics at Work"; and an annual report.

THE EXPERIMENT IN INTERNATIONAL LIVING
School for International Training
P.O. Box 676
Brattleboro, Vermont 05302-0676
(802) 257-7751

The Experiment in International Living (EIL) is a nonprofit organization that provides students with the knowledge, attitudes, and skills to enable them to contribute personally to international understanding and global development.

ORIGIN AND DEVELOPMENT

EIL was founded in 1932. EIL was the first to initiate the *homestay* concept of learning about the culture of another country in which students would live as a member of one of the families in that country. Homestays remain the basis of many of EIL's programs. According to its published material, EIL has grown into a diversified, worldwide organization that promotes international under-standing through citizen exchange, career-oriented higher education, language instruction, and projects in international development and training.

ORGANIZATION AND FUNDING

EIL is not a membership organization. It is governed by a 33-member board of trustees. The board also has fiduciary responsibilities. William Rotch is chair of the board, and Charles F. MacCormack is the president. EIL employs over 100 associates.

Recent operating budgets have surpassed $47 million. Approximately $11.4 million has come from tuition and fees, and the remainder has come from grants, contracts, gifts, and endowment income. Approximately $47 million was spent, $5 million on administrative services and the rest on program expenses.

POLICY CONCERNS AND TACTICS

EIL is concerned with a variety of international student exchange issues, and seeks to further its goals primarily through its exchange programs. The group also offers congressional testimony.

POLITICAL ACTIVITY

EIL offered supportive testimony at the hearings for the Foreign Language Competence for the Future Act of 1989, emphasizing the need for placing lan-guage training in a cultural context that is relevant to the age and experience of the student.

FURTHER INFORMATION

An annual report, brochures, and a ''Fact Sheet.''

F

/

THE FOREIGN STUDENT SERVICE COUNCIL

2337 18th Street, N.W.
Washington, D.C. 20009
(202) 232-4979   fax: (202) 667-9305

The Foreign Student Service Council (FSSC) is a nonprofit organization that helps connect foreign students studying in the United States with Americans. In doing so, foreign students learn more about American values, culture, and politics.

ORIGIN AND DEVELOPMENT

FSSC was founded in 1957.

ORGANIZATION AND FUNDING

FSSC is not a membership organization. It is governed by a board of directors. The chair has been Richard Murphy since 1989, and since 1987, Frances W. Bremer has been executive director. FSSC has a full-time staff of four employees. It accepts one student intern annually.

The 1992 operating budget was $200,000. Approximately 30 percent of the annual budget comes from private contributions, 25 percent comes from government, 15 percent from corporations, 10 percent from foundations, and 15 percent from earnings. Only 3 percent of the income comes from user fees. Approximately 15 percent of the costs are directed toward administration and 12 percent toward fund-raising. The remainder goes toward programs.

POLICY CONCERNS AND TACTICS

FSSC is concerned with increasing funding for nonsponsored international students. It does not try to affect legislation or public opinion.

POLITICAL ACTIVITY

None.

FURTHER INFORMATION

No information available.

G

/

GREAT LAKES COLLEGES ASSOCIATION
2929 Plymouth Road, Suite 207
Ann Arbor, Michigan 48105-3206
(313) 761-4833   fax: (313) 761-3939

The Great Lakes Colleges Association (GLCA) is designed to preserve and strengthen its member institutions as private colleges of liberal arts and sciences.

ORIGIN AND DEVELOPMENT

The GLCA was chartered in 1962 as a consortium of twelve Midwestern liberal arts colleges. The colleges came together on the basis of common characteristics: high academic standards and levels of achievement and a commitment to the liberal arts and sciences.

ORGANIZATION AND FUNDING

GLCA is governed by a board of directors, a dean's council, and an academic council. The board is comprised of the twelve member presidents, a chief academic officer selected by GLCA colleagues, and three faculty representatives. The board meets twice yearly and approves all projects undertaken by the association, as well as setting the annual budget. The dean's council is comprised of the chief academic officer of each member college. The dean's council oversees the academic quality of consortial programs and offers advice on the consortium's faculty development programs. The academic council includes two faculty members selected from each college, as well as the three faculty members who serve on the board. The academic council reviews matters of particular concern to the faculties of member colleges.

The president of the association since 1990 has been Dr. Carol J. Guardo.

GLCA employs a staff of eight (two part-time positions) and utilizes student interns (one or two per year) and volunteers to do program planning. GLCA is a 501(c)(3) organization with an annual operating budget of $600,000. Budget funding and allocation information is unavailable.

POLICY CONCERNS AND TACTICS

In general, GLCA is interested in fostering the educational quality and managerial effectiveness of its member institutions, as well as building public support for its mission. More specifically, GLCA serves its members through faculty development/assistance activities and programs, curriculum and community initiatives, off-campus and international learning programs, administrative cooperation, and public policy initiatives. GLCA sees federal policy as increasingly important for its member institutions, particularly in the areas of campus safety, retirement policies and pensions, athletic programs, tax incentives for private contributions, and other aspects of college life.

According to GLCA literature, the organization is attempting to meet its goals by means of workshops, conferences, "networking" on alternative strategies and approaches, and pressuring Congress to consider GLCA federal education policy concerns.

POLITICAL ACTIVITY

GLCA has been increasingly active in Washington, D.C., collectively pressing the concerns and needs of its member colleges. The GLCA board holds one of its meetings each year in Washington and devotes time to calls on federal officials, emphasizing to them the interests and problems of its members. Member presidents also present testimony to congressional committees about issues of importance. In addition, GLCA shares in the sponsorship of the Independent Colleges Office, which has represented the interest of the GLCA institutions in Washington for several years.

GLCA does not support or endorse candidates for political office.

FURTHER INFORMATION

No information available.

H
/

HEALTH EDUCATION FOUNDATION
600 New Hampshire Avenue, N.W., Suite 452
Washington, D.C. 20037
(202) 338-3501

The Health Education Foundation (HEF) is a nonprofit organization that develops public awareness of the individual's role in achieving and maintaining mental and physical well-being. HEF fosters health education as a preventative procedure.

ORIGIN AND DEVELOPMENT

HEF was founded in 1975 in response to rising health costs.

ORGANIZATION AND FUNDING

HEF is not a membership organization. A board of directors establishes policy. Since 1975, Morris E. Chafetz has been the executive director. It has a full-time staff of two employees and accepts one intern per year.

The 1992 operating budget was approximately $150,000. More than 90 percent of funding comes from corporations and individual sources. Approximately 15 percent of funding goes toward administration, with the remainder going toward dissemination of information.

POLICY CONCERNS AND TACTICS

HEF advocates moderation in the consumption of alcohol, sugar, and other products. It has created Training for Intervention Procedures (TIPS) by servers of alcohol, a nationwide program designed to train servers and sellers of alcohol in ways to prevent alcohol abuse.

HEF disseminates information to Congress. It is opposed to government involvement in health issues. It tries to increase public awareness of the responsibilities of the individual in maintaining good health.

POLITICAL ACTIVITY

None.

FURTHER INFORMATION

No information available.

THE HOME AND SCHOOL INSTITUTE, INC.
1201 16th Street
Washington, D.C. 20036
(202) 466-3633

The Home and School Institute, Inc. (HSI) is a nonprofit organization that offers programs designed to help families build children's achievement in school and beyond. HSI works with school districts, all levels of government, corporations, and community organizations.

ORIGIN AND DEVELOPMENT

HSI was founded in 1964.

ORGANIZATION AND FUNDING

HSI is not a membership organization. It has a five-member board of directors and a seventeen-member national advisory council. Dorothy Rich is president of the board. Staffing and funding information is unavailable.

POLICY CONCERNS AND TACTICS

Concerned with student achievement, HSI has developed systematic training and informational materials designed to gain total community involvement. The primary program is the MegaSkills Leader Training Program, a "train the trainer" strategy that trains workshop leaders who then conduct workshops throughout their community. The workshop programs contain strategies and techniques for parents to explore their own strengths and to work with their children to develop "MegaSkills"—the values, attitudes, and behaviors that determine individual achievement.

HSI is not involved with affecting public policy or public opinion.

POLITICAL ACTIVITY

None.

FURTHER INFORMATION

Series of brochures and pamphlets including *MegaSkills: How Families Can Help Children Succeed in School and Beyond, The Forgotten Factor in School*

Success—The Family, Survival Guide for Busy Parents, Get Smart: Advice for Teens with Babies, Special Solutions, Bright Idea, Job Success Begins at Home, Families Learning Together, and *Careers and Caring.*

HUMAN RESOURCES RESEARCH ORGANIZATION
66 Canal Center Plaza, Suite 400
Alexandria, Virginia 22314
(703) 549-3611

The Human Resources Research Organization (HRRO) is a nonprofit organization that conducts research in, and evaluation of, behavioral and social sciences with application toward improving human performance and organizational effectiveness.

ORIGIN AND DEVELOPMENT

Established in 1951 as a unit of The George Washington University, HRRO's first task was to carry out an integrated program of human resources for the Department of the Army. In 1967, HRO extended its research and development activities to other departments of the federal government, as well as to state and local governments and to private sector organizations. In 1969, HRRO separated from The George Washington University and became an independent organization.

ORGANIZATION AND FUNDING

HRRO is not a membership organization. It is governed by a board of governors. William C. Osborn is the president. HRRO has a full-time staff of 100 employees. HRRO receives funding from contracts from government and private industry.

POLICY CONCERNS AND TACTICS

HRRO is concerned with increasing organizational effectiveness and offers workshops on improving the capacity of human resources. It does not try to affect legislation or public opinion.

POLITICAL ACTIVITY

None.

FURTHER INFORMATION

Final reports for completed contracts.

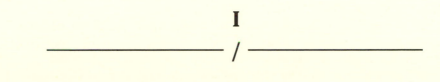

I

THE INSTITUTE FOR ALTERNATIVE FUTURES

108 North Alfred Street
Alexandria, Virginia 22314
(703) 684-5880   fax: (703) 684-0640

The Institute for Alternative Futures (IAF) is a nonprofit research and educational organization that develops techniques for assisting communities and organizations to choose their future more wisely.

ORIGIN AND DEVELOPMENT

IAF was founded in 1977 by Alvin Toffler, James Dator, and Clement Bezold. According to printed material, IAF works with state and local governments and the U.S. Congress to develop their foresight capabilities. It uses futures methods to assist associations and voluntary organizations in training, environmental scanning, and strategic planning. IAF has worked in a wide range of fields such as energy and natural resources, architecture, and child development.

ORGANIZATION AND FUNDING

IAF is governed by a board of directors. Since 1987, James Dator has been the president of IAF. Clement Bezold has been the executive director since 1977. There is a full-time staff of seven persons. Funding information is unavailable.

POLICY CONCERNS AND TACTICS

Information/communication, health, and aging are the areas in which IAF has done its most extensive work recently. It provides presentations, speeches, and workshops on strategic planning. It does not try to affect legislation.

POLITICAL ACTIVITY

None.

FURTHER INFORMATION

Numerous publications including two books, *The Future of Work and Health* by Clement Bezold, et al. (Alexandria, VA: IAF, 1986) and *Pharmacy in the 21st Century*, edited by Clement Bezold, et al. (Alexandria, VA: IAF, 1984).

THE INSTITUTE FOR EDUCATIONAL LEADERSHIP, INC.

1001 Connecticut Avenue, N.W., Suite 310
Washington, D.C. 20036
(202) 822-8405   fax: (202) 872-4050

The Institute for Educational Leadership, Inc. (IEL) is a nonprofit organization that develops and supports leaders who work together to improve educational opportunities and results for all children and youth. Operating nationwide, IEL's programs engage leaders from education and health/human services agencies, schools, school boards, advocacy groups, foundations, corporations, and all levels of government.

ORIGIN AND DEVELOPMENT

IEL was established in 1964 as a component of The George Washington University to run a Washington, D.C.–based federal education policy internship program for midcareer K-12 educators and administrators. IEL became independent in 1981 and within ten years developed leadership programs that, alone or in collaboration with other public and/or independent sector institutions, operate in every state. IEL is currently involved in collaborative efforts with the following organizations: The McKenzie Group, the Joint Center for Political and Economic Development, the U.S. Department of Education Office of Educational Research and Improvement, the National Commission to Prevent Infant Mortality, the Education Commission of the States, and the American Educational Research Association.

ORGANIZATION AND FUNDING

IEL is not a membership organization. It is governed by a twenty-member board of directors. The chair is William S. Woodside. Since 1981, Michael D. Usdan has been president. There are twenty-two full-time employees on staff. IEL accepts up to four student interns per year.

The 1992 operative budget was $2.6 million, of which 51 percent came from foundations, 15 percent from participant fees, 13 percent from corporations or individuals, 11 percent from government, and 10 percent from interest, publications, and fiscal agent fees. Seven percent of costs go toward administration and personnel, 6 percent toward publications, and 87 percent toward programs.

POLICY CONCERNS AND TACTICS

IEL is concerned with increasing the capacity of national, state, and local education policy makers; public school officials and administrators; school board members; and managers of other independent and other private organizations to create enlightened public policy and to respond effectively to the challenges facing public schools. It also promotes the concept that all of these individuals must learn to work together if systematic change in the school systems is to occur.

IEL addresses these issues by: (1) informing private and public sector officials about collaborative strategies and leadership skills through consultations, seminars, study groups, and conferences; (2) encouraging enlightened policy through forums where national, state, and local policy makers meet with their counterparts from the private and independent sectors; (3) designing, implementing, and facilitating multisector collaborations, coalitions, and partnerships at the national, state, and local levels; and (4) identifying and analyzing emerging trends and issues through demographic studies and research programs, disseminating findings through a national publications program.

POLITICAL ACTIVITY

IEL does not directly try to affect legislation or public policy.

FURTHER INFORMATION

Annual report.

INSTITUTE OF INTERNATIONAL EDUCATION
809 United Nations Plaza
New York, New York 10017-3580
(212) 883-8200

The Institute of International Education (IIE) is a nonprofit organization that administers international education, training, and research activities.

ORIGIN AND DEVELOPMENT

IIE was founded in 1918. It manages 200 programs that benefit nearly 10,000 men and women from over 140 nations.

ORGANIZATION AND FUNDING

IIE is not a membership organization. It is governed by a 37-member board of trustees. The 1992 chair was Henry Kaufman. Richard M. Krasno is president. Recent annual operating budgets have totaled more than $138 million. There are 350 full-time staff members. Direct expenses for sponsored program services have been $132.2 million. Total costs for IIE's educational and arts services and supportive services have been $6.4 million.

POLICY CONCERNS AND TACTICS

Involved in international student exchanges.

POLITICAL ACTIVITY

None.

FURTHER INFORMATION

Annual report.

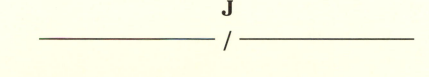

J

JOINT NATIONAL COMMITTEE FOR LANGUAGES
300 Eye Street, N.E., Suite 211
Washington, D.C. 20002
(202) 546-7855　　fax: (202) 546-7859

The Joint National Committee for Languages (JNCL) is a nonprofit organization that provides a forum for cooperation and discussion among language professionals.

ORIGIN AND DEVELOPMENT

JNCL was formed in 1976. It is affiliated with the National Council for Languages and International Studies, which shares its governance structure and staff. JNCL has a membership of thirty-five organizations encompassing all areas of the language profession.

ORGANIZATION AND FUNDING

JNCL operates under a three-tiered governance structure: the delegate assembly, consisting of one voting representative from each member organization; a sixteen-member board of directors; and an administrative steering committee composed of JNCL's officers and two at-large members of the board of directors. It has a full-time staff of three employees. JNCL is entirely member-funded. Budget information is unavailable.

POLICY CONCERNS AND TACTICS

JNCL is concerned with advancing the interests of its member organizations. These interests include foreign language instruction, bilingual education, the classics, linguistics, translation, research, and educational technology. In addition to providing information to the public and members about language issues, JNCL monitors relevant legislation. The group also produces an annual survey of state initiatives, providing an overview of the status of foreign education across the nation.

POLITICAL ACTIVITY

JNCL recently provided supportive testimony at hearings for the National Security Education Act, the Global Education Opportunities Act, Titles V and VI of the Higher Education Act, and the Foreign Language Competence for the Future Act.

FURTHER INFORMATION

Annual survey of state activities, a monthly newsletter, *EPIC EVENTS*, and a *Federal Funding Guide* detailing every government program providing assistance to foreign languages, bilingual education, and English as a second language.

JUNIOR STATESMEN FOUNDATION
650 Blair Island Road, Suite 201
Redwood City, California 94063
(800) 334-5353   fax: (415) 366-5067

The purpose of the Junior Statesmen Foundation (JSF) is to teach high school students about government, to help them develop and polish their leadership skills, to encourage critical thinking, and to transmit the knowledge necessary for active, informed participation in public affairs.

ORIGIN AND DEVELOPMENT

JSF was founded in 1934 as the Junior Statesmen of America. The organization was started by a professor and a group of high school students in California to inform young people about threats to democracy and liberty and about their citizenship responsibilities. JSF was chartered in 1938 in order to provide more formal and organized administrative support and guidance.

ORGANIZATION AND FUNDING

JSF is governed by a board of directors. The executive director since 1969 has been Richard Prosser; the president since 1991 has been Gary Fazzino. Within JSF is a student-run organization called The Junior State, also known as Junior Statesmen of America (JSA). JSF employs a full-time staff of ten (one clerical) and a part-time staff of thirty. The organization also relies on approximately thirty student interns per year, as well as numerous volunteer teacher advisors at the chapter level. JSF also utilizes outside professional marketing advice.

JSF operates on an annual budget of approximately $2 million. Roughly 80 percent of funding is derived from tuition, with the remainder divided primarily between foundation support, corporate support, and private contributions. Only 5 percent of the budget is allocated to administrative expenses, with the remainder allocated to publications, publicity, and conferences.

POLICY CONCERNS AND TACTICS

JSF is an educational group interested solely in issues of civics education, particularly the quality of such education. JSF pursues its goals through educational programs on 300 high school campuses, principally by means of the Junior State program. The organization encourages student participation in public affairs and runs voter registration drives on high school campuses.

POLITICAL ACTIVITY

JSF rarely attempts to influence legislation but does advocate better high school civics education, and legislation may impact on decision-making in this area. JSF does not support or endorse any political candidates.

FURTHER INFORMATION

Annual foundation report, Junior State Handbook, and JSA Report (newsletter).

K

—————————— / ——————————

THE KETTERING FOUNDATION
200 Commons Road
Dayton, Ohio 45459
(513) 434-7300

The Kettering Foundation is a nonprofit organization that finances and facilitates education and research to find and disseminate new ways of addressing fundamental problems in politics.

ORIGIN AND DEVELOPMENT

The Kettering Foundation was founded in 1927 by Charles F. Kettering.

ORGANIZATION AND FUNDING

The Kettering Foundation is not a membership organization. It has a ten-member board of trustees. David Mathews is president and chief executive officer. Its endowment of $130 million provides roughly a third of the resources for the programs.

POLICY CONCERNS AND TACTICS

According to printed material, the Kettering Foundation produces: (1) programs of nongovernmental diplomacy to supplement what is done in official diplomacy; (2) strategies for citizens and officials of governments to understand their respective roles and their relationship in the task of governing the country; (3) alternative ways to deal with political pathologies, like the polarization and fragmentation that undermine a community's efforts to deal effectively with systemic problems, like those that put young people at risk; (4) studies of the way decisions are made on policies that are characterized by significant scientific and technical complexity; (5) workbooks, discussion guides, and other tools for citizen groups to use in attacking the obstacles that stand in the way of community development and educational reform; and (6) new forums that help citizens to work through the difficult choices that the public must make on policy questions.

POLITICAL ACTIVITY

None.

FURTHER INFORMATION

A monthly newsletter, *The Kettering Foundation Connections*; and a quarterly journal, the *Kettering Review.*

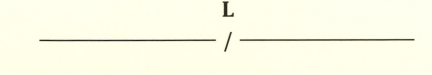

L

THE LINGUISTIC SOCIETY OF AMERICA
1325 18th Street, N.W., Suite 211
Washington, D.C. 20036-6501
(202) 835-1714

The Linguistic Society of America (LSA) is a nonprofit organization that provides a forum for the dissemination of ideas about linguistics teaching and research.

ORIGIN AND DEVELOPMENT

LSA was founded in 1924 and today has 5,000 individual members and 2,000 institutional members.

ORGANIZATION AND FUNDING

LSA is governed by an executive committee. The 1992 president was Arnold Zwicky. Since 1980, Margaret W. Reynolds has been executive director. Two employees comprise the full-time staff. The 1992 operating budget was $475,000, of which 70 percent came from membership fees and 30 percent from conference fees and publication sales.

POLICY CONCERNS AND TACTICS

LSA is primarily concerned with the dissemination of information about linguistics research and teaching. It is not involved with public policy.

POLITICAL ACTIVITY

None.

FURTHER INFORMATION

A journal and a newsletter.

M

---- / ----

MUJERES ACTIVAS EN LETRAS Y CAMBIO SOCIAL
c/o Ethnic Studies Program
Santa Clara University
Santa Clara, California 95053
(408) 554-4511

Mujeres Activas En Letras Y Cambio Social (MALCS) did not respond to our inquiries. According to the 1993 edition of the *Encyclopedia of Associations*, MALCS was founded in 1982 and has about ninety members. Its annual budget is approximately $25,000. Dr. Alma Garcia is the chairperson. The primary purpose of MALCS is to assist Latin-American women who conduct research on Chicano and Latino issues. It publishes a directory of members every three years and a newsletter, *Noticiera de MALCS*, three times a year.

MUSIC EDUCATORS NATIONAL CONFERENCE
1902 Association Drive
Reston, Virginia 22091
(703) 860-4000   fax: (703) 860-1531

The Music Educators National Conference (MENC) is a nonprofit organization that is dedicated to the advancement of music education.

ORIGIN AND DEVELOPMENT

MENC was founded in 1907 when 104 music teachers from 16 states answered an invitation to take part in a special conference for school music teachers in Keokuk, Iowa. It serves as an umbrella organization for all levels and interests in music education. It has 15 allied organizations as well as 52 state and international federated organizations, with a total of 62,000 members.

ORGANIZATION AND FUNDING

MENC is governed by a ten-member national executive board. Karl J. Glenn has been president since 1990. John J. Mahlmann has been executive director since 1983. MENC has forty-three full-time employees.

The 1992 operating budget was $4 million, about half of which came from membership fees and the other half from conference and publication fees. Approximately 30 percent of funding is directed toward administrative and personnel costs with the rest targeted toward membership services and publications.

POLICY CONCERNS AND TACTICS

According to its annual report, MENC is primarily concerned with conducting programs that build a "vital musical culture and an enlightened musical public." It does so by increasing public awareness (Music in Our Schools Month) and by sponsoring student honor societies. MENC does inform Congress about the concerns of music educators.

POLITICAL ACTIVITY

None.

FURTHER INFORMATION

Over 100 publications on music education.

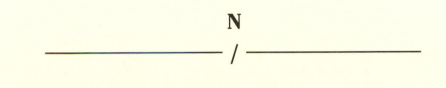

NATIONAL ALLIANCE OF BLACK SCHOOL EDUCATORS
2816 Georgia Avenue, N.W.
Washington, D.C. 20001
(202) 483-1549   fax: (202) 483-8323

The National Alliance of Black School Educators (NABSE) is a nonprofit organization representing African-American teachers and administrators at all levels of education. Its purpose is to advance education among African-Americans.

ORIGIN AND DEVELOPMENT

NABSE was founded in 1970, emerging out of a meeting of black superintendents in Chicago. There are over 20,000 members of NABSE and affiliate chapters in 35 states, Canada, Great Britain, Germany, and the Caribbean.

ORGANIZATION AND FUNDING

NABSE is governed by an executive board. No other information is available.

POLICY CONCERNS AND TACTICS

NABSE is concerned with all aspects of education for African-American students. In 1987 NABSE was instrumental in establishing the African American Education Week, and the introduction of commemorative resolutions in both the U.S. Senate and House of Representatives.

POLITICAL ACTIVITY

NABSE testifies on Capitol Hill on all education bills. The group has recently been active in education reappropriation bills and the renewal of the Civil Rights

Act. NABSE has also lobbied Congress on international issues, such as ending apartheid in South Africa. NABSE endorsed Bill Clinton for the presidency in 1992.

FURTHER INFORMATION

Several publications, including pamphlets titled "1 Shared Dream: 1970–1987," "Saving the African American Children," and "Blueprint for Action."

NATIONAL ART EDUCATION ASSOCIATION
1916 Association Drive
Reston, Virginia 22091-1590
(703) 860-8000   fax: (703) 860-2960

The National Art Education Association (NAEA) is a nonprofit organization dedicated to advancing knowledge, leadership, professional development, and service in art education. NAEA's purpose is to promote and maintain quality instruction in visual arts programs at all levels of learning.

ORIGIN AND DEVELOPMENT

NAEA was founded in 1947 when several smaller organizations merged. It has developed subsections in elementary, secondary, and higher education, as well as for art administrators and members associated with museums. There are approximately 15,000 members.

ORGANIZATION AND FUNDING

NAEA is governed by a twelve-member board of directors. The 1992 president was James Clarke. Since 1983, Thomas A. Hatfield has been executive director. NAEA has a full-time staff of twelve employees.

The 1992 operating budget was $2 million, of which 45 percent came from membership fees and 55 percent from conventions and publication sales. Approximately 40 percent of funding went toward membership services and another 40 percent toward publications. The remaining funds went toward administration and personnel costs.

POLICY CONCERNS AND TACTICS

NAEA is primarily concerned with the status of art education in American schools, specifically with standards in programs and facilities. It tries to affect legislation and public opinion through the dissemination of information. NAEA considers itself a "professional association, not a lobbying group."

POLITICAL ACTIVITY

None.

FURTHER INFORMATION

Several publications, including pamphlets "A Statement on Arts Education to Governors and State Legislators" and "NAEA Co-Sponsored Academies and Institutes"; and a monthly newsletter, *National Arts Placement.*

NATIONAL ASSOCIATION FOR CHICANO STUDIES

c/o Dr. Carlos S. Maldonado
Eastern Washington University
Chicano Education Program
Monroe Hall 198, MS-170
Cheny, Washington 99004
(509) 359-2404

The National Association for Chicano Studies (NACS) did not respond to our inquiries. According to the 1993 edition of the *Encyclopedia of Associations,* NACS was founded in 1971 and has 301 members. Its general coordinator is Dr. Carlos S. Maldonado. The primary purpose of NACS is to increase the visibility of Chicano issues. NACS publishes its *Annual Proceedings.*

NATIONAL ASSOCIATION FOR CORE CURRICULUM

404 Robert I. White Hall
Kent State University
P.O. Box 5190
Kent, Ohio 44242-0001
(216) 672-2580

The National Association for Core Curriculum (NACC) is a membership corporation designed to promote educational programs variously known as core, common learnings, integrative curriculum, unified studies, combined studies, block-time, humanities, or general education at all levels, from elementary through graduate school.

ORIGIN AND DEVELOPMENT

NACC began in 1953 as the result of a conference called by the University of West Virginia College of Education to consider the establishment of a national council of core teachers. Formal organization into present structure, as well as incorporation in the state of New York, occurred in 1964. Today the association has approximately 100 members.

ORGANIZATION AND FUNDING

The association is governed by an advisory committee that serves at the invitation of the executive secretary-treasurer. The executive director since 1961 has been Dr. Gordon F. Vars. The organization maintains a small part-time staff and relies almost entirely on the work of volunteers. Outside professionals are occasionally utilized for conferences, workshops, and "action labs."

NACC is a 501(c)(3) organization with an annual budget of approximately $1,000; 95 percent of the budget is funded by membership fees and 5 percent by the sale of publications. The entire budget is allocated to membership services: a quarterly newsletter, curriculum materials, monographs, and information services.

POLICY CONCERNS AND TACTICS

NACC is interested in taking advantage of the widespread interest in interdisciplinary and integrative curriculum to advocate a forward-looking approach that utilizes more completely the lessons learned from past attempts at integration. With this in mind, the association is interested in (1) teaching educators about the theoretical basis for and the historical roots of integration and (2) maintaining and publicizing research on integrative programs. The association seeks to meet these goals by means of publications; presentations at national, state, and regional conferences; and information services.

POLITICAL ACTIVITY

None.

FURTHER INFORMATION

Conference proceedings, 1953–1973; informational brochures; list of publications; and *The Core Teacher* (newsletter).

NATIONAL ASSOCIATION FOR EQUAL OPPORTUNITY IN HIGHER EDUCATION
Black Higher Education Center, Lovejoy Building
400 12th Street, N.E.
Washington, D.C. 20002
(202) 543-9111   fax: (202) 543-9113

The National Association for Equal Opportunity in Higher Education (NAFEO) is an association of historically black colleges and universities committed to the creation of successful higher education programs in its member institutions.

ORIGIN AND DEVELOPMENT

NAFEO was founded in 1969 and today consists of 117 institutions enrolling approximately 300,000 students.

ORGANIZATION AND FUNDING

The association is governed by a board of directors comprised of the presidents of select member institutions. Additional organizational/funding information is unavailable.

POLICY CONCERNS AND TACTICS

NAFEO's primary aim is to increase the flow of students from minority and lower-income families, mostly African-American, into the mainstream of U.S. society. According to association literature, NAFEO seeks to accomplish its goals by: (1) building the case for securing increased support from federal agencies, philanthropic foundations, and other sources; (2) increasing the active participation of African-Americans in the leadership of educational organizations together with memberships on federal boards and commissions relating to education; (3) providing periodic public information on member colleges in order to highlight their needs; (4) acting as a voice for historically African-American colleges; (5) acting as a coordinator for a variety of organizations and activities committed to similar goals; and (6) briefings to presidents of member institutions on national policy issues affecting African-Americans in higher education.

NAFEO relies on a full range of programs to meet its goals, including the coordinating and pooling views of member institution presidents and articulating them to policy makers on issues deemed significant to African-Americans in higher education.

POLITICAL ACTIVITY

None.

FURTHER INFORMATION

Brochure.

NATIONAL ASSOCIATION FOR GIFTED CHILDREN
1155 15th Street, N.W., Suite 1002
Washington, D.C. 20005
(202) 785-4268

The National Association for Gifted Children (NAGC) is designed to help parents, educators, and public officials recognize the abilities of gifted children and youth.

ORIGIN AND DEVELOPMENT

NAGC was founded in 1954, and today maintains a membership of approximately 7,000, including international members.

ORGANIZATION AND FUNDING

NAGC is governed by a board of directors consisting of five officers and twenty-four at-large members. The president since 1991 has been Dr. Barbara Clark, and the executive director since 1989 has been Peter D. Rosenstein. The association employs a full-time staff of six, and utilizes volunteers for a variety of projects. NAGC is broken down into fourteen divisions: computers and technology, conceptual foundations, counseling and guidance, creativity, curriculum, early childhood, futures, global awareness, parent and community, professional development, research and development, special populations, special schools/ programs, and visual/performing arts.

The association is a 501(c)(3) organization with an annual budget of between $600,000 and $1 million. Funding sources and allocation information are unavailable.

POLICY CONCERNS AND TACTICS

According to association literature, the primary concerns of NAGC are to (1) disseminate information related to gifted children; (2) serve as public advocate concerning the needs of the gifted; (3) promote research and development on the nature and education of the gifted; and (4) encourage the development of state and local organizations that support gifted education. Recently, specific areas of concern have included educational acceleration issues; identification of the gifted among lower income, handicapped, or non-English-speaking populations; and the practice of ''grouping'' students with advanced abilities. The association seeks to address these concerns and others through a variety of publications (including policy position statements), an annual education convention, and occasional political advocacy efforts.

POLITICAL ACTIVITY

According to NAGC literature, the association helped win passage of the Jacob K. Javits Act for Gifted and Talented Education. The act was designed in part to promote ways of identifying young people that are not currently being served in gifted programs. The association continues to provide relevant information to the media and public officials through its Washington, D.C.–based legislative liaison.

FURTHER INFORMATION

No information available.

NATIONAL ASSOCIATION FOR HUMANITIES EDUCATION
University of Minnesota–Duluth
208 Cina Hall
10 University Drive
Duluth, Minnesota 55812-2496
(218) 726-8237

The National Association for Humanities Education (NAHE) seeks to promote the integrated teaching and learning of the humanities in schools, universities, museums, and other public programs.

ORIGIN AND DEVELOPMENT

NAHE was founded in 1970 as a result of a New York State Education Department meeting in 1970 on the state of humanities education. Current membership is approximately 230.

ORGANIZATION AND FUNDING

NAHE is governed by a president, board of directors, and executive secretary. Presidential and board elections are held biennially. The 1993 president was Darrell Bourque, and the executive director since 1983 has been Fred E. H. Schroeder. NAHE is a federally tax-exempt organization with an annual budget that ranges between $3,000 and $4,000. The entire budget is funded through membership fees, and the entire budget is allocated to the publication of a quarterly journal.

POLICY CONCERNS AND TACTICS

NAHE has an ongoing concern with preparing teachers in interdisciplinary humanities and fine arts education. Teacher certification may be a future concern, depending on new leadership priorities. Goals are met through the publication of a journal and an annual conference.

POLITICAL ACTIVITY

None.

FURTHER INFORMATION

A quarterly journal.

NATIONAL ASSOCIATION FOR THE EDUCATION OF YOUNG CHILDREN

1834 Connecticut Avenue, N.W.
Washington, D.C. 20009
(202) 328-2614

The National Association for the Education of Young Children (NAEYC) is a nonprofit organization seeking to improve the quality of educational services available for young children and their families. It offers a wide range of services including a voluntary, national accreditation system for early childhood programs.

ORIGIN AND DEVELOPMENT

NAEYC was founded in 1926 as a result of the proliferation of nursery schools through the United States. Today the organization has more than 77,000 members.

ORGANIZATION AND FUNDING

NAEYC is governed by a board of trustees. Staff information is unavailable. The 1992 operating budget was $6.4 million, of which 20 percent came from publications receipts, 21 percent from membership fees, 20 percent from conference fees, and the remainder from accreditation and the sale of audiovisual items. Approximately 30 percent goes toward administrative and membership services and 30 percent toward publications and audiovisual items. The remainder goes toward conferences and accreditation.

POLICY CONCERNS AND TACTICS

NAEYC is concerned with enhancing the quality of child development. In addition to providing professional development opportunities and program accreditation services, NAEYC provides information to members about legislation affecting early childhood services.

POLITICAL ACTIVITY

None.

FURTHER INFORMATION

An annual report; a bimonthly journal, *Young Children*; and a thirty-one-page publication catalog.

NATIONAL ASSOCIATION FOR WOMEN IN EDUCATION
1325 18th Street, N.W., Suite 210
Washington, D.C. 20036-6511
(202) 659-9330   fax: (202) 457-0946

The National Association for Women in Education (NAWE) seeks the advancement and professional development of women who are college and university administrators.

ORIGIN AND DEVELOPMENT

NAWE was founded in 1916 at Columbia University Teachers' College by Kathryn Sissian Phillips and other deans of women at several U.S. colleges and universities. NAWE has ties to the National Education Association,* the American Council on Education, the National Coalition for Women and Girls in Education, the Association for Black Women in Higher Education, and the National Council for Research on Women. Current membership is approximately 2,000.

ORGANIZATION AND FUNDING

NAWE is governed by a fourteen-member elected executive board. The 1993 president was Dr. Augustine Pounds, and the executive director since 1979 has been Dr. Patricia Rueckel. The association employs a staff of four (all part-time) and relies on student interns and volunteers for a variety of projects.

NAWE is a 501(c)(3) organization with an annual operating budget of approximately $383,000. Approximately 50 percent of funding is derived from membership fees, 20 percent from endowment earnings, 20 percent from program revenues, and 10 percent from corporate contributions. Approximately 30 percent of the budget is allocated to membership services, 30 percent to publications, and less than 1 percent for lobbying activities. Additional budget allocation information is unavailable.

POLICY CONCERNS AND TACTICS

Policy concerns include pay equity, professional advancement, access issues, leadership development, and a variety of other women's issues and political causes (such as sexual harassment, sexual assault, AIDS, sex role stereotyping, retirement/pension benefits, equal opportunity employment practices, and disability issues). NAWE seeks to accomplish its goals through supportive networks, publications, various awards and issues programs, an annual conference, liaison work with other related organizations, and political lobbying.

POLITICAL ACTIVITY

According to association literature, NAWE maintains a strong presence in Washington, D.C. In the past NAWE has actively supported the enforcement of Title IX of the Civil Rights Act, the proposed Equal Rights Amendment, the Civil Rights Restoration Act, and proposals to increase AIDS funding and education. The association's political activity often takes the form of a resolution or a sign-on to key legislation and position papers, or working in conjunction with related groups. Although NAWE does not support or endorse particular candidates for office, it does support the advancement of women in politics in general.

FURTHER INFORMATION

Brochure, *Initiatives* (quarterly journal), "About Women on Campus" and "NAWE News" (newsletters), handbook, and periodic special-interest newsletters.

NATIONAL ASSOCIATION FOR YEAR-ROUND EDUCATION
P.O. Box 711386
San Diego, California 92171-1386
(619) 276-5296   fax: (619) 571-5754

The National Association for Year-Round Education (NAYRE) advocates improved K-12 education through the reorganization and expansion of the school year. NAYRE is the only national repository of information about year-round education.

ORIGIN AND DEVELOPMENT

NAYRE was founded in 1972 as a loosely organized, volunteer group. In 1986 the group absorbed the history, budget, most of the bylaws, conference structure, and officers of the National Council of Year-Round Education. Today NAYRE is a permanent association with eight state affiliates.

ORGANIZATION AND FUNDING

NAYRE is governed by a board of directors elected by the membership. The membership is composed of 1,516 individual members, 102 institutional members, and 2 commercial members. The 1993 president of NAYRE was Patrick McDaniel, and Charles E. Ballinger has been the executive director since 1980. NAYRE employs 3 full-time, nonclerical staff members and 2 part-time staff members.

NAYRE is a 501(c)(3) organization with an annual operating budget of approximately $531,200. A total of 82 percent of budget funding is from conference income, 11 percent from membership fees, and 7 percent from miscellaneous sources. Approximately 50 percent of the budget is allocated to administration, 33 percent to conference expenses, 6 percent to membership services including a quarterly newsletter and directories, 9 percent to publications and publicity, and 2 percent to lobbying activities.

POLICY CONCERNS AND TACTICS

According to association literature, NAYRE is interested in reorganizing the traditional school calendar, especially the length of the school year, in order to encourage a continuous learning process. In order to accomplish its goals, NAYRE seeks to build public support through education by means of conferences, seminars, and workshops, various publications, media appearances, and talks with local community groups.

POLITICAL ACTIVITY

NAYRE attempts to influence education policy by working with state legislators. NAYRE does not support or endorse political candidates.

FURTHER INFORMATION

Quarterly newsletter, directories.

NATIONAL ASSOCIATION OF CATHOLIC SCHOOL TEACHERS

1700 Sansom Street, Suite 903
Philadelphia, Pennsylvania 19103
(215) 665-0993

The National Association of Catholic School Teachers (NACST) did not respond to our inquiries. According to the 1993 edition of the *Encyclopedia of Associations*, it was founded in 1978 and has approximately 5,000 members. The president of NACST is John J. Reilly; the association has a staff of one. The primary purpose of NACST is to assist its members in collective bargaining. It also tries to influence education policy by promoting nonpublic and Catholic education issues. NACST publishes periodically an association newsletter, the *National Association of Catholic School Teachers—Newsworthy*.

NATIONAL ASSOCIATION OF COLLEGE ADMISSION COUNSELORS
1631 Prince Street
Alexandria, Virginia 22314-2818
(703) 836-2222   fax: (703) 836-8015

The National Association of College Admission Counselors (NACAC) seeks to promote understanding of the college transition process and to help counselors and admissions officers improve their effectiveness with students.

ORIGIN AND DEVELOPMENT

NACAC began in 1937 when a group of Midwestern colleges sought to create a code of conduct to guide institutions in their dealings with students in the transition process. Today the organization maintains a membership of 5,500 spread over 24 state and regional affiliates.

ORGANIZATION AND FUNDING

The association is governed by an executive board and assembly. The 1992–1993 president was Cleve Latham, and the executive director since 1986 has been Frank Burtnett. NACAC employs a full-time staff of twenty-nine, plus student interns and volunteers for a variety of tasks.

NACAC is a 501(c)(3) organization with an annual operating budget of approximately $4 million. Roughly 84 percent of funding is derived from program, service, and product revenues, and roughly 16 percent from membership fees. Approximately 52 percent of the annual budget is allocated to administrative and governing expenses, 42 percent to membership services (programs, services, and products), 5 percent to publications and dissemination of information, and 1 percent to governmental relations activities.

POLICY CONCERNS AND TACTICS

NACAC is concerned with upholding professional ethics within the field, creating professional development opportunities of members, maintaining program standards, studying and responding to human relations issues in the field, and responding to diversity issues. The association utilizes programs, conventions, public information campaigns, published standards guidelines, product development, and other member services as a means of accomplishing its goals. NACAC attempts to affect legislation through informing federal and state officials of student needs and how counselors and admissions officers address them, and by making officials aware of association positions, particularly on ethics issues.

POLITICAL ACTIVITY

None.

FURTHER INFORMATION

Resources guide that lists a full range of available publications, *Journal of College Admission*, and NACAC Bulletin.

NATIONAL ASSOCIATION OF COLLEGE AND UNIVERSITY ATTORNEYS

One Dupont Circle, N.W., Suite 620
Washington, D.C. 20036
(202) 833-8390   fax: (202) 296-8379

The National Association of College and University Attorneys (NACUA) is a nonprofit organization dedicated to improving the quality of legal assistance to colleges and universities by educating attorneys and administrators to the nature of campus issues.

ORIGIN AND DEVELOPMENT

NACUA was founded in 1960. A group of college and university attorneys got together in an informal setting to discuss issues of common concern. They decided to repeat the event the following year and thereafter. There are approximately 2,500 members in NACUA.

ORGANIZATION AND FUNDING

NACUA is governed by a fifteen-member board of directors. The 1991 president of NACUA was Beverly Ledbetter. Since 1980, the executive director has been Phillip M. Grier. NACUA has a full-time staff of nine employees. It accepts four student interns annually.

The 1992 operating budget was $1.1 million, of which 50 percent came from membership fees, 30 percent from meeting fees and publication sales, and the remainder from endowment earnings. Approximately 50 percent of expenditures is directed toward administrative and personnel costs, 30 percent toward membership services, and 20 percent toward publications.

POLICY CONCERNS AND TACTICS

NACUA is concerned with the cost of delivering legal services to colleges and universities. It is also concerned with ethical issues affecting college and university attorneys. It addresses these issues through Continuing Legal Education workshops, dissemination of information through the Legal Reference Service, and its publications. NACUA does not try to affect legislation or public opinion.

POLITICAL ACTIVITY

None.

FURTHER INFORMATION

A quarterly journal, *The College Law Digest*; and an annual report.

NATIONAL ASSOCIATION OF COLLEGE AND UNIVERSITY BUSINESS OFFICERS
One Dupont Circle, N.W., Suite 500
Washington, D.C. 20036
(202) 861-2500   fax: (202) 861-2583

The National Association of College and University Business Officers (NA-CUBO) is a nonprofit organization that is dedicated to anticipating the issues affecting higher education and to promoting sound management and financial administration of colleges and universities.

ORIGIN AND DEVELOPMENT

NACUBO was founded in 1962, but its roots reach back to the founding of the Central Association in 1912. The Central Association was the first regional association to be established. The Eastern Association was established in 1920, the Southern Association in 1928, and the Western Association in 1936. These four regional associations combined with the American Association of College and University Business Officers to form the National Federation of College and University Business Officers.

ORGANIZATION AND FUNDING

Membership is by institution, which includes 2,100 colleges and universities in the United States, Canada, and other foreign countries. NACUBO is governed by a 21-member board of directors. The 1992 board chair was Carl E. Hanes, Jr. Caspa L. Harris, Jr., has been the president since 1987. There are 51 full-time employees, and NACUBO accepts 1 student intern annually.

Recent operating budgets have approximated $6.5 million, of which 53 percent has come from membership fees and 7 percent from foundations, individuals, and corporations. The remaining 40 percent has come from publications and fees. Approximately 25 percent of the budget is directed toward administrative and personnel costs. The remainder goes toward membership services.

POLICY CONCERNS AND TACTICS

NACUBO seeks to represent colleges and universities by reflecting the management and financial interests of higher education at the national level. It is also concerned with issues such as direct lending, reimbursement bond regulations, minority scholarships, postretirement benefits, academic productivity, rightsizing, tuition discounting, and total quality management. NACUBO addresses these issues through dissemination of information both to member institutions and to lawmakers and through congressional testimony. It also offers professional development workshops and publications.

POLITICAL ACTIVITY

NACUBO testified in support of direct lending at the hearings for the Financial Aid for All Students Act of 1991. It also provided supportive testimony at the reauthorization hearings for the Stafford Loan Program and Title III and Title VIII of the Higher Education Act.

FURTHER INFORMATION

"Special Action Reports"; Special Advisory Reports"; and a newsmagazine, *Business Officer*.

NATIONAL ASSOCIATION OF EDUCATIONAL BUYERS, INC.

450 Wireless Boulevard
Hauppauge, New York 11788
(516) 273-2600   fax: (516) 273-2305

The National Association of Educational Buyers (NAEB) is a nonprofit organization designed to promote the development and use of ethical and effective purchasing management techniques among member institutions.

ORIGIN AND DEVELOPMENT

NAEB was founded in 1920 by educational institutions in order to share specialized information of concern to nonprofit organizations. In 1930 NAEB members founded the E & I Cooperative Service (higher education's purchasing co-op), and the two organizations remain closely linked. There are 1,900 NAEB members, divided among 20 regional groups.

ORGANIZATION AND FUNDING

NAEB is governed by a volunteer board elected annually by the membership at large. The current president is Soledad Harmon, and the executive director is Neil D. Markee. The association employs a staff of seven (one part-time) and relies on volunteers to assist with workshop instruction, writing, and publishing.

NAEB is a 501(c)(3) organization with an annual operating budget of $800,000. The annual meeting and other meetings generate approximately 85 percent of funding, with the remainder coming from endowment earnings, individual contributions, and other miscellaneous sources. Approximately 75 percent of the budget is allocated to membership services (booklets, newsletter, workshops, and electronic mail) and 25 percent to administrative expenses.

POLICY CONCERNS AND TACTICS

NAEB has inhouse policy concerns associated with developing a new relationship with its regional organizations. These changes will require a reworking of tax status, articles of incorporation, and by-laws. The association is also seeking to find more effective ways of providing members with the specialized information they need. Toward this end, the association has plans to increase computer use and enhance member communication, as well as occasional public relations work with campus residents, vendors, and the industry at large.

POLITICAL ACTIVITY

None.

FURTHER INFORMATION

A variety of informational booklets and a newsletter.

NATIONAL ASSOCIATION OF ELEMENTARY SCHOOL PRINCIPALS

1615 Duke Street
Alexandria, Virginia 22314
(703) 684-3345   fax: (703) 548-6024

The National Association of Elementary School Principals (NAESP) is a non-profit organization that is dedicated, according to its mission statement, to assuring that every student receive the world's best elementary and middle school education. NAESP's mission also includes representing the interests of, and providing professional development opportunities for, elementary school principals.

ORIGIN AND DEVELOPMENT

NAESP was founded in 1921. During the previous year, a group of elementary school principals attending a class in school administration and supervision at the University of Chicago became strongly interested in the idea of having a national organization for elementarv school principals. It is closely associated with the National Association of Secondary School Principals.* Currently both organizations disseminate and sell the presidential Academic Fitness Award Pins and the Study Skills Program. NAESP has 26,000 members.

ORGANIZATION AND FUNDING

NAESP is governed by a board of directors. The 1992 president was Lillian Brinkley. Since 1982 Samuel G. Sava has been executive director. There are thirty-six full-time employees. NAESP accepts two student interns per year.

The 1992 operating budget was approximately $4.9 million, of which 64 percent came from membership fees, 2 percent from corporations, 4 percent from endowment earnings, and the remainder from product sales and conference registration; 20 percent of the budget is directed toward administrative and personnel costs, 30 percent toward membership services, 17 percent toward publications, 12 percent toward lobbying activities, 89 percent toward product development, and 13 percent toward convention expenses.

POLICY CONCERNS AND TACTICS

NAESP is concerned with several issues: early childhood readiness to learn, national educational standards and assessments, professional development support from school administrators, and comprehensive health and social services for children and their families. NAESP addresses these issues by working with state and federal lawmakers.

POLITICAL ACTIVITY

NAESP provided testimony at the hearings for the America 2000 Excellence in Education Act, arguing for reductions in funding for the Leadership in Educational Administration program. It also testified at the hearings for the Education Excellence Act and the Equity and Excellence in Education Implementation Act. At the hearings, it encouraged Congress to provide full funding for Chapter 1, Blue Ribbon Schools, Head Start, magnet schools program, and Even Start. NAESP also encouraged Congress to redirect funds from alternative certification proposals to professional development programs, to increase recruitment funding for minority teachers, and to integrate health and social programs into education programs.

FURTHER INFORMATION

Publications and brochures on childhood education and professional development.

NATIONAL ASSOCIATION OF FOREIGN STUDENT ADVISORS' ASSOCIATION OF INTERNATIONAL EDUCATORS

1875 Connecticut Avenue, N.W., Suite 1000
Washington, D.C. 20009-5728
(202) 462-4811   fax: (202) 667-3419

The National Association of Foreign Student Advisors' Association of International Educators (NAFSA-AIE) is a nonprofit organization that provides professional development and service to individuals and organizations interested in offering educational exchange programs.

ORIGIN AND DEVELOPMENT

AIE was founded in 1948 as a professional association for individuals working with foreign students studying at U.S. colleges and universities. It has expanded into an organization that is also involved in study abroad programs and other dimensions of international education. AIE has about 6,500 members.

ORGANIZATION AND FUNDING

AIE is governed by a board of directors. The 1992 president was Richard Reiff. Since 1977, Jack Reichard has been the executive director. There are forty full-time staff members. AIE also accepts two to three student interns each year.

The 1992 operating budget was $3 million, with 40 percent from membership fees, 30 percent from user fees, and the remainder coming from foundations, corporations, and individual contributions. Approximately 20 percent is spent on administrative and personnel costs, 55 percent on membership services, 20 percent on publications, and 5 percent on lobbying activities.

POLICY CONCERNS AND TACTICS

AIE is concerned with a variety of issues that affect foreign students and American students studying abroad, including credentials, foreign student tax issues, and foreign student employment issues. It is currently interested in facilitating exchanges with the former Soviet Union and Eastern European nations. AIE believes that more funding should be available for study abroad programs and international exchanges. It addresses these issues through lobbying and advocacy activities, keeping members informed, and disseminating information through press releases.

POLITICAL ACTIVITY

AIE has lobbied Congress for increased funding of the Fulbright program.

FURTHER INFORMATION

An annual report and a monthly newsletter, *NAFSA: Association of International Educators Newsletter.*

NATIONAL ASSOCIATION OF INDEPENDENT COLLEGES AND UNIVERSITIES
122 C Street, N.W.
Washington, D.C. 20001
(202) 347-7512   fax: (202) 628-2513

The National Association of Independent Colleges and Universities (NAICU) is a nonprofit organization that informs the public and government about the accomplishments and concerns of independent higher education. NAICU is a lobbying organization, and affecting legislation is one of its primary purposes.

ORIGIN AND DEVELOPMENT

NAICU was founded in 1976. Prior to that date, NAICU was a subsection of the Association of American Colleges.*

ORGANIZATION AND FUNDING

There are 813 member institutions. NAICU is governed by a forty-four-member board of directors. The 1992 chair was William Cotter. Since 1988, the president has been Richard F. Rosser. There are twenty-three full-time staff members. NAICU accepts four student interns each year.

The 1992 operating budget was $2.5 million, with 80 percent derived from membership fees and the remainder from foundations, interest, publications, and conference fees. Approximately 30 percent of the budget is spent on research, and 40 percent is spent on lobbying activities. The remainder is spent on administration (10 percent) and membership services (20 percent).

POLICY CONCERNS AND TACTICS

NAICU is concerned with federal policies affecting independent colleges and universities, such as student aid, tax policy, science facilities, and regulatory issues. It addresses these issues through lobbying and through a public affairs program that highlights the contributions of independent colleges and universities.

POLITICAL ACTIVITY

During the reauthorization hearings for the Higher Education Act, NAICU testified in support of increasing the maximum Pell Grant to $4,000, expanding eligibility for Pell Grants to families with incomes up to $43,000, simplifying statutory definitions for dependent students, allowing the transfer of up to 25 percent of campus-based funds among programs, expanding loan payback alternatives and consolidation options, and revitalizing Part A of Title III and equity in Part A of Title III between two- and four-year institutions. NAICU also testified in support of the Education Excellence Act and the Equity and Excellence in Education Implementation Act, where it advocated changes in the needs analysis to permit the qualification of students from homes with modest income. NAICU also provided supportive testimony at the reauthorization hearings for the Carl D. Perkins Vocational Education Act.

FURTHER INFORMATION

Numerous reports.

NATIONAL ASSOCIATION OF INDEPENDENT SCHOOLS
1800 M Street, N.W., Suite 460 S.
Washington, D.C. 20036
(202) 833-4757   fax: (202) 833-4763

The National Association of Independent Schools (NAIS) is a nonprofit organization that speaks on behalf of independent elementary, middle, and secondary education. In serving its member schools, NAIS has a threefold purpose: (1) to advance high standards of educational quality and ethical behavior; (2) to preserve the independence of member institutions; and (3) to affirm the values of diversity, choice, and opportunity for all students.

ORIGIN AND DEVELOPMENT

NAIS was founded in 1962 by the merger of the Independent School Education Board, an organization of independent schools founded in 1925, and the Council of Independent Schools, an association of state and regional independent school associations founded in 1943. NAIS is a founding member of the Council for American Private Education.* NAIS also works closely with the Council for Advancement and Support of Education.* It is an institutional member of the American Council on Education, The College Board,* and the Education Writers Association.

ORGANIZATION AND FUNDING

NAIS has over 1,000 member schools. NAIS represents 369,285 students, 39,052 teachers, and 7,137 administrators. It is governed by a 24-member board of directors composed of school heads, trustees, and faculty members who are elected by active member schools and member associations. The 1992 chair was Karan A. Merry. Since 1991, Peter D. Relic has been president. NAIS has a full-time staff of 40 employees.

Recent operating budgets have approximated $5.2 million, the majority of which has been derived from membership dues, financial aid services, and fees from conferences, workshops, and publications. Approximately $5.2 million has been spent annually. About $2.6 million has gone toward administrative and personnel costs and the remainder toward membership services and publications.

POLICY CONCERNS AND TACTICS

NAIS is especially concerned about issues related to equity and access in education, tax treatment of charitable gifts, the recruitment of new teachers, compensation for teachers, gender equity, multicultural education, and professional development.

NAIS addresses these issues by working individually and in coalition with other nonprofit organizations. It has a government relations department that designs and implements an advocacy strategy and works to build a network of influential independent school proponents.

POLITICAL ACTIVITY

None.

FURTHER INFORMATION

An annual report and numerous publications, including pamphlets titled "Audio-Visual Marketing Handbook for Independent Schools," "Business Management for Independent Schools," and "A Legal Primer for Independent Schools."

NATIONAL ASSOCIATION OF PARTNERS IN EDUCATION, INC.

209 Madison Street, Suite 401
Alexandria, Virginia 22314
(703) 836-4880   fax: (703) 836-6941

The National Association of Partners in Education, Inc. (NAPE) is a nonprofit organization that provides leadership in the formation and growth of effective partnerships that ensure the success of all students.

ORIGIN AND DEVELOPMENT

NAPE was found in 1988. It was created from the merger of two organizations: National School Volunteer Programs, Inc. (begun in 1964) and National Symposium on Partnerships in Education (begun in 1984). The latter organization was formerly sponsored by the White House Office on Private Sector Initiatives. NAPE has more than 7,000 members.

ORGANIZATION AND FUNDING

NAPE is governed by a twenty-six-member board of directors. The 1992 president was David L. Goodman. Since 1981, Daniel W. Merenda has been the executive director. NAPE has two full-time staff members and accepts student interns.

The 1992 operating budget was $1.5 million, with approximately 60 percent from foundations and corporations, 20 percent from membership fees, and 20 percent from publication sales. Expenditures went toward membership services (80 percent), administration and personnel (15 percent), and fund-raising (5 percent).

POLICY CONCERNS AND TACTICS

NAPE is primarily concerned with disseminating information about the need for greater educational partnerships among government, business, and education groups.

POLITICAL ACTIVITY

None.

FURTHER INFORMATION

An annual report; a monthly newsletter, *Partners in Education*; and a series of guides and manuals, including *A Practical Guide to Creating and Managing School/Community Partnerships, How to Organize and Manage School Volunteer Programs*, and *How to Evaluate Your Educational Partnership*.

NATIONAL ASSOCIATION OF PRINCIPALS OF SCHOOLS FOR GIRLS
4050 Little River Road
Hendersonville, North Carolina 28739
(704) 693-8248   fax: (704) 693-1490

The National Association of Principals of Schools for Girls (NAPSG) seeks to advance the cause of education for women and girls and to provide a congenial environment in which common educational aims, ideals, and objectives may be shared.

ORIGIN AND DEVELOPMENT

NAPSG was founded in 1915, and today has a membership of 550.

ORGANIZATION AND FUNDING

The association is governed by an executive council. The 1993–1995 president is Agnes C. Underwood, and the executive director since 1980 has been Nancy E. Kussrow. NAPSG has no paid staff. The association is a nonprofit organization with an annual operating budget of $84,500 that is funded largely through membership fees.

POLICY CONCERNS AND TACTICS

NAPSG is concerned with the following: moral development of students and values education, effective learning styles, single-sex educational issues, school choice issues, and college admissions issues. The association addresses these concerns through a speakers' program and an annual meeting.

POLITICAL ACTIVITY

None.

FURTHER INFORMATION

Proceedings of annual meeting.

NATIONAL ASSOCIATION OF PRIVATE, NONTRADITIONAL SCHOOLS AND COLLEGES

182 Thompson Road
Grand Junction, Colorado 81503
(303) 243-5441

The National Association of Private, Nontraditional Schools and Colleges (NAPNSC) seeks to establish the validity, integrity, and international recognition of private, nontraditional education.

ORIGIN AND DEVELOPMENT

NAPNSC was founded in April 1974 as a means for assuring the quality of private, freestanding, nontraditional schools, colleges, and universities. NAPNSC has nine institutional members, twelve individual members, and fourteen commission members.

ORGANIZATION AND FUNDING

NAPNSC is governed by a board of trustees comprised of elected institutional representatives. The board appoints members to the NAPNSC Accrediting Commission. The president since 1989 has been N. Charles Dalton, and the executive director since 1974 has been H. Earl Heusser. NAPNSC employs a full-time staff of two.

The association is a 501(c)(3) organization with an annual budget of approximately $60,000. Approximately 50 percent of the budget is funded by membership fees, 40 percent by individual contributions, and 10 percent by user fees; 50 percent of the budget is allocated to administration, 30 percent to membership services, 10 percent to litigation, and 10 percent to publications.

POLICY CONCERNS AND TACTICS

Of immediate concern to NAPNSC are changes in recognition criteria resulting from the July 1992 amendments to the Higher Education Act of 1965. NAPNSC is currently revising and updating its petition for recognition by the U.S. Secretary of Education.

POLITICAL ACTIVITY

None.

FURTHER INFORMATION

No information available.

NATIONAL ASSOCIATION OF PRIVATE SCHOOLS FOR EXCEPTIONAL CHILDREN
1522 K Street N.W., Suite 1032
Washington, D.C. 20005
(202) 408-3338　　　fax: (202) 408-3340

The National Association of Private Schools for Exceptional Children (NAPSEC) seeks to promote excellence in educational opportunities for children and youths with disabilities by enhancing the role of private education as a vital component of the U.S. educational system.

ORIGIN AND DEVELOPMENT

NAPSEC was founded in 1971 by a small group of special educators in Florida who had a common interest in providing educational opportunities for children and youth with disabilities. Through this unified group and national organization the membership hoped to educate and serve students by creating a vehicle for networking about common problems and to influence public policy. Through the years NAPSEC has developed important ties with other organizations advocating children's interests, such as the Council for Exceptional Children, the Council of American Private Education, the Council of Administrators of Special Education, and the National Association of State Directors of Special Education.* Current NAPSEC membership is 207.

ORGANIZATION AND FUNDING

NAPSEC is governed by a fourteen-member volunteer board of trustees who are elected by the membership and serve a two-year term. The executive director reports to the executive committee of the board and is responsible for the effective operation of the NAPSEC office. The president since January 1993 has been Stanley Mopsik, and the executive director since September 1990 has been Sherry L. Kolbe. The association employs a full-time staff of three and utilizes volunteers extensively in the governing of the organization. NAPSEC has also used the donated services of graphic artists and legal counsel in the past.

NAPSEC is a 501(c)(4) social welfare organization with an annual budget of approximately $250,000. A total of 65 percent of funding is from membership fees, 25 percent from conferences, 5 percent from private/individual contributions, 3 percent from publication sales, and 2 percent from mailing list sales; 45 percent of the budget is allocated to administration, 25 percent to membership services (consultant database, insurance program, discounted furniture, referral service, reduced long distance rates, and reduced subscription rates), 20 percent to publications, and 10 percent to lobbying activities.

POLICY CONCERNS AND TACTICS

General policy interests include: (1) rights to appropriate education for children and youths with disabilities (inclusive education); (2) leadership roles for the private component in the development of special education; (3) quality and effectiveness in private special education; (4) public understanding of the role and contributions of special education in serving children and youth with disabilities; (5) intercommunication between private special education facilities; (6) cooperation between public and private education in meeting the needs of children and youths with disabilities; and (7) tax code issues regarding charities.

NAPSEC seeks to accomplish its goals by means of educational seminars and conferences; newsletters and monthly publications; timely information on legislative, regulatory, and judicial developments; and a free public referral service.

POLITICAL ACTIVITY

According to its 1992 annual report, NAPSEC's Governmental Affairs Committee was quite active during 1992. The committee worked with Senator Paul Simon's (D-Ill.) office to rewrite the Chapter 1 Handicapped Program (P.L. 89-313) in an effort to improve the program before its reauthorization in 1993. The committee also kept abreast of developments at the Department of Education by representing NAPSEC at a meeting held by Dr. Robert Davila, Assistant Secretary of Special Education and Rehabilitation Services, to discuss issues of concern to the private special education community. In addition, the association sent participants to Washington, D.C., on Governmental Affairs Day to voice concerns about the 3 percent floor on charitable tax deductions, and appropriation levels for fiscal year 1993 special education programs. The 1993 Governmental Affairs Day was lengthened due to the attendees' request for more time to cover the issues.

FURTHER INFORMATION

Annual report, brochures, *Journal of Emotional and Behavioral Problems in Children and Youth*, directory, quarterly newsletter, and monthly legislative report.

NATIONAL ASSOCIATION OF PROFESSIONAL EDUCATORS
412 1st Street, S.E.
Washington, D.C. 20003
(202) 484-8969

The National Association of Professional Educators (NAPE) is a nonprofit organization that advocates that strikes are unethical. NAPE promotes only voluntary membership in all organizations and believes in "public control" of education.

ORIGIN AND DEVELOPMENT

NAPE was founded in 1972 after the National Education Association* and the American Federation of Teachers* sanctioned a teachers strike in Los Angeles. Many teachers opposed to the principle of strike left both organizations and formed NAPE.

ORGANIZATION AND FUNDING

NAPE membership figures are unavailable. The association is governed by an elected board of directors. Since 1987, Jo Ann Hewitt has been president. Philip Strittmatter has been executive director since 1985. Information on staffing and budget is also unavailable.

POLICY CONCERNS AND TACTICS

NAPE is an antiunion, antistrike organization. According to its annual report, it believes that: (1) Congress should not try to be a "national school board" and dictate how teaching should be done; (2) state legislators should remove from current legislation any regulations that could be better determined at the school district level; (3) members of a state board of education should be chosen in some way to reflect public control of education; (4) state superintendents should be appointed by the state board and be responsible to it; (5) local boards should delegate as much authority as practical to each local school; (6) district and school administrators' priority should be to help teachers develop their skills and use their unique personalities in the best way to educate the children, and never to impose their own ideas of instruction on all teachers; and (7) teachers should be able to devote the school day to preparation and teaching duties and not be required to leave their classes to substitutes in order to attend meetings or perform duties that could be done by others.

NAPE relies on individual members to express these views to the public and to lawmakers.

POLITICAL ACTIVITY

None.

FURTHER INFORMATION

Annual report.

NATIONAL ASSOCIATION OF SCHOOL PSYCHOLOGISTS
8455 Colesville Road, Suite 1000
Silver Springs, Maryland 20910
(301) 608-0500   fax: (301) 608-2514

The National Association of School Psychologists (NASP) is a nonprofit organization that seeks to advance the rights, welfare, education, and mental health of children and youth. It also seeks to promote the profession of school psychology.

ORIGIN AND DEVELOPMENT

NASP was founded in 1969, and today there are 16,000 members.

ORGANIZATION AND FUNDING

NASP is governed by a delegate assembly, elected by membership. Members also elect national officers and regional directors who serve as NASP's executive board. The 1992 president was Kathy Durbin. Since 1989, Margaret Gibelman has been the executive director. There are fourteen full-time members in NASP.

The 1992 operating budget was $2.5 million, with 52 percent from membership fees and 15 percent from user fees. The remainder comes from publications and conference fees. Approximately 20 percent of the budget goes toward administrative and personnel costs and 40 percent toward membership services. The remaining portions of the budget are directed toward publications and lobbying.

POLICY CONCERNS AND TACTICS

NASP is concerned with a number of public policy issues, including corporal punishment in schools, psychological help for the handicapped, school psychology training, and early childhood education.

POLITICAL ACTIVITY

According to its annual report, NASP is a very active lobbying group. One of its top priorities is to ban corporal punishment in the schools. It assisted in building a coalition of over thirty national organizations that advocated the abolition of physical punishment through congressional action. NASP was instrumental in including psychological services as part of the 1990 reauthorization of the Education of the Handicapped Act. School psychology training scholarships were written into the proposed National Teacher Act of 1990. It was also a participant in the passage of the 1987 Hawkins-Stafford Elementary and Secondary Education Amendments. NASP also plays a role in supporting increased federal funds for Head Start, Chapters 1 and 2. It is an active member of the

Committee for Education Funding. It recently employed a full-time government and professional relations staff.

FURTHER INFORMATION

Annual reports and numerous publications and position papers; a newsletter, *Communique*, eight times a year; and a quarterly journal, *The School Psychology Review*, dealing with research, theoretical perspectives, and critical issues.

NATIONAL ASSOCIATION OF SCHOOLS OF MUSIC

11250 Roger Bacon Drive, Suite 21
Reston, Virginia 22090
(703) 437-0700   fax: (703) 437-6312

The National Association of Schools of Music (NASM) is an agency responsible for the accreditation of music curricula. The services of the association are available to all types of degree-granting institutions in higher education and to non-degree-granting institutions offering preprofessional programs or general music training programs.

ORIGIN AND DEVELOPMENT

According to association literature, NASM was founded by 6 schools in 1924 for the purpose of securing a better understanding among institutions of higher education engaged in music, of establishing a more uniform method of granting credit, and of setting minimum standards for the granting of degrees and other credentials. The work of the association in its early years was financed largely by the Carnegie Corporation of New York. In November 1975, representatives of member institutions ratified proposals creating a category of membership for non-degree-granting institutions. Currently there are 549 member institutions.

ORGANIZATION AND FUNDING

The officers of NASM are the president, vice-president, treasurer, secretary, and nine regional chairmen, all of whom are elected by the membership. These thirteen individuals, along with the immediate past president and the leadership of the accrediting commissions, constitute the board of directors. The executive director is an officer and an *ex officio* member of the board. The executive body of the board of directors is the executive committee, whose members are the president, vice-president, treasurer, secretary, chairman and associate chairman of the Commission on Accreditation, and executive director (*ex officio*). Members of the commissions are elected by members of the association. The president since 1991 has been Frederick Miller. The executive director since 1975 has been Samuel Hope. NASM employs a full-time staff of eight and a part-time staff of one. The association also relies on volunteers to assist with accreditation visits.

NASM is a 501(c)(3) organization with an annual operating budget of approximately $1 million. A full 95 percent of the budget is financed by membership fees and 5 percent by publications. A total of 25 percent of the budget is allocated to administration; 70 percent to the annual meeting, workshops, and other membership services; and 5 percent to accreditation materials, reports, and other publications.

POLICY CONCERNS AND TACTICS

According to NASM literature, the general aims and objectives of the organization are: (1) to provide a national forum for the discussion and consideration of concerns relevant to the preservation and advancement of standards in the field of music in higher education; (2) to develop a national unity and strength for the purpose of maintaining the position of music study in the family of fine arts and humanities in our universities, colleges, and schools of music; (3) to maintain professional leadership in music training and to develop a national context for the professional growth of the artist; (4) to establish minimum standards of achievement in music curricula without restricting an administration or school in its freedom to develop new ideas, to experiment, or to expand its program; (5) to recognize that inspired teaching may rightly reject a "status quo" philosophy; and (6) to establish that the prime objective of all educational programs in music is to provide the opportunity for every music student to develop individual potential to the utmost. NASM seeks to achieve these objectives through the accreditation process.

POLITICAL ACTIVITY

None.

FURTHER INFORMATION

Directory and handbook.

NATIONAL ASSOCIATION OF SCHOOLS OF PUBLIC AFFAIRS AND ADMINISTRATION
1120 G Street, N.W., Suite 520
Washington, D.C. 20005
(202) 628-8965   fax: (202) 626-4978

The National Association of Schools of Public Affairs and Administration (NASPAA) is a nonprofit organization committed to improving the quality of education for public service.

ORIGIN AND DEVELOPMENT

NASPAA was formed officially in 1970. It is the result of continued informal meetings of university and college deans and directors of graduate-level public administration programs that began in the 1950s. NASPAA was formed to help guide developing public administration programs. It has evolved into an accrediting body for programs offering the master's degree in public administration

(MPA). NASPAA maintains close ties with the American Society for Public Administration (ASPA). There are 220 institutional members in NASPAA.

ORGANIZATION AND FUNDING

NASPAA is governed by a nineteen-member executive council elected by the membership. The 1992 president was Frank Thompson. Since 1983, Alfred M. Zuck has been executive director. NASPAA has a full-time staff of six employees and occasionally accepts student interns.

The 1992 operating budget was $640,000, with 57 percent from membership fees, 27 percent from government, and 16 percent from endowment earnings. Approximately 40 percent of the budget goes toward administrative and personnel costs, and 50 percent goes toward membership services (conferences, accreditation, clearinghouse on curriculum, and faculty information); 10 percent goes toward the dissemination of information about member institutions to prospective students and prospective employers of students.

POLICY CONCERNS AND TACTICS

NASPAA is primarily an accreditation agency, although it does take positions that advance the condition of public servants at all levels of government. It is primarily concerned with issues relating to the evaluation of education quality, curriculum standards, and increasing diversity of students and faculty.

NASPAA addresses these issues by conference activities and workshops, speeches, and op-ed pieces in newspapers. It does not try to affect legislation.

POLITICAL ACTIVITY

None.

FURTHER INFORMATION

Standard guidelines for a variety of academic issues, including curriculum, diversity, and internships.

NATIONAL ASSOCIATION OF SCHOOLS OF THEATRE
11250 Roger Bacon Drive, Suite 21
Reston, Virginia 22090
(703) 437-0700   fax: (703) 437-6312

The National Association of Schools of Theatre (NAST) is an accrediting body designed to foster a closer relationship among schools of theatre in order to improve educational standards.

ORIGIN AND DEVELOPMENT

NAST was founded in 1969, and today has a membership of eighty-four.

ORGANIZATION AND FUNDING

NAST is governed by a board of directors and the officers of the association. The board is comprised of the officers (president, vice-president, secretary, treasurer, and executive director), the chair of the Commission on Accreditation, the immediate past president, and four directors elected by the membership. The executive director is appointed by the board, and the officers are elected by the membership at large. The Commission on Accreditation reviews membership applications and consists of a chairman, two public members, and five representatives. The association also maintains a committee on ethics, a committee on research, and a committee on nominations.

The 1993 president was R. Keith Michael, and the executive director since 1975 has been Samuel Hope. NAST maintains a staff of nine (one part-time), and utilizes volunteers to assist with accreditation visitations.

The association is a 501(c)(3) organization with an annual budget of $110,000. A full 95 percent of funding is from membership fees, and 5 percent is from publications. A total of 25 percent of the budget is allocated to administration, 70 percent to the annual meetings, workshops, and other membership services; and 5 percent to accreditation materials, reports, and other publications.

POLICY CONCERNS AND TACTICS

According to association literature, the objectives of NAST are: (1) to establish a national forum to stimulate interest in creative arts education; (2) to establish a variety of educational and institutional standards for theatre arts programs; (3) to encourage the development of high-quality and creative instruction; (4) to evaluate the quality of schools of theatre; (5) to assure students and parents that accredited programs provide a sound education; (6) to assist institutions in program development; (7) to encourage the cooperation of theatre professionals in the educational and accreditation process; and (8) to maintain a national voice to be heard in matters pertaining to theatre and member institutions.

POLITICAL ACTIVITY

None.

FURTHER INFORMATION

Handbook, directory.

NATIONAL ASSOCIATION OF SECONDARY SCHOOL PRINCIPALS
1904 Association Drive
Reston, Virginia 22091
(703) 860-0200   fax: (703) 476-5432

The National Association of Secondary School Principals (NASSP) is a nonprofit organization of middle-level and high school administrators that addresses school quality and professional leadership needs of school administrators. NASSP also advances the development of student leadership through the sponsoring of activities like the National Honor Society, the National Junior Honor Society, and the National Association of Student Councils.

ORIGIN AND DEVELOPMENT

NASSP was founded in 1916 as a result of a small group of principals believing that they could share ideas to improve schools. NASSP works closely with other major education associations. It also works closely with business groups, such as the Business Roundtable. NASSP also sponsors the National Honor Society and the National Association of Student Councils. The association has 43,000 members.

ORGANIZATION AND FUNDING

NASSP is governed by an eighteen-member board of directors with the majority of members elected regionally. The 1992 president was Robert Blaine. Since 1989, Timothy J. Dyer has been the executive director. There are seventy-eight full-time staff members.

The 1992 operating budget was $18 million, with 28 percent from special services, 26 percent from membership, 22 percent from student services, and the remainder from grants and contracts and professional development activities. Approximately 25 percent of expenditures go toward administration and personnel, 29 percent toward membership services, 19 percent toward professional development activities, and 16 percent toward student services. The remainder goes toward grants and contracts.

POLICY CONCERNS AND TACTICS

According to its brochure *Goals for the 21st Century*, NASSP is concerned with six issues: (1) reconceptualizing middle and high schools with specific emphasis on new technologies, multicultural sensitivities, international developments, and social issues; (2) advocating equal opportunities for all students; (3) establishing an optimum climate for effective teaching and learning in all schools; (4) creating strategies to increase public recognition that education should be the nation's number one priority; (5) professional development for membership; and (6) financial stability of schools.

NASSP addresses these issues through conference activities, workshops, and publications. Through a state-based Federal Relations Network and daily activities by a federal relations staff, NASSP tries to affect legislation and the opinions of lawmakers. It testified during the hearings of the Twenty-First Century Teachers Act, in support of making professional development courses available to assistant principals and principals, linking the improvement of school-based management with the enhancement of the skills of teachers and principals, developing a principals recognition program, emphasizing the recruitment of minorities into the teaching profession, and improving teaching in urban schools.

POLITICAL ACTIVITY

None.

FURTHER INFORMATION

An annual report, a membership guide, and a brochure *Goals for the 21st Century.*

NATIONAL ASSOCIATION OF STATE BOARDS OF EDUCATION

1012 Cameroon Street
Alexandria, Virginia 22314
(703) 684-4000

The National Association of State Boards of Education (NASBE) is a nonprofit organization that represents state and territorial boards of education. In doing so, NASBE seeks to accomplish four tasks: to strengthen state leadership in educational policy making; to promote excellence in the education of all students; to advocate equality of access to educational opportunity; and to assure continued citizen support for public education.

ORIGIN AND DEVELOPMENT

NASBE was founded in 1936.

ORGANIZATION AND FUNDING

Membership consists of boards of education in all fifty states, Guam, and Puerto Rico. NASBE is governed by an elected fourteen-member board of directors. The 1992 president was Patricia Hamner. Gene Wilhoit is executive director. NASBE has a full-time staff of nineteen employees. The 1992 operating budget was over $2.1 million, of which $1.4 million came from grants and contracts, $600,000 from membership dues, and the remainder from registration fees, publications, and interest. Total expenses were $2 million. Administrative and personnel costs consumed almost $1.5 million, and the rest went toward membership services.

POLICY CONCERNS AND TACTICS

According to its annual report, NASBE is concerned with all aspects of elementary and secondary education, from AIDS education to math education. It holds an annual legislative conference that permits members to exchange views with congressional leaders. It also has a governmental affairs division designed to help state board members understand, influence, and plan for federal education policies that affect them.

POLITICAL ACTIVITY

NASBE has been active on Capitol Hill in testifying on a number of education issues, including the reauthorization of appropriation bills, the reauthorization of the early intervention programs under the Individuals with Disabilities Education Act, and preliminary hearings on creating a Children's Trust. It testified at the hearings for the Education Excellence Act and the Equity and Excellence in Education Implementation Act, questioning the need for new programs that duplicate existing state and federal programs and whether special recognition and scholarship programs are an effective use of limited federal funds. NASBE's input was also sought by the Bush administration's America 2000 education strategy.

FURTHER INFORMATION

An annual report and numerous publications, including *The State Board Connection*, a quarterly newsletter; *Issues in Brief*, a quarterly newsletter devoted to a specific educational issue; and a series of textbooks on a wide range of topics in education policy.

NATIONAL ASSOCIATION OF STATE DIRECTORS OF SPECIAL EDUCATION

King Street Station I
1800 Diagonal Road, Suite 320
Alexandria, Virginia 22314
(703) 519-3800   fax: (703) 519-3808

The National Association of State Directors of Special Education (NASDSE) operates for the purpose of providing services to state agencies in order to facilitate their efforts to educate individuals with disabilities.

ORIGIN AND DEVELOPMENT

NASDSE was founded in 1938. The organization began as an offshoot of the Council for Exceptional Children Association. NASDSE established an office in Washington, D.C., in 1972, and since that time has worked closely with a vareity of organizations involved in the education of the disabled, including parent groups, institutions of higher education, and the federal government.

ORGANIZATION AND FUNDING

NASDSE is governed by a board of directors elected out of the membership ranks on a staggered term basis. Members are typically state department of education employees, particularly division of special education personnel. The 1992–1993 president was Dr. John Heskett, and the executive director since mid-1993 has been Martha J. Fields. NASDSE employs a full-time staff of twenty (4 clerical).

NASDSE is a 501(c)(3) organization with an annual operating budget of approximately $3 million. Approximately 50 percent of funding comes from membership fees and 50 percent from grants and contracts. Budget allocation information is not available.

POLICY CONCERNS AND TACTICS

According to association literature, all NASDSE activities relate to the following general objectives: (1) to expand the capabilities of state education agencies with respect to individuals with disabilities; (2) to provide leadership in the development of national policy related to services that produce successful education outcomes; (3) to be the best national source of information regarding education for individuals with disabilities; (4) to create and maintain a productive and supportive work environment for NASDSE staff; and (5) to become financially stable and develop the resources necessary to achieve goals.

More specifically, association literature expresses a commitment to the following by the year 2000: (1) meeting the needs of all children without reference to assigned labels or categories of severity of disability; (2) assisting schools in providing information, health care, and preschool learning opportunities; (3) assisting schools in providing adult life preparation, including internship programs, multilevels of school-exit points that are outcome-based, educational attendance options, and potential postsecondary options; (4) encouraging schools to treat diversity as a strength so that instruction is adapted to the natural variability of all learners; (5) encouraging schools to make education a lifelong experience for all learners; (6) encouraging schools to provide multiagency, community-based counseling, recreation, and rehabilitation services; and (7) encouraging federal, state, and local governments to provide adequate funding to meet the needs of all students.

NASDSE seeks to achieve these goals by addressing educational issues in conjunction with the membership, related agencies, the federal government, and parent groups. The association is also interested in keeping the public informed by collecting, validating, and disseminating research relating to education of the disabled.

NASDSE attempts to influence legislation at both state and federal levels by supplying timely and accurate data to public officials.

POLITICAL ACTIVITY

NASDSE testified at the hearings for reauthorization of Part H of the Individuals with Disabilities Education Act. At those hearings, it argued for allowing the continued participation of states that had been unable to meet Part H requirements in the fourth or fifth years yet have demonstrated good faith efforts. Further, it advocated that a greater share of Part H appropriations be allocated to states that provide required services to infants and small children. It also testified about the need for technical assistance in order to establish statewide systems of early intervention services for infants and toddlers with disabilities.

FURTHER INFORMATION

Publications ("Counterpoint," "Liaison Bulletin," brochures) and frequent SpecialNet news and bulletins (SpecialNet is an online computer network that services the special education community).

NATIONAL ASSOCIATION OF STATE DIRECTORS OF VOCATIONAL/TECHNICAL EDUCATION

1420 16th Street, N.W.
Washington, D.C. 20036
(203) 528-0216   fax: (202) 797-3756

The National Association of State Directors of Vocational/Technical Education (NASDVTE) is a nonprofit organization committed to advancing leadership and outstanding performance in vocational and technical education.

ORIGIN AND DEVELOPMENT

NASDVTE was founded in 1920 as a result of a need for professional development and experience-sharing.

ORGANIZATION AND FUNDING

NASDVTE has 200 members and is governed by a board of directors. The 1992 president was Roy Peters. Since 1986, Madeleine Hemmings has been executive director. There are 2 full-time staff members. NASDVTE accepts student interns annually.

The 1992 operating budget was $350,000, with 85 percent from membership fees and 15 percent from individual contributions. Approximately 10 percent of funding is directed toward administrative and personnel costs and 80 percent toward membership services. The remainder goes toward publications and lobbying activities.

POLICY CONCERNS AND TACTICS

NASDVTE is concerned with a variety of issues relating vocational and adult education policy, and it advances its interests through member programs, publications, and governmental lobbying.

POLITICAL ACTIVITY

NASDVTE provided supportive testimony at the reauthorization hearings of the Carl D. Perkins Vocational Education Act and at the hearings for the Applied Technology Education Act, the Job Training Partnership Act, and the Adult Literacy and Employability Act. At the hearings for the Perkins Act, it argued for increased funding for new research on vocational education. It also testifies on Capitol Hill in support of other proposals, such as School- to-Work Transition Proposal, Employer Standards Proposal, and performance measures in education.

FURTHER INFORMATION

Annual report.

NATIONAL ASSOCIATION OF STATE UNIVERSITIES AND LAND-GRANT COLLEGES

One Dupont Circle, N.W., Suite 710
Washington, D.C. 20036
(202) 778-0818   fax: (202) 296-6456

The National Association of State Universities and Land-Grant Colleges (NASULGC) is a nonprofit organization that promotes the land-grant mission and impacts national policies and programs on behalf of major research universities.

ORIGIN AND DEVELOPMENT

NASULGC was founded in 1887. Its origins stretch back to 1871 when twenty-nine land-grant campus representatives met in Chicago to discuss mutual problems. A committee was authorized to urge Congress and the state legislatures to establish agricultural experimental stations. A permanent land-grant organization was discussed but not formed. Further informal meetings were held in Washington, D.C. (1872), Columbus, Ohio (1877), and again in Washington, D.C. (1882 and 1883).

Since 1887 NASULGC has expanded to include nonagricultural, state research universities. It also has a subsection, the Office for the Advancement of Public Black Colleges (OAPBC), which represents thirty-five predominantly African-American state universities.

ORGANIZATION AND FUNDING

NASULGC has a membership that includes 148 public research universities. It is governed by a 21-member executive committee. Donald Langenberg was the 1992 chair. Robert L. Clodius is president and chief executive of NASULGC. There are 30 full-time employees. Budget information is unavailable.

POLICY CONCERNS AND TACTICS

NASULGC is concerned with all aspects of teaching, research, and outreach as they affect state and land-grant universities. According to its annual report, NASULGC focuses on several broad policy areas: agricultural and natural resources, higher education research, international affairs, tax and fiscal policy, and the advancement of public African-American colleges. Almost one-third of the full-time staff work in the federal relations division. This division keeps membership informed about developments in Washington and keeps lawmakers informed about the needs of research and land-grant universities.

POLITICAL ACTIVITY

NASULGC testified at the reauthorization hearings of the Higher Education Act of 1965, specifically in support of restructuring loan programs to increase payment flexibility and the elimination of the Income Contingent Loan Program.

FURTHER INFORMATION

Annual report and position papers.

NATIONAL ASSOCIATION OF STUDENT PERSONNEL ADMINISTRATORS, INC.

1875 Connecticut Avenue, N.W., Suite 418
Washington, D.C. 20009-5728
(202) 265-7500   fax: (202) 797-1157

The National Association of Student Personnel Administrators, Inc. (NASPA) is a nonprofit organization that serves colleges and universities by providing leadership and professional growth opportunities for the chief student affairs officer and other professionals who consider higher education and student affairs issues from an institutional perspective.

ORIGIN AND DEVELOPMENT

NASPA was founded in 1919 as a result of several meetings initiated by deans of men at Midwestern universities. The early association, known as the National Association of Deans and Advisors of Men, conducted annual meetings to discuss and clarify the role of deans of men and to exchange pertinent information related to their functions. The name was changed to NASPA in 1951 to broaden the base of the association and to respond to the growing number of women in the profession. There are 6,090 members, including 1,067 institutional members and 4,923 individual members.

ORGANIZATION AND FUNDING

NASPA is governed by an eighteen-member board of directors. The 1992 president was Joan M. Claar. Since 1987, Elizabeth M. Nuss has been executive director. There are five full-time employees. NASPA accepts one student intern each year.

The 1992 operating budget was approximately $1.4 million, of which 56 percent came from membership fees, 36 percent from corporations, 4 percent from endowment earnings, and 4 percent from miscellaneous sources. Administrative and personnel costs account for 47 percent of the budget, membership services account for 37 percent, publications account for 10 percent, and 6 percent is for miscellaneous expenses.

POLICY CONCERNS AND TACTICS

NASPA maintains a general interest in policy issues that affect the lives of college students, such as harassment, risk management, minority scholarships, sexual assault, and campus security. It is also concerned with institutional issues like downsizing, budget and staff reduction, student diversity and multicultural issues, campus discipline, and litigation.

NASPA monitors legislation and informs members of Congress on its position.

POLITICAL ACTIVITY

None.

FURTHER INFORMATION

An annual report, member handbook, occasional papers, monograph series, *The NASPA Forum* (monthly newsletter), and *The NASPA Journal* (quarterly).

NATIONAL CATHOLIC BUSINESS EDUCATION ASSOCIATION

c/o Richard F. Reicherter
Box 982
Emporia, Kansas 66801
(316) 343-8463

The National Catholic Business Education Association (NCBEA) did not respond to our inquiries. According to the 1993 edition of the *Encyclopedia of Associations*, NCBEA was founded in 1945 and currently has 1,000 members. Richard F. Reicherter is its executive director. The primary purpose of NCBEA is to encourage business education research among its members, as well as to assist in curriculum efforts. It maintains an archive and publishes the *Review* on a quarterly basis.

NATIONAL CATHOLIC EDUCATION ASSOCIATION

1077 30th Street, N.W., Suite 100
Washington, D.C. 20007
(202) 337-6232   fax: (202) 333-6706

The National Catholic Education Association (NCEA) did not respond to our inquiries. According to the 1993 edition of the *Encyclopedia of Associations*, NCEA was founded in 1904 and currently has approximately 20,000 members. It employs forty-five staff members, and its budget is about $3 million annually. Catherine T. McNamee is the president of NCEA.

NCEA is concerned with a wide variety of issues. It conducts workshops and conferences for its members, and it tries to affect public policy by working with government agencies. It also maintains a database on Catholic education in the United States.

NCEA offers several publications: *Current Issues in Catholic Higher Education* and *Forum* (both published semiannually), *Data Bank Report* (published annually), and *Momentum* (published quarterly).

NATIONAL CHRISTIAN EDUCATION ASSOCIATION

c/o National Evangelical Association
450 Gunderson Drive
Carol Stream, Illinois 60188
(708) 665-0500   fax: (708) 665-8575

The National Christian Education Association (NCEA) enables evangelical Christians to coordinate ideas, programs, research, and promotion of Christian education at the local church level.

ORIGIN AND DEVELOPMENT

The NCEA was founded in 1942. The association is a commission of the 50,000 member National Evangelical Association, which was founded in 1846 to advance the evangelical view of the Christian faith.

ORGANIZATION AND FUNDING

The NCEA is governed by a 180-member board of administration. The board is composed of representatives from member denominations, state chairmen, commission chairmen, and at-large members. The 1992 president was Dr. Don Argue; the executive director since 1967 has been Dr. Billy Melvin. The NCEA relies on a full-time staff of 16, a part-time staff of 2, 1 student intern, and board, commission, and network volunteers. The NCEA is a nonprofit organization deriving its funding from membership fees and private contributions.

POLICY CONCERNS AND TACTICS

No information available.

POLITICAL ACTIVITY

None.

FURTHER INFORMATION,

Available through the National Association of Evangelicals.

NATIONAL COMMITTEE FOR CITIZENS IN EDUCATION
c/o Center for Law in Education
1875 Connecticut Avenue, N.W., Suite 510
Washington, D.C. 20009
(202) 986-3000   fax: (202) 986-6648

The National Committee for Citizens in Education (NCCE) is a nonprofit organization that seeks to build public support for effective public schools and excellence in education.

ORIGIN AND DEVELOPMENT

Through a grant from the Ford Foundation, NCCE was established in 1973. NCCE has a membership of 500 grass-roots citizens groups.

ORGANIZATION AND FUNDING

NCCE has a nineteen-member governing board. Since 1990, Anne Carlson Hallet has been the president, and, since 1989, J. William Rioux has been the executive director. There is a full-time staff of twelve employees. NCCE accepts two student interns per year.

The 1992 operating budget was $1.4 million, of which 80 percent came from foundations, 12 percent from publication sales, and the remainder from corporate and individual contributions and membership fees. Only 4 percent of the budget goes toward administrative and personnel costs, and the remainder goes toward publication and the dissemination of information.

POLICY CONCERNS AND TACTICS

NCCE is primarily interested in building broad support for public schools. In doing so, it has been active in providing information both to citizens and lawmakers, as well as offering testimony to Congress.

POLITICAL ACTIVITY

NCCE testified in support of the passage of the Family Educational Rights and Privacy Act of 1974. The group was also instrumental in the creation of the Office of Public Participation and Consumer Affairs within the U.S. Department of Education. NCCE conducted a study of state compliance with parent participation aspects of the Handicapped Act, the results of which prompted the U.S. Department of Education to agree in 1981 to accelerate the review of state program administration. With lobbying by NCCE, the U.S. Department of Education strengthened parent participation requirements in Chapter 1 during 1986.

FURTHER INFORMATION

An annual report and numerous publications, including Jocelyn Garlington, *Helping Dreams Survive: The Story of a Project Involving African-American Families in the Education of Their Children*, (Washington, D.C.: NCCE, 1991); *One School at a Time* (informational booklet), and *Parents and Learning Disabilities* (informational booklet).

NATIONAL COMMUNITY EDUCATION ASSOCIATION
801 North Fairfax Street, Suite 209
Alexandria, Virginia 22314-1757
(703) 683-6232   fax: (703) 683-0161

The National Community Education Association (NCEA) seeks to create renewed communities committed to providing lifelong learning opportunities that recognize each individual as both learner and teaching resource.

ORIGIN AND DEVELOPMENT

NCEA was founded in 1966 in Flint, Michigan, as the National Community School Association. The original purposes of the organization were: (1) to promote parent and community involvement in public education, (2) to form community partnerships to address community needs, and (3) the expansion of lifelong learning opportunities for all community residents. The name of the organization was changed in 1974, and today NCEA has a membership of 1,400. The organization maintains ties with the International Community Education Association.

ORGANIZATION AND FUNDING

NCEA is governed by a fourteen-member board of directors, including a president, president-elect, secretary-treasurer, past president, two at-large members, and eight regional directors. The officers are elected by the entire voting membership, and the regional directors are elected by the voting members in their respective regions. The at-large members are elected by the board. The president since 1992 has been R.P.M. Bowden, and the executive director since 1989 has been Starla Jewell-Kelly. NCEA maintains a staff of four (one part-time position), and relies on student interns (approximately three per year), volunteers, and outside professionals for computer work, conference work, and a variety of special projects.

NCEA is a 501(c)(3) organization with an annual operating budget of $563,000; 42 percent of funding is derived from user fees, 24 percent from membership fees, 20 percent from foundation support, 12 percent from endowment earnings, and 2 percent from individual contributions. A total of 49 percent of the budget is allocated to administration, 22 percent to membership services, 26 percent to conferences and workshops, and 3 percent to publications and the dissemination of information.

POLICY CONCERNS AND TACTICS

Current areas of concern include community and parent involvement, service learning, improved facilities for community learning, lifelong "learning literacy," interagency cooperation, and public policy in the area of community education. The association is seeking to tie community education directly to educational reform. Specifically, NCEA seeks to help people understand social change by means of community organization and community education, especially among school-based individuals who might use community education as a problem-solving tool. The association attempts to influence congressional action by providing information on community needs and the programs coordinated by the members of NCEA.

POLITICAL ACTIVITY

According to association literature, NCEA seeks to accomplish its goals by means of task force work designed to target state legislators who are supportive of community education or who have worked in the field. At the national level, NCEA seeks to advance the cause of community education through the Department of Education and Congress. The association does not support or endorse particular candidates for office.

FURTHER INFORMATION

No information available.

NATIONAL COUNCIL FOR ACCREDITATION OF TEACHER EDUCATION

2010 Massachusetts Avenue, N.W., Suite 200
Washington, D.C. 20036-1023
(202) 466-7496   fax: (202) 296-6620

The National Council for Accreditation of Teacher Education (NCATE) is a nonprofit organization that seeks to advance, and encourage institutions to adopt, high standards of professional education. NCATE tries to ensure that requirements for accreditation are related to best professional practice.

ORIGIN AND DEVELOPMENT

NCATE was founded in 1954 by five educational groups: the American Association of Colleges for Teacher Education (AACTE),* the National Association of State Directors of Teacher Education and Certification, the National Commission on Teacher Education and Professional Standards of the National Education Association,* the National Council of Chief State School Officers, and the National School Boards Association.* NCATE became an independent accrediting agency, replacing the accreditation function within teacher education previously conducted by AACTE. There are twenty-seven constituent members in NCATE.

ORGANIZATION AND FUNDING

NCATE's constitution establishes four boards with responsibility for different aspects of the organization's activities: the executive board, which oversees all NCATE standards, policies, and fiscal matters; the unit accreditation board, which determines the accreditation status of professional education units at colleges and universities; the state recognition board, which recognizes states with program approval systems that meet national standards of quality; and the specialty areas studies board, which approves professional education guidelines that institutions are required to address as part of the preconditions process.

The 1992 president of NCATE was Arthur E. Wise. Since 1986, the vice-president has been Donna Gollnick. There are fourteen full-time staff members. The 1992 operating budget was approximately $1.6 million, with about 28 percent coming from foundations, 64 percent from membership fees, and the remainder from publication sales and honorarium fees. Approximately 76 percent of the budget goes toward administrative and personnel expenses, 22 percent toward membership services, and the remainder toward publications.

POLICY CONCERNS AND TACTICS

NCATE is concerned with accreditation standards. It does not try to affect legislation, nor does it try to shape public opinion on educational issues.

POLITICAL ACTIVITY

None.

FURTHER INFORMATION

Standards, Procedures, and Policies for the Accreditation of Professional Education Units (Washington, DC: NCATE, 1993).

NATIONAL COUNCIL FOR THE SOCIAL STUDIES
3501 Newark Street, N.W.
Washington, D.C. 20016
(202) 966-7840   fax: (202) 966-2061

The National Council for the Social Studies (NCSS) is a nonprofit organization dedicated to bringing greater cooperation among historians, sociologists, economists, political scientists, and geographers. As a service organization, the primary functions of NCSS include: (1) providing assistance to the classroom teacher through publications and other services; (2) providing communication and exchange among the various professional groups and individuals associated with the field; (3) supporting investigation into areas of ongoing and current importance to the teaching of social studies; and (4) developing programs dealing with the real social world and encouraging participation in it as part of the social studies program.

ORIGIN AND DEVELOPMENT

NCSS was founded in 1921 as the National Council of Teachers of the Social Studies. NCSS was affiliated with the National Education Association* from 1925 until 1973 when it severed formal ties with that association. Today the group has 29,398 members.

ORGANIZATION AND FUNDING

NCSS is governed by an elected board of directors. The 1992 president was Charlotte Anderson. Since 1984, Frances Haley has been executive director. There are nineteen full-time staff members in NCSS.

The 1992 operating budget is $1.8 million, of which roughly 50 percent comes from membership fees and 50 percent from annual meeting fees, exhibit fees, advertising, and publication sales.

POLICY CONCERNS AND TACTICS

NCSS is concerned with enhancing the quality of social studies teaching. It does so through conferences and publications. It does not to try to affect legislation, nor does it try to shape public opinion.

POLITICAL ACTIVITY

None.

FURTHER INFORMATION

A quarterly journal, *Social Education*.

NATIONAL COUNCIL OF TEACHERS OF ENGLISH

1111 Kenyon Road
Urbana, Illinois 61801
(217) 328-3870   fax: (217) 328-9645

The National Council of Teachers of English (NCTE) seeks to improve the teaching of English and the language arts at all levels of education, to provide an array of opportunities for teachers to continue their professional growth throughout their careers, and to provide a forum for cooperation in order to deal with issues relating to the teaching of English.

ORIGIN AND DEVELOPMENT

NCTE was founded in 1911 when a group of secondary and college-level educators saw the need to discuss important issues relating to the secondary school English curriculum. The group expanded in 1912 to include the concerns of elementary level educators. Currently, NCTE is cooperating on a variety of projects with The College Board,* the International Reading Association, and the Center for the Study of Reading at the University of Illinois. Current NCTE membership is approximately 90,000.

ORGANIZATION AND FUNDING

The executive committee directs the work of a council, following the general policies determined by the board of directors. NCTE operates with three conferences: the Conference on College Composition and Communication, the Conference on English Education, and the Conference on English Leadership. The current president is Jesse Perry (since November 1992), and the current executive director is Miles Myers (since April 1990). NCTE employs a staff of ninety-six (seventy-nine full-time).

NCTE is a 501(c)(3) organization with an annual budget of approximately $7.6 million. A total of 46.8 percent of the budget is derived from user fees, 43.7 percent from membership fees, 7.5 percent from endowment earnings, and 2.0 percent from foundation support; 39.7 percent of the budget is allocated to publications and dissemination of information, 38.7 percent to membership services (including conventions, conferences, committees, and other miscellaneous professional activities), and 21.6 percent to administrative expenses.

POLICY CONCERNS AND TACTICS

NCTE is broadly interested in many policy issues affecting its membership. Recently, the group has focused on national standards debates, testing reform, class sizes, censorship issues, and teacher certification. Specifically, the group has attempted to help teachers in censorship battles, encourage state legislation on class size, assisted in developing credible standards and alternative assessment for English and language arts, and influenced teacher certification efforts. NCTE utilizes affiliate-based "action programs," specific project grants, publications, conventions, conferences, an Education Services program, and federal and state informational liaisons as means for achieving organizational goals.

POLITICAL ACTIVITY

None.

FURTHER INFORMATION

No information available.

NATIONAL COUNCIL OF THE CHURCHES OF CHRIST IN THE U.S.A.—EDUCATION, COMMUNICATION, AND DISCIPLESHIP UNIT
475 Riverside Drive
New York, New York 10115
(212) 870-2227   fax: (212) 870-2030
The Education, Communication, and Discipleship Unit of the National Council of the Churches of Christ in the U.S.A. (NCCC) seeks to advance the teachings of the Church of Christ through educational activities.

ORIGIN AND DEVELOPMENT

NCCC was founded in 1950 by the action of twenty-nine denominations and by the merger of a dozen ecumenical agencies.

ORGANIZATION AND FUNDING

NCCC has 32 member communions. The top policy-making body is the general board, which meets once a year. It is made up of 270 delegates. Each member communion selects its own delegates according to its own procedures, within agreed-upon guidelines. The number of delegates is based on the communion's size.

The current president is Reverend Dr. Syngman Rhee, and the current executive director is Reverend Dr. Joan B. Campbell. NCCC has a staff of 334 professionals and accepts student interns each year.

NCCC is a 501(c)(3) organization with a total operating budget of over $47 million. Funding comes from contributions of church members.

POLICY CONCERNS AND TACTICS

NCCC believes that the schools have a responsibility to include religious information in teaching activities but believes that the Bible should not be used for devotional purposes in the schools. NCCC Washington Office pursues these policies through visiting legislators, presenting testimonies at congressional hearings, and disseminating positions through a newsletter.

POLITICAL ACTIVITY

NCCC provides periodic congressional testimony.

FURTHER INFORMATION

Annual reports, a newsletter, and a set of policy statements in *Policy*.

NATIONAL COUNCIL OF UNIVERSITY RESEARCH ADMINISTRATORS
One Dupont Circle, N.W., Suite 220
Washington, D.C. 20036
(202) 466-3894   fax: (202) 223-5573

The National Council of University Research Administrators (NCURA) is a nonprofit organization that assists individuals with professional interests in the administration of sponsored programs primarily at colleges and universities.

ORIGIN AND DEVELOPMENT

NCURA was founded in 1959. Federal support for research at colleges and universities mushroomed after the launching of Sputnik by the Soviet Union in 1957, and no satisfactory vehicle existed for research administrators to interpret clauses and regulations; nor was there a way for these administrators to confer with colleagues in the academic community. NCURA was established to fulfill the need for information exchange and for an opportunity to discuss mutual problems. There are 2,600 individual members in NCURA.

ORGANIZATION AND FUNDING

NCURA is governed by an executive committee. The 1992 president was Ardis M. Savory. Since 1979, Natalie Kirkman has been the executive director. There are four full-time staff members.

The 1992 operating budget was $471,300, with 57 percent from membership fees and the remainder from workshops and conferences. Approximately 60 percent of the budget goes toward administrative and personnel costs, 24 percent toward membership services, and the remainder toward publications.

POLICY CONCERNS AND TACTICS

NCURA is primarily concerned with regulations and compliance issues affecting the administration of research. It does not try to affect legislation, nor does it try to impact public opinion.

POLITICAL ACTIVITY

None.

FURTHER INFORMATION

A newsletter, a quarterly journal, monographs, and a membership directory.

NATIONAL COUNCIL ON MEASUREMENT IN EDUCATION
1230 17th Street, N.W.
Washington, D.C. 20036-3078
(202) 223-9318

The National Council on Measurement in Education (NCME) is a nonprofit organization that is committed to the continual improvement of testing and measurement practices in education.

ORIGIN AND DEVELOPMENT

NCME was founded in 1927. It is affiliated with the American Educational Research Association. Many members are involved in either the construction and uses of educational tests or the development and evaluation of measurement models and methods. There are approximately 2,000 members of NCME.

ORGANIZATION AND FUNDING

NCME is governed by a board of directors. The 1992 president was Larry Cuban. William J. Russell is the executive officer. There are eleven full-time employees. Budget information is unavailable.

POLICY CONCERNS AND TACTICS

NCME is primarily concerned with the preparation of instructional materials for teachers of educational measurement. It has also developed a resource bank, containing major sources of information on measurement.

NCME does not try to affect legislation, nor does it try to shape public opinion.

POLITICAL ACTIVITY

None.

FURTHER INFORMATION

Journal of Educational Measurement, with articles on technical and theoretical developments in measurement and improvements in the application of measurement methods in educational settings; and *Educational Measurement: Issues and Practice*, featuring articles that deal with the practical aspects of testing in educational settings.

NATIONAL EARTH SCIENCE TEACHERS ASSOCIATION
2000 Florida Avenue, N.W.
Washington, D.C. 20009
(202) 462-6910   fax: (202) 328-0566

The National Earth Science Teachers Association (NESTA) is involved in the advancement, stimulation, extension, improvement, and coordination of earth science education at all levels.

ORIGIN AND DEVELOPMENT

In April 1983, members of the National Association of Geology Teachers and the Michigan Earth Science Teachers Association met at the annual meeting of the National Science Teachers Association (NSTA)* and chartered NESTA. Current membership is 1,000.

ORGANIZATION AND FUNDING

NESTA elects presidential and association officers for two-year terms. Most actions of the association take place at an annual board and membership meeting held in conjunction with the NSTA meeting. Daily business is conducted by the president and executive advisor with input from the president-elect. Major issues are settled by mail or phone votes involving the elected officers. The president since 1992 has been Walter Sharp, and the executive advisor since 1991 has been M. Frank Watt Ireton. NESTA has no paid staff.

The association is a 501(c)(3) organization with an annual operating budget of $11,600. A total of 86 percent of revenues is derived from membership fees, 9 percent from slide sales, 2 percent from rock raffles, and 3 percent from private/individual donations; 85 percent of the budget is allocated to publications, 10 percent to membership services, and 5 percent to administration.

POLICY CONCERNS AND TACTICS

NESTA is concerned with the adoption of national standards for science teaching and how these standards might apply to earth science education. Also of interest are the reform efforts of other science-oriented organizations and how they will impact the earth science classroom. NESTA addresses its concerns through publications, conferences, meetings, and networking.

POLITICAL ACTIVITY

None.

FURTHER INFORMATION

No information available.

NATIONAL EDUCATION ASSOCIATION
1201 16th Street, N.W.
Washington, D.C. 20036-3290
(202) 833-4000

The National Education Association (NEA) is a nonprofit organization that seeks to advance the status, profession, process, and content of education.

ORIGIN AND DEVELOPMENT

NEA was founded in 1857. It is the largest professional and the largest employee organization in the nation. Fifty state-level associations, the Overseas

Education Association,* and associations in Puerto Rico and the District of Columbia are affiliated with NEA. There are more than 12,500 local associations affiliated with NEA. There are more than 2 million members in NEA. Membership includes elementary and secondary school teachers, higher education faculty, educational support personnel, retired education professionals, and students who intend to enter the teaching profession.

ORGANIZATION AND FUNDING

NEA is governed by delegates to the association's annual Representative Assembly. The Representative Assembly consists of over 8,000 delegates representing local and state affiliates, student members, and retirement members. Between the annual assemblies the approximately 130 members of the board of directors meet at least 5 times a year to determine general association policies. A 9-member executive committee acts on association general policies and professional interests between board meetings about 10 times a year.

Recent budgets have averaged around $150 million, with all but $200,000 having come from membership dues. The remainder comes from fees and services. Nearly one-third of the budget is spent on membership services and $30 million on administrative and personnel costs. The remainder is spent on NEA programs.

POLICY CONCERNS AND TACTICS

The NEA is perhaps the most active educational association. It is involved in professional development but also contributes to affecting the opinions of lawmakers and the general public. It invests over $8 million in lobbying Congress and other legislatures.

POLITICAL ACTIVITY

NEA has testified on practically every piece of educational legislation. It has provided testimony in support of the Twenty-First Century Teachers Act, emphasizing the need to attract qualified individuals into the teaching profession. At the hearings for reauthorization of the Carl D. Perkins Vocational Education Act, it supported increasing funding for vocational education that would assist the efforts of local educational agencies in keeping at-risk students in school. At the Perkins hearings, it urged Congress to invest tax dollars to upgrade vocational curriculum.

At the congressional hearings for the Community Collaborative for Early Childhood Development (Smart Start) Act, NEA argued that funds currently directed toward existing programs should not be used to establish new programs. Hence, NEA pointed to the need for coordination of Smart Start services with those found in similar programs. NEA offered testimony in support of funding for teacher preparation, certification, and inservice standards. Here it emphasized the need to include parents in the design and implementation of such activities.

NEA also testified at the hearings for the Education Excellence Act and the

Equity and Excellence in Education Implementation Act. At these hearings, it emphasized the need to expand and enhance the Head Start program and to increase funding for Chapter 1 compensatory education for disadvantaged students, programs which assist in educating the handicapped, the Pell Grant Program, and the Eisenhower Math and Science Program. It also called for raising standards and compensation for education professionals, as well as for funding to enhance recruitment of minority teachers. Further, NEA called for additional funding in the area of adult education.

At the hearings for the Regulatory Impact on Student Excellence Act, NEA supported efforts to modify and enhance the educational system but only if specific modifications were in line with the views of local educational authorities and were consistent with current efforts to assure excellence and equity for all students. NEA expressed opposition to all efforts by the federal government to restrict the discretion of state and local authorities in developing and implementing locally based solutions to education problems.

NEA also testified at the hearings for the National Education Report Card Act. Here NEA argued that only one assessment panel be developed, focusing on the accomplishment of national educational goals.

At the hearings for the reauthorization of discretionary programs in the Education of the Handicapped Act, NEA supported increasing the level of financial assistance to college students enrolled in special education programs, as well as increasing funding for research in this area.

NEA also provided supportive testimony at the hearings for the reauthorization of Impact Aid or Expiring Federal Elementary and Secondary Education Programs.

At the hearings on the Computer Education Assistance Act, NEA also provided supportive testimony. Here it suggested that the federal government should provide direct assistance to local school districts for the acquisition of computer equipment and software, but it should do so in an equitable way. Furthermore, NEA argued that teachers should be involved in each step of acquiring computer technology. NEA emphasized that computers should assist, but not replace, teachers in the classroom.

The NEA also offered supportive testimony at the hearings for the Jacob K. Javits Gifted and Talented Children and Youth Education Act and the Office of Comprehensive School Health Education Act. NEA suggested that the Office of Comprehensive School Health should assist in coordinating technical assistance to school nurses and others responsible for the health of students while at school.

NEA was also active in the reauthorization of the Higher Education Act. It argued on Capitol Hill for an additional $25 million (over the current $5 million) to fund research activities of the National Board of Professional Teaching Standards. It emphasized the need to create and maintain programs that would support individuals pursuing careers in the teaching field, including the reauthorization of the Paul Douglas Teacher Scholarship Program, the Christa McAuliffe Fellowship Program, and the Midcareer Teacher Training Program.

NEA also argued for expansion in the loan forgiveness provisions of the Carl D. Perkins Vocational Education Act.

At the Higher Education Act hearings, NEA also argued for $100 million to establish professional development schools or academies and that the reauthorization bill should include continuation and expansion of funding ($20 million) for the School, College, and University Partnership Program. NEA expressed support for reauthorization of the Leadership in Educational Administration Program, including increasing the authorization to $15 million for fiscal year 1992.

According to Federal Election Commission data, the NEA Political Action Committee contributed during the 1992 calendar year a total of $2,258,897 to 375 Democratic candidates, $87,175 to 32 Republican candidates, and $19,000 to 2 unaffiliated or independent candidates. The association endorsed Bill Clinton in the 1992 presidential elections.

FURTHER INFORMATION

An annual financial report and numerous publications, including *The National Education Association: The Power Base for Education*. Books about or relating to the NEA and its activities:

Berube, Maurice. *Teacher Politics: The Influence of Unions*. Westport, CT: Greenwood Press, 1988.

Cresswell, Anthony, Michael Murphy, and Charles Kerchner. *Teacher's Unions and Collective Bargaining in Public Education*. Berkeley, CA: McCutchan Publishing Corporation, 1980.

Eberts, Randall, and Joe Stone. *Unions and Public Schools*. Lexington, MA: Lexington Books, 1984.

Johnson, Susan. *Teachers' Unions in Schools*. Philadelphia: Temple University Press, 1984.

Murphy, Marjorie. *Blackboard Unions: The AFT and the NEA*. New York: Cornell University Press, 1990.

Selden, David. *The Teacher's Rebellion*. Washington, DC: Howard University Press, 1985.

Urban, Wayne. *Why Teachers Organized*. Detroit: Wayne State University Press, 1982.

West, Allan M. *The National Education Association: The Power Base for Education*. New York: The Free Press, 1988.

NATIONAL HEAD START ASSOCIATION

1309 King Street, Suite 200
Alexandria, Virginia 22314
(703) 739-0875   fax: (703) 739-0878

The National Head Start Association (NHSA) is a nonprofit organization that seeks to: (1) be an advocate for poor and at-risk young children and their families; (2) provide the Head Start community with the opportunity to express their concerns; (3) define strategies on pertinent issues affecting Head Start; (4) serve as an advocate for the Head Start Program; (5) provide training and professional development for the Head Start community; and (6) develop a networking system with other organizations whose efforts are consistent with those of NHSA.

ORIGIN AND DEVELOPMENT

NHSA was created in 1973. A small group of Head Start directors caucused during the annual conference of the national Head Start Community Action Agencies' executive directors about the need to form a Head Start Association. NHSA works closely with the Children's Defense Fund, the National Association of Young Children, and the National Association of Community Action Agencies.

ORGANIZATION AND FUNDING

NHSA has 7,000 members, consisting of Head Start program directors, staff members, and parents. It is governed by a 49-member board of directors, which is comprised of staff members, a friend, a director, and a parent from each of the 12 regions, plus the past president. The 1992 president was Arvern Moore. Since 1992, Sarah M. Greene has been executive director. There are 7 full-time staff members. NHSA accepts 2 student interns per year.

The 1992 operating budget was $1 million, of which 65 percent came from conference fees, 25 percent from membership fees, and the remainder from foundations and corporations. A total of 12 percent of the budget goes toward administration and personnel costs, 30 percent toward membership services, 48 percent toward publications, and 10 percent toward lobbying activities.

POLICY CONCERNS AND TACTICS

NHSA's primary concern is with providing an opportunity for networking and building local support of Head Start programs. The organization is also interested in influencing public policy in areas of immediate concern.

POLITICAL ACTIVITY

NHSA played a key role in the reauthorization of Head Start, part of the Human Services Reauthorization Act of 1990. It also played an active role in the appropriation process which resulted in a $399.8 million increase in fiscal year 1991, up 25 percent over 1990. NHSA also worked closely on the development of legislation (S. 911) that would entitle all eligible children to be served and increase funding to $8 billion by 1997. At the hearings of Smart Start: The Community Collaborative for Early Childhood Development Act of 1988, NHSA argued for increasing funding for teacher training and teacher salaries, enhancing the social service component through training of social workers, and extending the length of class time.

FURTHER INFORMATION

Several position papers, including "Standards for Training Programs in Head Start" and "Adult Training Programs for Head Start Family Members"; a quarterly journal, *Alerts*; and an annual report.

NATIONAL HOME STUDY COUNCIL
1601 18th Street, N.W.
Washington, D.C. 20009
(202) 234-5100   fax: (202) 332-1386

The National Home Study Council (NHSC) is a nonprofit organization that serves as a clearinghouse of information about the home study (correspondence) field. NHSC is also an accrediting agency for home study programs.

ORIGIN AND DEVELOPMENT

NHSC was founded in 1926 under the cooperative leadership of the Carnegie Corporation of New York and the national Better Business Bureau. In 1955, a seven-member accrediting commission was established.

ORGANIZATION AND FUNDING

NHSC has approximately sixty-five schools in its membership. It is governed by a nine-member board of trustees. The 1992 president was William H. Hunding. Since 1992, Michael P. Lambert has been executive director. There are four full-time staff members. The 1992 operating budget was approximately $500,000, all of whick came from membership fees. Approximately 75 percent of the budget goes toward accreditation activities and 25 percent toward trade association activities.

POLICY CONCERNS AND TACTICS

NHSC is primarily concerned with moving from voluntary to mandatory accreditation in the United States, and its programs and publications are geared toward this end. The group also testifies before Congress on important relevant legislation.

POLITICAL ACTIVITY

NHSC provided supportive testimony at the reauthorization hearings of the Higher Education Act, emphasizing the need for federal assistance for correspondence schools. It also testified in support of the Veterans' Education and Disability Compensation Act.

FURTHER INFORMATION

NHSC Accreditation Overview and *Directory of Accredited Home Study Schools.*

THE NATIONAL LEARNING CENTER
Capital Children's Museum
800 Third Street, N.E.
Washington, D.C. 20002
(202) 543-8600   fax: (202) 675-4140

The National Learning Center (TNLC) is a nonprofit organization that is concerned with the development of new educational structure, methods, and materials.

ORIGIN AND DEVELOPMENT

TNLC was founded in 1984 to develop and showcase a range of progressive programs that have included informal environments for lifelong learning, individualized instruction in a formal school setting, the use of computers as personal tools for learning, teacher training programs, and the development of prototype exhibits, science labs, books, software, video, and other media. TNLC has 7,500 members.

ORGANIZATION AND FUNDING

TNLC is governed by a thirty-four-member board of trustees. Since 1984, Ann W. Lewin has been president, and she has also been executive director since 1977. There are eighty full-time staff members. TNLC accepts ninety-five student interns each year.

The 1992 operating budget was $3.5 million, of which 30 percent came from foundations, 45 percent from government, 15 percent from corporations, and the remainder from membership fees and individual contributions. Approximately $1 million goes toward administrative and personnel costs, $1.4 million toward museum programs, and the remainder toward educational programs.

POLICY CONCERNS AND TACTICS

According to printed material, TNLC is involved with three activities: (1) a Capital Children's Museum; (2) the Option School, a full-day program for Washington, D.C., seventh graders whose academic performance is two years or more below grade level and who have been identified by the school system as requiring intensive intervention; and (3) the Model Early Learning Center, which provides a full-day academic program for three- and four-year-old children in order to explore age-appropriate curriculum for the D.C. public schools.

TNLC does not try to affect legislation, nor does it try to shape public opinion.

POLITICAL ACTIVITY

None.

FURTHER INFORMATION

Annual report.

NATIONAL PARENTS-TEACHERS ASSOCIATION

National Headquarters:
700 North Rush Street
Chicago, Illinois 60611-2571
(312) 787-0977   fax: (312) 787-8342

Office of Governmental Relations:
2000 L Street, N.W., Suite 600
Washington, D.C. 20036
(202) 331-1380   fax: (202) 331-1406

The National Parents-Teachers Association (NPTA) is a nonprofit organization with a threefold mission: (1) to support and speak out on behalf of children and youth in the schools, the community, and before government agencies and other organizations that make decisions affecting children; (2) to assist parents in developing the skills they need to raise and protect their children; and (3) to encourage parent and public involvement in the public schools of this nation. Furthermore, NPTA strives for intelligent cooperation between teachers and parents in the education of children and youth.

ORIGIN AND DEVELOPMENT

NPTA was founded in 1897. Alice McLellan Birney and Phoebe Apperson Hearst were concerned about the vast numbers of children in the United States who were ill-housed, poorly educated, hungry, sick, or otherwise suffering and wanted to mobilize caring adults to act on behalf of these children. They formed the national Congress of Mothers, which, after a series of name changes, became the National Congress of Parents and Teachers in 1924.

Concerned also about the needs of parents and children forced by law to attend racially segregated schools, NPTA helped Selena Sloan Butler to form the Georgia Congress of Colored Parents and Teachers in 1919, and in 1926 helped create the National Congress of Colored Parents and Teachers. The two associations merged in 1970. There are 7 million members in 29,000 local units.

ORGANIZATION AND FUNDING

NPTA is governed by a board of directors, which consists of the national officers, the president of each state PTA, members of PTA commissions, consultants, and the immediate past national president. The 1992 president was Pat S. Henry. Since 1992, Gene Honn has been executive director. There are sixty-one full-time staff members.

The 1992 operating budget was $6.1 million, of which 71 percent came from membership fees, 15 percent from grants and donations from foundations and corporations, 5 percent from endowment earnings, and the remainder from subscriptions and conference fees. Approximately 37 percent of the budget goes toward administrative and personnel costs, 57 percent toward membership services, and the remainder toward governance.

POLICY CONCERNS AND TACTICS

NPTA's major concerns include professional development issues and activities, as well as public policy measures that are likely to affect the interests of members. Monitoring legislative activities is one of its most important services. It keeps membership informed about legislation that is needed, proposed, or passed for the care and protection of children and youth. NPTA analyzes and shares with its members the impact of such legislation. The NPTA Legislative Program is implemented through the work of the vice-president for legislative activity, the Legislative Program Committee, the NPTA board of directors, the staff of the Office of Governmental Relations, the Washington Area Legislative Service Volunteers, the state legislative chairmen, the NPTA Member-to-Member Network, and the state, district, council, and local PTA membership.

POLITICAL ACTIVITY

NPTA lobbies before Congress on education legislation and offers testimony to government agencies.

FURTHER INFORMATION

An annual report; a magazine, *PTA Today*; and a newsletter on legislative developments, *What's Happening in Washington.*

NATIONAL RURAL EDUCATION ASSOCIATION
230 Education Building
Colorado State University
Fort Collins, Colorado 80523-0001
(303) 491-7022   fax: (303) 491-1317

The mission of the National Rural Education Association (NREA) is to provide a unified national voice to address the unique and diverse needs and concerns of rural education.

ORIGIN AND DEVELOPMENT

Formerly known as the REA, the association traces its origins back to 1907 when it was originally founded as the Department of Rural Education. According to NREA literature, through the years the association has evolved as a strong and respected organization of rural school administrators, teachers, board members, regional service personnel, researchers, business and industry representatives, and others interested in maintaining the vitality of rural school systems across the country.

ORGANIZATION AND FUNDING

The NREA is directed by an elected executive committee consisting of representatives of rural school administrators, teachers, and school boards, as well as representatives from state education agencies, higher education, educational service agencies, and at-large constituencies. In addition to the executive committee, the NREA has a delegate assembly that is made up of two representatives from each of the fifty states. The assembly hears reports from standing committees and passes on resolutions, policy matters, and other procedural aspects of the association. The 1992 president of the association was Gerald Hanson, and the executive director since 1981 has been Dr. Joe Newlin. The association employs four part-time staff members and relies on volunteers to stuff envelopes and help with mailings. The legal department at Colorado State University assists NREA at no cost.

NREA has an annual operating budget of $70,000, of which 80 percent is from membership fees, 18 percent from the annual convention, and 2 percent from miscellaneous income, including the sale of mailing labels and booklets; 50 percent of the budget is allocated to administration, and 50 percent is allocated to membership services, including publication of periodicals.

POLICY CONCERNS AND TACTICS

According to NREA literature, the association's 1992 National Congress on Rural Education convened in order to discuss the most disabling and chronic barriers to the improvement of rural education in America and to discuss possible solutions and strategies for addressing these barriers. Policy concerns include image/attitude problems associated with rural life; a lack of rural consciousness among policy makers; resource allocation fairness at the federal, state, and local levels; the erosion of population and economic bases in rural America; a loss of local control in rural areas; and various problems with curricula, staff, materials, technology, family structure, and values in rural schools and communities.

The NREA seeks to accomplish its goals by means of member activities, publications, committee work, coalition forming, and networking. The association writes letters to elected officials and encourages its members to do the same.

POLITICAL ACTIVITY

None.

FURTHER INFORMATION

National Congress proceedings, membership brochure, membership roster, journal, newsletter.

NATIONAL SCHOOL BOARDS ASSOCIATION
1680 Duke Street
Alexandria, Virginia 22314
(703) 838-6722   fax: (703) 683-7590

The National School Boards Association (NSBA) is a nonprofit organization that strives to foster excellence and equity in public education through school board leadership.

ORIGIN AND DEVELOPMENT

NSBA was founded in 1940 under the name of the National Council of State School Boards Association. Membership was limited to officers or regularly elected delegates of established state associations of school trustees and school board members.

ORGANIZATION AND FUNDING

NSBA represents 49 state board associations, the Hawaii state board of education, and the boards of education of the District of Columbia, the Virgin Islands, and Puerto Rico. Membership also includes 2,000 local-level affiliates. It is governed by a 150-member delegate assembly (elected by membership) and a 24-member board of directors (elected by the delegate assembly.) The 1992 president was E. Harold Fisher. Since 1977, Thomas A. Shannon has been executive director. NSBA has 120 full-time staff members.

The 1992 operating budget was $16 million, of which 80 percent came from user fees, 17 percent from membership fees, and 3 percent from foundations, rents, and interest. Information about expenditures is not available.

POLICY CONCERNS AND TACTICS

The NSBA is concerned primarily with providing professional development opportunities for its members and with affecting public policy in areas of interest to members. The group is particularly interested in First Amendment issues, tax and voucher issues, school finance issues, early childhood development, and other issues related to educational quality. To secure its goals, the group relies on inhouse programs as well as a variety of political activities.

POLITICAL ACTIVITY

NSBA is particularly active in filing *amicus curiae* briefs at either the U.S. Supreme Court or the U.S. Court of Appeals. Recent briefs include *Doe v. Taylor* in which NSBA's brief urged the U.S. Court of Appeals to rule that action charging that a school district failed to protect students from abuse should be filed under state negligence laws rather than the U.S. Constitution. Another case was *Lee v. Weisman* in which NSBA urged the Court to retain the *Lemon* test as its standard for determining violations of the Establishment Clause. The *Lemon* test asks if an invocation (1) has a secular purpose, (2) neither advances nor inhibits religion, and (3) does not result in excessive entanglement of government and religion. Another case is *Luthens v. Blair* in which NSBA joined the Iowa Association of School Boards to file an *amicus curiae* brief challenging the constitutionality of the Iowa tax-credit statute.

NSBA is also a frequent visitor to Capitol Hill. It has testified at the hearings to reauthorize the Carl D. Perkins Vocational Education Act, arguing for increasing funding to $1.5 billion and giving more discretion in its expenditure to local school districts. In hearings for the Smart Start: Community Collaborative for Early Childhood Development Act, NSBA informed Congress about state initiatives in early childhood legislation. At hearings on the Education Excellence Act, NSBA argued that special recognition programs and scholarship programs do not effectively utilize limited federal funds. At hearings on the Regulatory Impact on Student Excellence Act, it argued for more studies on improving education and youth services through deregulation.

At the National Education Report Card Act hearings, NSBA argued that the program could neither be controlled and funded solely by the federal government nor rely on threats of withholding federal funds as a means of securing participation of states and local school districts. Further, it advocated that national assessment should only include nationwide testing if it explicitly avoids suppressing diversity and innovation through the imposition of a national curriculum. It also provided supportive testimony for the Computer Education Assistance Act, especially provisions that give local discretion in the allocation of funds for hardware, software, and inservice training for students. NSBA also supported the reauthorization of Part H of the Individuals with Disabilities Education Act.

FURTHER INFORMATION

Numerous publications, including a fortnightly newspaper, *School Board News*; a monthly journal, *The American School Board Journal*; a monthly journal for superintendents, *Executive Educator*; a quarterly newspaper, *School Board Leadership News*; and the *Annual Report and Events Calendar*.

NATIONAL SCHOOL HEALTH EDUCATION COALITION

1000 Vermont Avenue, N.W., Suite 400
Washington, D.C. 20005
(202) 682-3050   fax: (202) 789-2590

The National School Health Education Coalition (NASHEC) is a nonprofit organization that strives to ensure that every student in grades K-12 receives a comprehensive school health education experience. A comprehensive school health education refers to the development, delivery, and evaluation of a planned, multiple-topic curriculum with goals, objectives, content sequence, and specific classroom lessons.

ORIGIN AND DEVELOPMENT

NASHEC was founded in 1982 by a group of representatives from national voluntary organizations concerned with the health of children and youth and who were advocates for health education programs in schools. NASHEC developed into a national coalition of over sixty national organizations and agencies that work to promote comprehensive school health education.

ORGANIZATION AND FUNDING

NASHEC is governed by a five-member executive committee. Since 1990, Maureen Corry has been president, and, since 1991, Stephen H. Kreimer has been executive director. There are two full-time staff members. The 1992 operating budget was $325,000, of which 90 percent came from government and 10 percent from membership fees. Revenues were directed toward administrative and personnel costs (33 percent), membership services (66 percent), and publication and dissemination of a newsletter (1 percent).

POLICY CONCERNS AND TACTICS

NASHEC is concerned with the quality of health education in the schools. It addresses this issue by providing technical assistance to member institutions and through several manuals and handbooks.

With a limited staff, NASHEC also monitors relevant legislation in Congress. This is done through a committee called the NASHEC Legislative Action Group, which informs member institutions of such congressional activities. NASHEC provides a "federal liaison" membership to the following agencies: Bureau of Maternal and Child Health and Resources Development; Centers for Disease Control (CDC); Centers for Health Promotion Education; Department of Defense; Drug Enforcement Agency; Department of Justice; Food and Nutrition Information Center; National Highway Traffic Safety Administration; National Agricultural Library; National Cancer Institute; National Commission on Correctional Health Care; National Heart, Lung, and Blood Institute; National Highway Traffic Safety Administration; National Institute of Alcohol Abuse and Alcoholism; National Institute of Dental Research; Office of Disease Prevention and Health Promotion; Office of Elementary and Secondary Education; Office for Substance Abuse Prevention; Office on Smoking and Health—CDC; Department of Education; and U.S. Department of Agriculture—Nutrition and Tech Services.

POLITICAL ACTIVITY

NASHEC testified on Capitol Hill in support of the Jacob K. Javits Gifted and Talented Children and Youth Education Act and the Office of Comprehensive School Health Education Act.

FURTHER INFORMATION

NASHEC *Newsletter.*

NATIONAL SCIENCE TEACHERS ASSOCIATION
1742 Connecticut Avenue, N.W.
Washington, D.C. 20009
(202) 328-5800   fax: (202) 328-0974

The National Science Teachers Association (NSTA) seeks to improve the quality of science education at all levels, from preschool through college.

ORIGIN AND DEVELOPMENT

NSTA was founded in 1944 when the American Council of Science Teachers and the American Science Teachers Association merged to become a department of the National Education Association.* NSTA later became its own independent association and is today an affiliate of the American Association for the Advancement of Science. NSTA works closely with the National Science Foundation, the Department of Education, and other related groups on a variety of projects. The association maintains a current membership of approximately

50,000, with members distributed among 12 national districts, 50 state chapters, 7 division affiliates, and 11 associated groups.

ORGANIZATION AND FUNDING

The association is governed by an elected board of directors comprised of officers, division directors, district directors, and presidents of each affiliate group. The 1993 president was Gerry Madrazo, and the current executive director is Bill G. Aldridge. NSTA employs a full-time staff of 105 and utilizes volunteers for convention and committee work.

NSTA is a 501(c)(3) organization with an annual budget of approximately $14 million. Approximately 19 percent of funding is derived from membership fees, 5 percent from advertising, 38 percent from grants and contracts, 6 percent from the sale of publications, 26 percent from convention revenues, and 6 percent from miscellaneous sources. Approximately 9 percent of the budget is allocated to administration, 2 percent to member services, 20 percent to publications, 38 percent to grants and contracts, 15 percent to convention expenses, 3 percent to board expenses, 10 percent to building maintenance and fees; and the remainder (3 percent) is unspecified.

POLICY CONCERNS AND TACTICS

NSTA's primary concerns center around addressing subjects of critical interest to science educators. According to NSTA literature, the association is involved in many programs and services for science teachers, including awards and scholarships, teacher training workshops, educational tours, an employment registry, information services, and a variety of internally and externally funded professional development projects. NSTA is also currently involved in national standards issues and curriculum reform issues, particularly those involving grades 7 through 12, and maintains an ongoing interest in science-related public policy issues: teacher preparation, laboratory science, the use of animals in the classroom, laboratory safety, and elementary- and middle-level science.

POLITICAL ACTIVITY

According to association literature, NSTA disseminates results from nationwide surveys and reports and offers testimony to Congress on science-education-related legislation and other issues. The organization publishes position statements on a variety of issues related to science instruction.

FURTHER INFORMATION

Many publications of interest to members and *NSTA Reports!* magazine.

**NATIONAL SOCIETY FOR INTERNSHIPS AND
EXPERIENTIAL EDUCATION**
3509 Haworth Drive, Suite 207
Raleigh, North Carolina 27609
(919) 787-3263   fax: (919) 787-3381

The National Society for Internships and Experiential Education (NSIEE) is a professional association and national resource center that supports the use of learning through experience.

ORIGIN AND DEVELOPMENT

NSIEE was founded in 1971 as the National Center for Public Service Internship Programs and the Society for Field Experience Education. NSIEE currently has 800 institutional members and 1,300 individual members.

ORGANIZATION AND FUNDING

NSIEE is governed by a board of directors elected by a vote of the general membership. The current president is Hymon Johnson, and the current executive director is Allen Wutzdorff. The society employs a staff of nine (two part-time), and relies on student interns, volunteers, and outside professionals for a variety of projects.

NSIEE is a 501(c)(3) organization with an annual operating budget of approximately $670,000. Funding comes from foundation support (61 percent), membership fees (14 percent), publications (8 percent), and consulting services and interest revenue (9 percent); 35 percent of the budget is allocated to membership services, 35 percent to publications and dissemination of information, 15 percent to conferences, 10 percent to consulting services, and 5 percent to administration.

POLICY CONCERNS AND TACTICS

According to its literature, NSIEE's goals are: (1) to advocate for the effective use of experiential learning throughout the educational system and the larger community; (2) to disseminate information on principles of good practice and innovations in the field; (3) to enhance professional growth and leadership development in the field; and (4) to encourage the development and dissemination of related research and theory.

NSIEE attempts to accomplish its goals by (1) offering national and regional conferences and workshops where experiential educators can gather for substantive discussions, information exchange, and professional development; (2) providing ''special interest groups'' for educators with similar interests to meet for professional support, information exchange, and advocacy; (3) offering technical assistance; (4) providing consultants who can assist with program development, evaluation, strategies for gaining institutional support, increasing faculty involvement, and other aspects of effective programs and courses; (5) publishing a variety of books that examine key issues and sound practices in experiential education; and (6) working with high school educators in leadership development programs.

POLITICAL ACTIVITY

Affecting legislation is not a major activity of the organization, but NSIEE is prepared to work with other groups in the future on any legislation related to experiential education.

FURTHER INFORMATION

Brochure, publications list with items of interest to members, membership directory, and *Experiential Education* (newsletter).

NATIONAL STUDENT NURSES' ASSOCIATION
555 West 57th Street
New York, New York 10019
(212) 581-2211   fax: (212) 581-2368

The National Student Nurses' Association (NSNA) seeks to organize, represent, train, and mentor students preparing for nursing careers.

ORIGIN AND DEVELOPMENT

NSNA was founded in 1952 as a result of a major reorganization of national nursing associations, particularly the American Nurses Association (ANA). Since its founding NSNA has had a close working relationship with the ANA, as well as the National League for Nursing. Current NSNA membership is 35,000.

ORIGIN AND DEVELOPMENT

NSNA is governed by a board of directors composed of ten student members, nine of whom are elected by a House of Delegates annually and one who is elected by the Council of State Presidents to serve in an *ex officio* capacity. The House of Delegates meets annually to vote on amendments to by-laws, to hear and vote on resolutions, to elect new officers, and to elect members to a nominating and elections committee. The current president is Julie A. McGee (since 1991), and the current executive director is Robert V. Piemonte (since 1985). NSNA employs a staff of twelve and utilizes volunteers to serve on resolutions committees and to assist with conferences and meetings.

NSNA is a 501(c)(3) organization with an annual budget of approximately $2.27 million. Approximately 32 percent of 1993 revenues was derived from advertising and publications, 29 percent from membership dues, 20 percent from exhibit fees, 9 percent from royalties, 7 percent from convention and conference fees, and 3 percent from interest. The 1993 budget called for an allocation of 35 percent to administration, 32 percent to publications, 11 percent to conventions and conferences, 7 percent to exhibit expenses, 7 percent to membership promotion, 4 percent to board activities, and 4 percent to income tax provisions.

POLICY CONCERNS AND TACTICS

According to organization by-laws, NSNA's major concern is with socializing nursing students into the nursing profession, in order to assist the profession in providing the highest possible quality health care. More specifically, the association maintains an interest in professional development, educational standards, health care legislation, community health issues, and student recruitment. Local chapters have expressed concerns with more particular issues, such as those relating to AIDS/HIV research, prenatal care, rehabilitation nursing recruitment, tuberculosis research, drug and alcohol addiction among nurses and pregnant women, medication error prevention, basic life support training, lead poisoning, childhood immunization, and childhood accidents. The association as a whole addresses these concerns through various community programs and activities, conferences and conventions, publications, resolutions, and letter writing/public pressure campaigns before elected officials.

POLITICAL ACTIVITY

None.

FURTHER INFORMATION

Imprint magazine, a variety of brochures and other informative publications, and an annual convention report.

NATIONAL WOMEN'S LAW CENTER

1616 P Street, N.W.
Washington, D.C. 20036
(202) 328-5160   fax: (202) 328-5137

The National Women's Law Center (NWLC) is a nonprofit organization that advocates the rights of women. In the area of education, it strives to achieve equity for women and girls in all facets of education.

ORIGIN AND DEVELOPMENT

NWLC was founded in 1981. It began as the Women's Rights Project of the Center for Law and Social Policy. NWLC became an independent entity to affect public- and private-sector politics and practices so they better reflect the needs and rights of women, with special emphasis on how poor women are affected.

ORGANIZATION AND FUNDING

NWLC is not a membership organization. It is governed by a fourteen-member board of directors. Since 1981, Marcia D. Greenberger and Nancy Duff Campbell have been co-presidents. There are sixteen full-time staff members. NWLC accepts a varying number of student interns each year.

Recent budgets have approximated $1.2 million, almost all of which has come from grants, contributions, and legal fees. NWLC spends about 20 percent on administrative and personnel costs and the remainder on specific programs. Among these programs, $85,046 was spent in the area of education.

POLICY CONCERNS AND TACTICS

NWLC is concerned with enforcement of Title IX of the Higher Education Act, specifically gender bias in testing, athletic discrimination, minority scholarships, and general access to education for women. NWLC addresses these issues by providing technical assistance to lawmakers, as well as by litigation. The group is working on a law review article that will provide a blueprint for exploring legal issues raised by gender bias in standardized testing.

POLITICAL ACTIVITY

In the case *Pfeiffer v. Marion Center Area High School*, NWLC won on appeal the case of a pregnant, unmarried high school student who was expelled from her school's honor society. When another circuit heard a similar case, *Franklin v. Gwinnett County Public Schools*, NWLC filed an *amicus* brief in the appeals court and again in the Supreme Court on behalf of scores of organizations. In *Hafer v. Temple University*, it obtained a ground-breaking settlement that challenged broad-based sex discrimination in Temple's intercollegiate athletics program.

NWLC also completed two decade-long cases against the Department of Education, challenging the department's failure to enforce Title IX and other laws barring discrimination. These cases—*Women's Equity Action League v. Cavazos* and *Adams v. Cavazos*—had resulted in improved enforcement of government regulations requiring the handling of all complaints received.

FURTHER INFORMATION

An annual report; an informational fact sheet entitled "Education for All," in which NWLC exposed the failure of policy makers to consider the needs of women and girls in formulating the National Education Goals and policies to achieve them; and other publications that include "Federal Laws and Regulations Prohibiting Sex Discrimination in Educational Institutions," "Comments on the Title IX Athletics Investigator's Manual," "Update on Sex Discrimination in Education: The Bush Record," and "How Does the SAT Score for Women?"

NEW ENGLAND ASSOCIATION OF SCHOOLS AND COLLEGES, INC.

The Sanborn House
15 High Street
Winchester, Massachusetts 01890
(617) 729-6762   fax: (617) 729-6762

The New England Association of Schools and Colleges, Inc. (NEASC) is an accrediting association involved in the evaluation of schools and colleges in New England and selected areas abroad.

ORIGIN AND DEVELOPMENT

NEASC was founded in 1885, and today maintains a membership of 1,680.

ORGANIZATION AND FUNDING

NEASC is governed by an executive committee. The 1992-1993 president was John C. Davis, and the executive director is Richard J. Bradley. NEASC employs a full-time staff of twenty-seven and a part-time staff of two, and it occasionally utilizes student interns and volunteers in the evaluation process.

NEASC is a nonprofit 501(c)(3) organization with an annual operating budget of $2.3 million, 92 percent of which comes from membership fees, 1 percent from government sources, and an undisclosed percentage from interest payments, publication sales, accreditation fees, and workshops. A full 80 percent of the budget is allocated to administrative expenses and 20 percent to accreditation services.

POLICY CONCERNS AND TACTICS

Current policy concerns related to the organization include issues of public accountability, issues of cost containment, and the realignment of commission and committee structures.

POLITICAL ACTIVITY

None.

FURTHER INFORMATION

Membership roster.

NORTH AMERICAN COUNCIL OF AUTOMOTIVE TEACHERS

11956 Bernardo Plaza Drive
Department 436
San Diego, California 92128-9713
(619) 487-8126   fax: (619) 487-3617

The North American Council of Automotive Teachers (NACTA) seeks to improve automotive education at all levels in both the United States and Canada.

ORIGIN AND DEVELOPMENT

NACTA, formerly the National Association of College Automotive Teachers, was founded in 1973.

ORGANIZATION AND FUNDING

NACTA is governed by officers (president, vice-president, secretary, treasurer, and historian) and a board of directors. The officers and board meet twice yearly. The president since 1991 has been Chane Bush, and the executive director since 1992 has been Alfred Goodyear. The council employs one full-time staff worker and relies on volunteers and industry experts for a variety of problem-solving projects and ideas.

NACTA is a tax-exempt organization with an annual operating budget of $50,000. A full 90 percent of the budget is funded by membership fees, 5 percent by mailing list sales, and 5 percent by advertising revenues. Budget allocation figures are not available.

POLICY CONCERNS AND TACTICS

Currently the council is seeking increased industry support for educational equipment in schools and is seeking to become more involved in field-level technician training. A major concern is the ever-increasing gap between the technician's knowledge and changing automotive technology. NACTA seeks to accomplish its goals by hosting an annual conference with seminars and a trade show, disseminating publications, and working closely with a variety of private and government organizations that share similar concerns.

POLITICAL ACTIVITY

NACTA does no lobbying and does not support or endorse any candidates for office. However, the organization does align itself with other organizations in promoting policies that would improve technician training. Of particular concern are the policies of the federal Environmental Protection Agency.

FURTHER INFORMATION

Newsletter.

NORTH AMERICAN PROFESSORS OF CHRISTIAN EDUCATION

850 North Grove Avenue, Suite C
Elgin, Illinois 60120
(303) 761-2482   fax: (303) 761-8060

North American Professors of Christian Education (NAPCE) seeks to advance the professional development of college and seminary professors in the field of Christian education.

ORIGIN AND DEVELOPMENT

NAPCE was founded in 1950 out of a desire on the part of Christian educators to articulate an educational philosophy, develop appropriate textbooks, and do research in the field of Christian education. The organization has a membership of approximately 200.

ORGANIZATION AND FUNDING

NAPCE is governed by a ten-member board of directors elected by the membership and by five officers elected by the board. The president since 1992 has been Fred Wilson, and the executive administrator since 1985 has been Dennis E. Williams. NAPCE is a 501(c)(3) organization with an annual operating budget of approximately $26,000, 39 percent of which is derived from convention fees, 25 percent from membership fees, 34 percent from private/individual contributions, and 2 percent from interest earnings. A total of 27 percent of the budget is allocated to administration and 23 percent to publications and research (the remainder of expenditures is unspecified).

POLICY CONCERNS AND TACTICS

NAPCE is interested solely in the professional development of its members. The organization meets its goals by means of research presentations, task force groups, and lectures and dialogue in order to share ideas, syllabi, and resources for teaching and research improvement. NAPCE holds an annual conference, publishes a journal, and offers a yearly student scholastic award.

POLITICAL ACTIVITY

None.

FURTHER INFORMATION

Christian Education Journal (published three times yearly) and a brochure.

NORTHWEST ASSOCIATION OF SCHOOLS AND COLLEGES
Commission on Schools
Boise State University
Education Building
1910 University Drive
Boise, Idaho 83725
(208) 334-3226   fax: (208) 334-3228

The Northwest Association of Schools and Colleges (NASC) is an accrediting body that seeks to advance the cause of education in its member institutions.

ORIGIN AND DEVELOPMENT

NASC was founded in 1917 during a meeting of the Inland Empire Teachers Association. The group on secondary and higher education devoted a section of its meeting to the organization of NASC. The association has a current membership of 1,317 schools and 150 colleges. NASC maintains ties with the National Study of School Evaluation, the Council of Regional School Accrediting Commissions, and the American Council on Education.

ORGANIZATION AND FUNDING

NASC is composed of two commissions—the Commission on Schools and the Commission on Colleges. The organization is governed by an eleven-member board of trustees. The board consists of a president, first vice-president (who also serves as chair of the Commission on Schools), second vice- president (who also serves as chair of the Commission on Colleges), the executive director of each commission, and six appointed members (three representatives from each of the commissions). The president since 1992 has been Stowell Johnstone, and the executive directors are David Steadman (Commission on Schools, since 1988) and Joseph Malik (Commission on Colleges, since 1990). NASC employs a staff of three and utilizes one student intern per year as well as volunteers to assist with on-site visitations.

The association is a 501(c)(3) organization with an annual operating budget of approximately $50,000. A total of 77 percent of funding is from membership fees, 17 percent from the annual meeting, and 6 percent from miscellaneous sources; 75 percent of the budget is allocated to administration, 20 percent to publications, and 5 percent to membership services, particularly staff development.

POLICY CONCERNS AND TACTICS

The concerns of the association are exclusively educational. NASC is interested in developing educational policies, evaluation criteria, and other activities that will extend and improve educational opportunities. Current issues include cultural diversity, international standards and accreditation of foreign schools, and membership growth.

POLITICAL ACTIVITY

None.

FURTHER INFORMATION

Proceedings of the annual meeting; directory.

O
/

OVERSEAS EDUCATION ASSOCIATION
1201 16th Street, N.W.
Washington, D.C. 20036
(202) 822-7850   fax: (202) 822-7867

The Overseas Education Association (OEA) is a nonprofit organization that represents teachers employed by the U.S. Department of Defense, Office of Dependents Schools (DODDS), on military bases overseas and some Section Six Schools in the U.S. Atlantic, Germany, and Pacific Regions. OEA participates in the negotiated agreement with DODDS.

ORIGIN AND DEVELOPMENT

OEA was founded in 1956.

ORGANIZATION AND FUNDING

OEA represents approximately 9,000 teachers (exclusive bargaining rights) and has more than 7,500 members. Teachers may become unified members of an affiliated local association, OEA, and the National Education Association* by simply paying combined dues.

OEA is governed by an eleven-member board of directors. Since 1980, Jack Rollins has been president, and, since 1976, Ron Austin has been executive director. OEA employs twenty full-time staff members. The 1991 operating budget is $214,000, all of which came from membership fees. Approximately 25 percent went toward administrative and personnel costs, and the remainder went toward membership services.

POLICY CONCERNS AND TACTICS

OEA is primarily concerned with protecting the rights of teachers who work on overseas military bases. According to its annual report, this is accomplished in three ways: (1) contract negotiations; (2) litigation; and (3) influencing legislation. OEA helped shape legislation on issues ranging from the weight allowance for shipment of goods to unlimited accumulation of teacher leave.

POLITICAL ACTIVITY

OEA provided testimony on Capitol Hill at the hearings of the Overseas Teachers Act of 1987 where it recommended the filling of teaching vacancies with qualified members of military personnel and opposed decreases in travel allowances.

FURTHER INFORMATION

Annual report.

P

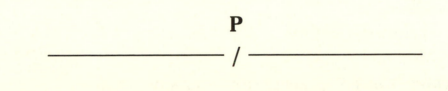

PRESIDENTIAL CLASSROOM FOR YOUNG AMERICANS

441 North Lee Street
Alexandria, Virginia 22314-2346
(703) 683-5400   fax: (703) 548-5728

Presidential Classroom for Young Americans (PC) is a nonprofit organization that engages high school juniors and seniors in seminars and dialogues with national leaders.

ORIGIN AND DEVELOPMENT

PC was founded in 1968. It was inspired by two Kennedy administration pilot programs, "Widening Horizons" and "White House Seminars." During the Johnson administration, a similar program was developed, "Washington Briefings," which was directed by Vice-President Hubert Humphrey. The White House eventually transferred the concept and responsibility of this program to an independent board of directors. Seminars feature a wide variety of government officials, including cabinet members, senators, representatives, military and diplomatic officers, political correspondents, and business leaders.

ORGANIZATION AND FUNDING

PC is not a membership organization. In 1991, nearly 3,000 students attended the program, representing 50 states, the District of Columbia, Puerto Rico, and several foreign countries. It is governed by a 14-member board of directors. Since 1989, George B. Wilkes III has been chair and Nila A. Vehar has been executive director. There are 10 full-time staff members. PC accepts 30 student interns each year.

Recent operating budgets have been about $2 million, of which over $1.7

million comes from student fees. Over $500,000 goes toward administration and personnel expenses, $1.4 million goes toward the Senior High School Program, and the remainder goes toward other PC programs.

POLICY CONCERNS AND TACTICS

Through the Senior High School Program, participants gain insight into leadership styles by observing and interacting with key members of the federal community. PC does not try to influence public policy, nor does it try to shape public opinion.

POLITICAL ACTIVITY

None.

FURTHER INFORMATION

Annual report.

PROJECT ON EQUAL EDUCATION RIGHTS OF THE NOW LEGAL DEFENSE AND EDUCATION FUND
99 Hudson Street
New York, New York 10013
(212) 925-6635   fax: (212) 226-1066

The National Organization of Women (NOW) Legal Defense and Education Fund is a nonprofit organization that works to end sex discrimination in the classroom, workplace, family, and courts. The fund's mission is the achievement of full equality for all women via legal reform and educational campaigns.

The fund's Project on Equal Education Rights (PEER) works to promote equity in education for women and girls. PEER's programs help train today's girls for the workplaces of tomorrow and provide a focus for the efforts of concerned parents, teachers, and policy makers to ensure quality public education for girls.

ORIGIN AND DEVELOPMENT

PEER was founded in 1974.

ORGANIZATION AND FUNDING

As part of the fund, PEER has forty-nine members. It is governed by a twenty-four-member board of directors. Since 1990, Phyllis N. Segal has been president of the fund, and, since 1989, Helen R. Neuborne has been executive director. Walteen Grady Truely became PEER director in 1990. There are twenty-three full-time staff members, and fifteen student interns are accepted each year.

The 1992 operating budget was $2.4 million, of which 48 percent came from individual contributions, 31 percent from foundations, 7 percent from corporations, and the remainder from special events and endowment earnings. About 16 percent of funding goes toward personnel and administrative costs and the remainder goes toward programs. PEER receives 12.5 percent of the fund's budget.

POLICY CONCERNS AND TACTICS

PEER is concerned about the needs of girls from largely low-income urban communities whose educational and vocational needs are virtually ignored by the current educational reform movement. It strives to establish an effective school-to-work transition program that will enable young mothers to move off welfare and into employment. PEER reports to Congress on the status of women and girls in education and the impact of sex-role stereotyping of girls of color on teen pregnancy and school drop-out rates.

POLITICAL ACTIVITY

Through NOW, PEER endorsed Bill Clinton for the 1992 presidential campaign.

FURTHER INFORMATION

An annual report and several publications, including "Report on the Status of Women and Girls in Education," "Sex-Role Stereotyping and Early Parenting: Cause and Effect," and "In Their Own Voices."

PUSH LITERACY ACTION NOW
1332 G Street, S.E.
Washington, D.C. 20003
(202) 547-8903

Push Literacy Action Now (PLAN) is a nonprofit organization that strives to meet the literacy and human development needs of low-literate adults and their families. PLAN also strives to challenge the conditions that cause and perpetuate illiteracy.

ORIGIN AND DEVELOPMENT

PLAN was founded in 1972 by a mission group of the Church of the Savior to provide one-on-one literacy training to Washington, D.C.–area residents. It became an independent organization in 1976.

ORGANIZATION AND FUNDING

PLAN is not a membership organization. It is governed by an eighteen-member board of directors comprised of teachers, adult learners, and community members. Since 1990, George D. Hager has been president of the board. Since 1992, Anthony A. Knoll, Jr., has been executive director. There are two full-time staff members. PLAN accepts one student intern each year.

The 1992 operating budget was $103,000, of which 15 percent came from foundations, 12 percent from corporations, 24 percent from publications, 23 percent from student fees, and 26 percent from private individuals. Approximately 16 percent of the budget goes toward administration and personnel costs, 60 percent toward program services, and the remainder toward dissemination of information and marketing.

POLICY CONCERNS AND TACTICS

PLAN is concerned with (1) funding of community-based literacy programs, (2) literacy traiing, (3) future funding for public libraries, and (4) allocation of state funds to literacy programs. While providing several programs that increase the literacy of individuals, PLAN does not directly try to affect legislation on these issues.

POLITICAL ACTIVITY

None.

FURTHER INFORMATION

An annual report and a bimonthly newsletter, *The Ladder*.

S
/

SCHOOL SCIENCE AND MATHEMATICS ASSOCIATION
Curriculum and Foundations
Bloomsburg University
Bloomsburg, Pennsylvania 17815
(717) 389-4915   fax: (717) 389-3894

The School Science and Mathematics Association (SSMA) produces publications and organizes conventions for teachers of mathematics and science.

ORIGIN AND DEVELOPMENT

SSMA was founded in 1901 as a vehicle for teachers of mathematics and science to share common interests. Today SSMA has approximately 1,100 members. The organization is affiliated with the American Association for the Advancement of Science.

ORGANIZATION AND FUNDING

SSMA is governed by a president (Jerry P. Becker in 1992) and a board of six directors. The 1993 executive director was Donald L. Pratt. SSMA employs a part-time staff of four and relies on volunteer work for a variety of administrative tasks.

SSMA is a 501(c)(3) organization with an annual operating budget of $100,000. A full 99 percent of budget funding comes from membership fees and 1 percent from endowment earnings; 60 percent of the budget is allocated to a journal and a newsletter, 30 percent to record keeping, and 10 percent to other administrative expenses.

POLICY CONCERNS AND TACTICS

No information available.

POLITICAL ACTIVITY

None.

FURTHER INFORMATION

Journal and newsletter.

SOCIETY FOR HEALTH AND HUMAN VALUES
6728 Old McLean Village Drive
McLean, Virginia 22101
(703) 556-9222

The Society for Health and Human Values (SHHV) is a nonprofit organization that strives to promote the inclusion of humanities disciplines in the curricula and educational ambience of health professional schools.

ORIGIN AND DEVELOPMENT

SHHV was founded in 1969, and today has 950 members.

ORGANIZATION AND FUNDING

SHHV is governed by an eight-member council. The 1992 president was David Barnard. Since 1982, George K. Degnon has been executive director. There are no full-time staff members. SHHV accepts one student intern per year. Financial information is unavailable.

POLICY CONCERNS AND TACTICS

SHHV is primarily concerned with including humanities in the curricula of medical schools. It does not try to affect legislation, nor does it try to shape public opinion.

POLITICAL ACTIVITY

None.

FURTHER INFORMATION

A monthly newsletter, *Bulletin*; and a quarterly journal *Medical Humanities Review*.

SOCIETY OF PROFESSORS OF CHILD AND ADOLESCENT PSYCHIATRY
3615 Wisconsin Avenue, N.W.
Washington, D.C. 20016
(202) 966-7300

The Society of Professors of Child and Adolescent Psychiatry (SPCAP) is a nonprofit organization that provides a forum for discussion and exchange of ideas among the child and adolescent psychiatry program directors in medical schools.

ORIGIN AND DEVELOPMENT

SPCAP was founded in 1975, and today there are 168 members.

ORGANIZATION AND FUNDING

SPCAP is governed by an executive committee. Since 1990, Bennet Leventhal has been president. There are no full-time staff members. The 1992 operating budget was $20,000, of which 95 percent came from membership fees and 5 percent from government. Expenses are directed toward administrative costs (10 percent), membership services (20 percent), dissemination of information (10 percent), and the annual meeting (60 percent).

POLICY CONCERNS AND TACTICS

SPCAP is concerned with strengthening graduate and postgraduate medical education in the area of child and adolescent psychiatry. It addresses this issue through annual meetings. It does not try to affect legislation, nor does it try to influence public opinion.

POLITICAL ACTIVITY

None.

FURTHER INFORMATION

No information available.

SOUTHERN ASSOCIATION OF COLLEGES AND SCHOOLS
1866 Southern Lane
Decatur, Georgia 30033-4097
(404) 679-4500   fax: (404) 679-4556

The Southern Association of Colleges and Schools (SACS) is one of six regional associations in the United States. SACS has as its central purpose the improvement of education in the South through the process of accreditation. Accreditation is a nongovernmental and voluntary process of evaluation concerned with improving educational quality and assuring the public that member institutions meet established standards.

ORIGIN AND DEVELOPMENT

SACS originated in 1895 as the result of a resolution developed by Vanderbilt University faculty members. The resolution led to a meeting of representatives from six southern colleges and universities. According to SACS literature, the purposes of the meeting were: (1) to organize Southern schools and colleges for cooperation and mutual assistance; (2) to elevate the standard of scholarship and to effect uniformity of entrance requirements; and (3) to develop preparatory schools to enhance college preparedness. Incorporation as a nonprofit organization was authorized in 1962. There are currently 12,000 members.

ORGANIZATION AND FUNDING

SACS is comprised of four commissions: the Commission on Elementary Education, the Commission on Secondary Schools, the Commission on Occupational Education Institutions, and the Commission on Colleges. SACS is governed by a board of trustees composed of representatives from the four commissions and the public. Since 1992 the president of SACS has been Jack D. Rose, and the chief administrative officer has been John M. Davis. SACS employs three student interns per year and relies on a full-time staff of fifty (twenty-five nonclerical). SACS also relies on volunteers and outside professionals for special projects.

SACS is a nonprofit, federal-tax-exempt organization with an annual budget of $4 million. A full 99 percent of the budget is from membership fees, and 1 percent is from user fees.

POLICY CONCERNS AND TACTICS

SACS is concerned solely with accreditation standards for the purpose of improving education in the South.

POLITICAL ACTIVITY

None.

FURTHER INFORMATION

Bimonthly published proceedings.

SPEECH COMMUNICATION ASSOCIATION
Building E
5105 Backlick Road
Annandale, Virginia 22003
(703) 750-0533   fax: (703) 914-9471

The Speech Communication Association (SCA) is a nonprofit organization that promotes the study, research, teaching, and application of the artistic, humanistic, and scientific principles of communication.

ORIGIN AND DEVELOPMENT

SCA was founded in 1914 as the National Association of Academic Teachers of Public Speaking. SCA was incorporated in 1950 as the Speech Association of America. SCA adopted its present name in 1970. Today there are 6,500 members of SCA.

ORGANIZATION AND FUNDING

It is governed by a legislative council and an administrative council. The 1992 president was Dale G. Leathers. Since 1989, James G. Gaudino has been executive director. There are twelve full-time staff members. SCA accepts one student intern each year. The 1992 operating budget was $1.4 million. Budget allocation information is unavailable.

POLICY CONCERNS AND TACTICS

SCA is strictly concerned with the advancement of communications as a discipline. It addresses this issue through discussions and presentations at annual conventions. It does not affect legislation, nor does it try to give shape to public opinion.

POLITICAL ACTIVITY

None.

FURTHER INFORMATION

No information available.

STUDENT PRESS LAW CENTER, INC.
1735 Eye Street, N.W., Suite 504
Washington, D.C. 20006
(202) 466-5242

The Student Press Law Center, Inc. (SPLC) is a nonprofit organization that educates high school and college journalists about their legal rights and responsibilities in relationship to a free press and supports the student media in achieving press freedom.

ORIGIN AND DEVELOPMENT

SPLC was founded in 1974. A national commission of inquiry into high school journalism found censorship to be a major problem for student publications. The commission recommended a national center to educate and defend the rights of student journalists. SPLC resulted from the recommendation.

ORGANIZATION AND FUNDING

SPLC is not a membership organization. It is governed by a twenty-three-person board of directors. The 1992 president of the board was J. Marc Abrams. Since 1985, Mark Goodman has been the executive director. There are two full-time staff members. SPLC accepts four to six student interns each year.

The 1992 operating budget was $110,000, of which 40 percent came from foundations, 40 percent from individuals, 10 percent from corporations, 5 percent from publications, and 5 percent from endowment earnings. Approximately

20 percent of the budget goes toward administration and personnel, 60 percent toward providing legal advice to members, and 20 percent to publications.

POLICY CONCERNS AND TACTICS

SPLC is concerned with free expression for students, access to campus crime information, and restrictions to limit politically incorrect speech. It addresses these issues through publications, education and providing legal advice and representation. It does not try to affect legislation.

POLITICAL ACTIVITY

None.

FURTHER INFORMATION

The SPLC *Report*, published three times a year, with features on First Amendment issues, practical advice on news gathering and reporting, and the latest cases involving the student press and what they mean; *Law of the Student Press*, a complete manual for the student journalist, which includes model publications guidelines.

U

/

UNITED NEGRO COLLEGE FUND
500 East 62nd Street
New York, New York 10021
(212) 326-1100

The United Negro College Fund (UNCF) is a nonprofit organization that acts as a consortium of private, historically black colleges and universities.

ORIGIN AND DEVELOPMENT

UNCF was founded in 1944 to seek financial support nationally for private, historically black colleges.

ORGANIZATION AND FUNDING

UNCF represents forty-one colleges. It is governed by a forty-eight-member board of directors. Since 1973, Christopher F. Edley has been president and chief executive officer. The 1992 annual campaign resulted in revenues of $45.8 million.

POLICY CONCERNS AND TACTICS

UNCF is concerned with student scholarships and other financial needs of black colleges, such as faculty salaries, buildings, and academic programs. It addresses these issues through fund-raising and publicizing black colleges, as well as congressional testimony.

POLITICAL ACTIVITY

UNCF testified in the reauthorization hearings of the Higher Education Act, arguing for Pell Grant entitlements with $20 million being reserved for historically African-American universities. At the hearings for the Access to Higher Education Act, UNCF argued for the creation of the Augustus F. Hawkins Fellowship Program for minority students who seek to enter the profession of higher education. It also argued to increase the number of Patricia Roberts Harris awards and to increase the amount of the award to $15,000.

FURTHER INFORMATION

An annual report and a quarterly magazine, *Amindis*.

URBAN AFFAIRS ASSOCIATION
University of Delaware
Newark, Delaware 19716-4706
(302) 831-2395   fax: (302) 831-3587
The Urban Affairs Association (UAA) is the international professional organization for urban scholars, researchers, and public service personnel.

ORIGIN AND DEVELOPMENT

UAA was founded in 1969 as the successor to the Council of University Institutes for Urban Affairs. The name was changed in 1981. Current membership includes 75 institutional members, 300 individual members, and 50 student members.

ORGANIZATION AND FUNDING

UAA is governed by a fifteen-member board elected by the UAA membership. Officers are elected by and from the governing board. The current president is Marvel Lang (since 1993), and the current executive director is Mary Helen Callahan (since 1983). The association utilizes a part-time staff of two and uses volunteers for a variety of committee projects.

The association is a 501(c)(3) organization with an annual operating budget of $40,000. A total of 84 percent of revenues is derived from membership fees, 12 percent from endowment earnings, and 4 percent from user fees; 40 percent of the budget is allocated to membership services, 40 percent to publications, and 20 percent to administration.

POLICY CONCERNS AND TACTICS

UAA is concerned primarily with the dissemination of information about urban issues and with the support of university education, research, and service programs in urban affairs. The association also seeks to provide leadership in promoting urban affairs as a professional and academic field. The group attempts to accomplish its goals by means of publications, an annual meeting, and other member services (including a clearinghouse for information, technical program advice, and liaison with other related professional and educational organizations).

POLITICAL ACTIVITY

None.

FURTHER INFORMATION

Journal of Urban Affairs (refereed scholarly quarterly), *Urban Affairs* (newsletter), and *University Urban Programs* (directory).

U.S. ENGLISH
818 Connecticut Avenue, N.W., Suite 200
Washington, D.C. 20006-2790
(202) 833-0100   fax: (202) 833-0108

U.S. English USE) is a nonprofit organization that seeks to have English designated as the official language of government, and promotes opportunities for all people to learn English.

ORIGIN AND DEVELOPMENT

USE was founded in 1983. Former U.S. senator and noted linguist S. I. Hayakawa founded USE after evoking support in 1981 when he introduced the first English Language Amendment to the Constitution. There are 400,000 members of USE.

ORGANIZATION AND FUNDING

USE is governed by an eight-member board of directors. Since 1992, Norman D. Shumway is acting executive director. He is also chair of the board. USE has eleven full-time staff members. It accepts two student interns per year.

The 1992 operating budget was over $5.8 million, of which 93 percent came from membership fees and the remainder from foundations and corporations. Approximately 28 percent goes toward administrative and personnel expenses, 38 percent toward membership services, 31 percent toward dissemination of information, and the remainder toward lobbying activities.

POLICY CONCERNS AND TACTICS

USE is concerned with the establishment of a national comprehensive language policy, with a common language at its core. It supports this position ''for the preservation of the unity of our country.''

POLITICAL ACTIVITY

USE lobbies Congress to enact legislation to affirm English as the common language, as well as to increase funding for English education in schools.

FURTHER INFORMATION

An annual report and a magazine, *U.S. English.*

APPENDIX A: QUESTIONNAIRE

————————— / —————————

The questionnaire included the following items:

I. Background Information
1. Date founded:
2. Short description of circumstances surrounding the founding:
3. Historical or current ties with other organizations:
4. Subsections or special groups within the organization:
5. Number of members in your organization:
6. How is your organization governed?
7. Name of current organization president:
8. How long has he/she held this position?
9. Name of current executive director:
10. How long has he/she held this position?
11. Do you use student interns?   Number per year:
12. Number of full-time staff members:
    Number nonclerical:
13. Number of part-time staff members:
14. Do you use volunteers?   In what capacity?
15. Do you rely on free services provided by outside professionals (lawyers, etc.)?
    In what capacity?
16. IRS tax status:
17. Annual operating budget:
18. Proportion of budget coming from:
    foundations: corporations:
    membership fees: user fees:
    endowment earnings: government:
    private/individual contributions: other (specify):
19. Proportion of budget allocated to:
    administration:

    membership services:
      specify:
    publications/dissemination of information:
      specify:
    lobbying activities:
      specify:
    litigation:
      specify:
    other (specify):

II. Education Issues and Strategies
1. What is the overall mission of your organization?
2. What policy issues currently concern your organization?
3. What specific goals and objectives are you pursuing?
4. How does your organization try to accomplish these goals?
5. Does your organization try to affect legislation?   How?
6. Does your organization support/endorse political candidates? Which candidates do you support?
7. Does your organization try to affect public opinion?
8. Other important information about your organization:

APPENDIX B:
ORGANIZATIONS
PARTICIPATING IN THE
STUDY

——————————— / ———————————

Academic Collective Bargaining Information Service

The Advocacy Institute

Aerospace Education Foundation

Alexander Graham Bell Association for the Deaf, Inc.

American Academy of Teachers of Singing

American Association for Adult and Continuing Education

American Association for Higher Education

American Association of Christian Schools

American Association of Colleges for Teacher Education

American Association of Colleges of Osteopathic Medicine

American Association of Collegiate Registrars and Admissions Officers

American Association of Community Colleges

American Association of Retired Persons

American Association of School Administrators

American Association of State Colleges and Universities

American Association of Teachers of French

American Association of Teachers of German

American Association of Teachers of Spanish and Portuguese

American Association of University Affiliated Programs for Persons with Developmental
   Disabilities

American Association of University Professors

American Association of University Women

American Association of Women in Community Colleges

American College Health Association

American College Testing Program

American Conference of Academic Deans

American Council for Drug Education

American Council of the Blind

American Education Finance Association

American Federation of Teachers

American Home Economics Association

American Political Science Association

American School Counselor Association

American Society for Training and Development

American Studies Center

Americans United for Separation of Church and State

Associated Colleges of the Midwest

Association for Childhood Education International

Association for Community-Based Education

Association for Gerontology in Higher Education

Association for the Advancement of Health Education

Association for the Behavioral Sciences and Medical Education

Association for the Education of Teachers in Science

Association of Academic Health Centers

The Association of American Colleges

Association of American Law Schools

Association of American Medical Colleges

Association of American Veterinary Medical Colleges

Association of Collegiate Schools of Architecture

Association of Episcopal Colleges

Association of Higher Education Facilities Officers

Association of Jesuit Colleges and Universities

Association of Mercy Colleges

Association of Presbyterian Colleges and Universities

Association of School Business Officials International

Association of Schools of Public Health

Association of Teacher Educators

Association of Teachers of Japanese

Association of Teachers of Technical Writing

Association of Theological Schools

Association of University Programs in Health Administration

Association of Higher Education and Disability

Atlantic Council of the United States

Augustinian Secondary Education Association

Board of Jewish Education

Broadcast Education Association

The Business–Higher Education Forum

The California Association for Counseling and Development

Career College Association

The Center for Applied Linguistics

The Christian College Coalition

Citizens for Educational Freedom

The Coalition for the Advancement of Jewish Education

College and University Personnel Association

The College Board

Council for Advancement and Support of Education

Council for American Private Education

The Council for International Exchange of Scholars

The Council of Chief State School Officers

Council of Colleges of Arts and Sciences

Council of Graduate Schools

Council of Independent Colleges

The Council of the Great City Schools

The Council on Education of the Deaf

The Council on Governmental Relations

The Educational Excellence Network

The Education Commission of the States

The Ethics Resource Center, Inc.

The Experiment in International Living

The Foreign Student Service Council

Great Lakes Colleges Association

Health Education Foundation

The Home and School Institute, Inc.

Human Resources Research Organization

The Institute for Alternative Futures

The Institute for Educational Leadership, Inc.

Institute of International Education

Joint National Committee for Languages

Junior Statesmen Foundation

The Kettering Foundation

The Linguistic Society of America

Mujeres Activas En Letras Y Cambio Social

Music Educators National Conference

National Alliance of Black School Educators

National Art Education Association

National Association for Chicano Studies

National Association for Core Curriculum

National Association for Equal Opportunity in Higher Education

National Association for Gifted Children

National Association for Humanities Education

National Association for the Education of Young Children

National Association for Women in Education

National Association for Year-Round Education

National Association of Catholic School Teachers

National Association of College Admission Counselors

National Association of College and University Attorneys

National Association of College and University Business Officers

National Association of Educational Buyers, Inc.

National Association of Elementary School Principals

National Association of Foreign Student Advisors' Association of International Educators

National Association of Independent Colleges and Universities

National Association of Independent Schools

National Association of Partners in Education, Inc.

National Association of Principals of Schools for Girls

National Association of Private, Nontraditional Schools and Colleges

National Association of Private Schools for Exceptional Children

National Association of Professional Educators

National Association of School Psychologists

National Association of Schools of Music

National Association of Schools of Public Affairs and Administration

National Association of Schools of Theatre

National Association of Secondary School Principals

National Association of State Boards of Education

National Association of State Directors of Special Education

National Association of State Directors of Vocational/Technical Education

National Association of State Universities and Land-Grant Colleges

National Association of Student Personnel Administrators, Inc.

National Catholic Business Education Association

National Catholic Education Association

National Christian Education Association

National Committee for Citizens in Education

National Community Education Association

National Council for Accreditation of Teacher Education

National Council for the Social Studies

National Council of Teachers of English

National Council of the Churches of Christ in the U.S.A.—Education, Communication, and Discipleship Unit

National Council of University Research Administrators

National Council on Measurement in Education

National Earth Science Teachers Association

National Education Association

National Head Start Association

National Home Study Council

The National Learning Center

National Parents-Teachers Association

National Rural Education Association

National School Boards Association

National School Health Education Coalition

National Science Teachers Association

National Society for Internships and Experiential Education

National Student Nurses' Association

National Women's Law Center

New England Association of Schools and Colleges, Inc.

North American Council of Automotive Teachers

North American Professors of Christian Education

Northwest Association of Schools and Colleges

Overseas Education Association

Presidential Classroom for Young Americans

Project on Equal Education Rights of the NOW Legal Defense and Education Fund

Push Literacy Action Now

School Science and Mathematics Association

Society for Health and Human Values

Society of Professors of Child and Adolescent Psychiatry
Southern Association of Colleges and Schools
Speech Communication Association
Student Press Law Center, Inc.
United Negro College Fund
Urban Affairs Association
U.S. English

APPENDIX C: PRIMARY GOVERNMENT PARTICIPANTS IN EDUCATION POLICY

————————— / —————————

I. Congressional Standing Committees
   1. House of Representatives
      a. Committee on Appropriations
      b. Committee on Education and Labor
   2. Senate
      a. Committee on Appropriations
      b. Committee on Labor and Human Resources
II. Department of Education
   1. Private Education Staff
   2. Corporate and Community Liaison Staff
   3. Office of Elementary and Secondary Education
   4. Office of Postsecondary Education
   5. Office of Educational Research and Improvement
   6. Office of Special Education and Rehabilitative Services
   7. Office of Vocational and Adult Education
   8. Office of Bilingual Education and Minority Languages Affairs

APPENDIX D: U.S. LEGISLATIVE HEARINGS IN EDUCATION, 1987–1992

———————— / ————————

Access to Higher Education: Increase Pell Grant and Widening Opportunities

Adult Education Act (reauthorization)

Adult Literacy and Employability Act

America 2000 Excellence in Education Act

Carl D. Perkins Vocational Education Act (reauthorization)

Computer Education Assistance Act

Discretionary Programs—Education of the Handicapped Act (reauthorization)

Education and Training for American Competitiveness Act

Education Excellence Act

Education of the Handicapped Act (reauthorization)

Equal Remedies Act

Equity and Excellence in Education Implementation Act

Expiring Federal Elementary and Secondary Education Programs, Chapter 2 of the Education Consolidation and Improvement Act (first set of reauthorizations)

Expiring Federal Elementary and Secondary Education Programs, Chapter 2 of the Education Consolidation and Improvement Act (second set of reauthorizations)

Expiring Federal Elementary and Secondary Education Programs—Impact Aid (reauthorization)

Federal Direct Student Loans, Part D of Title IV of the Higher Education Act (reauthorization)

Financial Aid for All Students Act

Foreign Language Competence for the Future Act

Head Start Act (reauthorization)

Health Professions Educational Assistance Act

Higher Education Act (reauthorization)

Jacob K. Javits Act for Gifted and Talented Education

Miscellaneous Programs of the Federal Elementary and Secondary Education Programs, Chapter 2 of the Education Consolidation and Improvement Act (reauthorization)

National Demonstration Program for Educational Performance Agreements for School Restructuring

National Education Report Card Act

Office of Comprehensive School Health Education Act

Overseas Teachers Act

Part H of the Individuals with Disabilities Education Act (reauthorization)

Prekindergarten Early Dropout Intervention Act

Regulatory Impact on Student Excellence Act

Smart Start: The Community Collaborative for Early Childhood Development Act

Stafford Loan Program of the Higher Education Act (reauthorization)

Tech-Prep Education Act

Title III, Title V, Title VIII, and Title IX of the Higher Education Act (reauthorization)

Twenty-First Century Teachers Act

Veterans' Education and Disability Compensation Act

SELECTED BIBLIOGRAPHY

————————— / —————————

BOOKS

Adams, Gordon. *The Politics of Defense Contracting: The Iron Triangle*. New York: Council on Economic Priorities, 1981.

Berry, Jeffrey M. *The Interest Group Society*. New York: HarperCollins, 1989.

Browne, William P. *Private Interests, Public Policy, and American Agriculture*. Lawrence: University of Kansas Press, 1988.

Browne, William P. and Allan J. Cigler. *U.S. Agricultural Groups: Institutional Profiles*. Westport, CT: Greenwood Press, 1990.

Burek, Deborah M., ed. *Encyclopedia of Associations*. Detroit: Gale Research, Inc., 1993.

Elmore, Richard F. *Restructuring Schools: The Next Generation of Education Reform*. San Francisco: Jossey-Bass, 1990.

Finifter, David H., Roger G. Baldwin, and John R. Thelen. *The Uneasy Public Policy Triangle in Higher Education: Quality, Diversity, and Budgetary Efficiency*. New York: American Council on Education, Macmillan Publishing, 1991.

Graham, Hugh Davis. *The Uncertain Triumph: Federal Education Policy in Kennedy and Johnson Years*. Chapel Hill: University of North Carolina Press, 1984.

Haskins, Ron and James J. Gallagher, eds. *Care and Education of Young Children in America: Policy, Politics, and Social Science*. Norwood, NJ: Ablex Publishing Company, 1980.

Lieberman, Ann and Milbrey W. McLaughlin, eds. *Policy Making in Education*. Chicago: National Society for the Study of Education, University of Chicago Press, 1982.

Lowi, Theodore J. *The End of Liberalism: The Second Republic of the United States*. New York: W. W. Norton & Company, 1979.

Marcus, Laurence R. and Benjamin D. Stickney. *Politics and Policy in the Age of Education*. Springfield, IL: C. C. Thomas.

Matthews, Joan M., Ronald G. Swanson, and Richard M. Kerker, eds. *From Politics to Policy: A Case Study in Educational Reform*. New York: Praeger, 1991.

Odden, Allan R., ed. *Education Policy Implementation*. Albany: State University of New York Press, 1991.

Salomone, Rosemary C. *Equal Education Under Law: Legal Rights and Federal Policy in the Post-Brown Era*. New York: St. Martin's Press, 1986.

Shaiko, Ronald G. "More Bang for the Buck: The New Era of Full-Service Public Interest Organizations," in Allan J. Cigler and Burdett A. Loomis, eds., *Interest Group Politics*. Washington, DC: Congressional Quarterly Inc., 1991, pp. 109-129.

Slack, James D. "Education Policy in the United States," in Frederic N. Bolotin, ed., *International Public Policy Sourcebook: Education and Environment*. Westport, CT: Greenwood Press, 1989, pp. 159-186.

Strike, Kenneth A. *Educational Policy and the Just Society*. Urbana: University of Illinois Press, 1982.

Van Tassel, David D. and Jimmy Elaine Wilkinson Meyer, eds. *U.S. Aging Policy Interest Groups: Institutional Profiles*. Westport, CT: Greenwood Press, 1992.

Washington Information Directory. Washington, DC: Congressional Quarterly, Inc., 1991.

Washington Representative. Washington, DC: Columbia Books, 1991.

JOURNALS

American Educational Research Journal. Washington, DC: American Educational Research Association.

American Journal of Education. Chicago: University of Chicago Press.

Changing Education: A Journal of the American Federation of Teachers. Detroit: MI: American Federation of Teachers.

History of Education Quarterly. New York: New York State University.

Journal of Education. Boston, MA: Boston University, School of Education.

Journal of Education Finance. Gainesville, FL: Institute of Education Finance.

Journal of Education Research. Bloomington: University of Illinois.

Journal of General Education. University Park: Pennsylvania State University Press.

Journal of Higher Education. Columbus: Ohio State University.

Journal of Research and Development in Education. Athens, GA: College of Education.

Journal of the National Education Association. Washington, DC: National Education Association.

INDEX

/

Page numbers in **bold** indicate main entries.

Academic Collective Bargaining Information Service, **3–4**

Accrediting organizations, 11, 13, 15, 16, 37, 52, 55, 62, 64, 66, 77, 79, 92, 129, 148, 150, 151, 163, 174, 187, 189–90, 199

Administration: admissions officers, 14–15, 133–34; business officers, 60–61, 135–37; college and university personnel, 18–19, 81–82, 86–87, 158–59; counselors, 39, 133–34; deans, 30–31; facilities officers, 57–58; health services, 28–29, 65–66; registrars, 14–15; research officers, 167

Adult education, 9–10, 156, 171

Adult Literacy and Employability Act, 9, 156

Advocacy Institute, **4–5**

Aerospace Education Foundation, **5–6**

AFL-CIO, 34

Afro-American concerns, 123–24, 126–27, 130–31, 157, 203–4

Alexander Graham Bell Association for the Deaf, Inc., **6–7**

American Academy of Teachers of Singing, **8–9**

American Association for Adult and Continuing Education, xvi, **9–10**

American Association for Higher Education, **10–11**

American Association of Christian Schools, **11–12**

American Association of Colleges for Teacher Education, xvi, **12–13**

American Association of Colleges of Nursing, xvi

American Association of Colleges of Osteopathic Medicine, **13–14**

American Association of Colleges of Pharmacy, xvi

American Association of Collegiate Registrars and Admissions Officers, **14–16**

American Association of Community Colleges, xvi, 3, **16–17**, 28

American Association of Retired Persons, **17–18**

American Association of School Administrators, xvi, **18–19**

American Association of State Colleges and Universities, xvi, **19–21**

American Association of State Colleges

of Agriculture and Renewable Re-
sources, 20
American Association of Teachers of
French, **21–22**
American Association of Teachers of
German, **22–23**
American Association of Teachers of
Spanish and Portuguese, **23–24**
American Association of the Deaf-Blind,
xvi
American Association of University Affil-
iated Programs for Persons with Devel-
opmental Disabilities, **24–25**
American Association of University Pro-
fessors, xvi, 3, **25–26**
American Association of University
Women, **26–27**
American Association of Women in
Community Colleges, **27–28**
American College Health Association,
28–29
American College Testing Program, **29–
30**
American Conference of Academic
Deans, **30–31**
American Council for Drug Education,
31–32
American Council of the Blind, **32–33**
American Council on Education, 3–4,
130
American Education Association, xvi
American Education Finance Association,
33–34
American Federation of Teachers, xvi, 4,
34–36
American Foundation for the Blind, xvi
American Home Economics Association,
36–37
American Political Science Association,
37–38
American Veterinary Medical Associa-
tion, 54
American Vocation Association, xvi
American School Counselor Association,
39–40
American Society for Training and De-
velopment, **40–41**
American Studies Center, **41**

Americans United for Separation of
Church and State, **41–42**
Americans with Disabilities Act, 32, 33,
82
America 2000, 9, 35, 42, 138, 154
Applied Technology Education Act, 156
Architecture, education and, 54–55
Art, education and, 124–25
Associated Colleges of the Midwest, **42–
43**
Association for Black Women in Higher
Education, 130
Association for Childhood Education In-
ternational, **43–44**
Association for Community-Based Educa-
tion, **44–45**
Association for Gerontology in Higher
Education, **45–46**
Association for the Advancement of
Health Education, xvi, **46–47**
Association for the Behavioral Sciences
and Medical Education, **47–48**
Association for the Education of Teachers
in Science, **48–49**
Association of Academic Health Centers,
xvi, **49–50**
Association of Accredited Cosmetology
Schools, xvi
Association of American Colleges, 4, **50–
51**
Association of American Law Schools,
51–52
Association of American Medical Col-
leges, xvi, **52–53**
Association of American Military Col-
leges and Schools of the U.S., **53**
Association of American Universities, xvi
Association of American Veterinary Med-
ical Colleges, xvi, **53–54**
Association of Collegiate Schools of Ar-
chitecture, **54–55**
Association of Community College Trus-
tees, xvi
Association of Episcopal Colleges, **55–56**
Association of Governing Boards of Uni-
versities and Colleges, 4
Association of Higher Education Facili-
ties Officers, **57–58**

Association of Jesuit Colleges and Universities, xvi, **58**

Association of Mercy Colleges, **58–59**

Association of Minority Health Professional Schools, xvi

Association of Presbyterian Colleges and Universities, **59–60**

Association of School Business Officials International, **60–61**

Association of Schools of Public Health, xvi, **61**

Association of Teacher Educators, xvi, **61–62**

Association of Teachers of Japanese, **62–63**

Association of Teachers of Technical Writing, **63–64**

Association of Theological Schools, **64–65**

Association of University Programs in Health Administration, xvi, **65–66**

Association of Urban Universities, xvi

Association on Higher Education and Disability, **66–67**

Athletics, education and, 15, 104

Atlantic Council of the United States, **67–68**

Augustinian Secondary Education Association, **68–69**

Board of Jewish Education, **71–72**

Boards of education, 153–54, 178–79

Broadcast Education Association, **72–73**

Business education, 73, 159

Business–Higher Education Forum, **73**

Business officers, 60–61, 135–36

California Association for Counseling and Development, **75–76**

Career College Association, **76–77**

Carl D. Perkins Vocational Education Act, 21, 36, 37, 140, 156, 170, 172, 179

Center for Applied Linguistics, **78**

Center for Law and Education, xvi

Christian College Coalition, **78–79**

Christian education: Catholic, 58–59, 68–69, 132, 159; Church of Christ, 166–67; Episcopal, 55–56; Evangelical, 159–60; general, 11–12, 64–65, 78–79, 188–89

Citizens for Educational Freedom, **79–80**

Civics, education and, 114–15, 117–18, 193–94. *See also* Political science

Civil rights, education and, 123–24, 131

Clinton, Bill, 36, 124

Coalition for Adult Education Organizations, 9

Coalition for the Advancement of Jewish Education, **80–81**

College and University Personnel Association, 4, **81–82**

The College Board, xvi, **82–83**

Colleges and Universities of the Anglican Communion, 56

Columbia University Teacher's College, **84**

Communication, education and, 200–201

Community-based education, 44–45, 90–91, 106–7, 146–47, 155, 161–62, 196

Community colleges, 16–17, 27–28, 67

Comprehensive School Health Education Act, 181

Computer Education Assistance Act, 171, 180

Consulting, organizational, 5

Council for Advancement and Support of Education, **84–85**

Council for American Private Education, **85**

Council for Basic Education, xvi

Council for International Exchange of Scholars, **86**

Council of Chief State School Officers, **86–87**

Council of Colleges of Arts and Sciences, **87–88**

Council of Exceptional Children, xvi

Council of Graduate Schools, **88–89**

Council of Independent Colleges, **89–90**

Council of the Great City Schools, xvi, **90–91**

Council on Education of the Deaf, **91–92**

Council on Governmental Relations, **92–93**

Council on Post-Secondary Accreditation, xvi
Counseling, 5, 39–40, 75–76, 78
Cultural values, xiii

Deans, academic, 30–31
Democracy, education groups and, xv
Disability concerns, 18, 19, 24–25, 32–33, 66–67, 91–92, 128, 131, 144–45, 147–48, 154–55
Diversity: in education, 44, 140, 150, 158, 190; education groups and, xv; in the workplace, 28, 62, 82, 133, 150
Drug abuse, 31–32, 35, 91, 155, 185

Earth science, education and, 168–69
Educate America Act (Goals 2000), 11
Education, Department of, 9, 12, 15, 16, 47, 62, 72, 77, 110, 145, 161, 162, 181, 186
Educational Excellence Network, **95–96**
Education Commission of the States, 4, **96–97**
Education Consolidation and Improvement Act, 19, 35, 91
Education Excellence Act, 13, 19, 35, 91, 138, 140, 154, 170–71, 179
Education of All Handicapped Children Act, 7
Education of the Handicapped Act, 33, 147, 171
Education Writers Association, 141
Elementary and childhood education, 43, 91, 129–30, 137–38, 175
Elementary and Secondary Education Act, 62
Encyclopedia of Associations, ix
English language education, 205
Environmentalism, 59, 188
Episcopal colleges, 55–56
Equal Remedies Act, 27
Equity and Excellence in Education Implementation Act, 13, 19, 35, 91, 138, 140, 154, 170–71
Ethics Resource Center, Inc., **97–98**
Even Start, 19, 91, 138
Experiment in International Living, xvi, **98–99**

Facilities officers, 57–58
Family life and values, 11, 36, 107, 161, 178
Federal Direct Student Loan Program, 66
Federated Associations of Schools of the Health Professions, 54
Finance education, 33–34
Financial Aid for All Students Act, 136
Foreign Language Competency for the Future Act, 99, 114
Foreign language education, 99, 113–14. *See also specific languages*
Foreign Student Service Council, **101–2**
French language education, 21

General education, 51, 125–26
German language education, 22
Gerontology, 45–46
Gifted child education, 127–28
Global Education Opportunities Act, 114
Graduate schools, 88–89
Great Lakes Colleges Association, **103–4**

Head Start, 36, 138, 147, 171, 172–73
Health and medical concerns, 46–50, 105–6, 109, 198; health administration, 65–66; health education, 180–81; nursing, 184–85; osteopathic medicine, 13; public health schools, 61; student health care services, 28
Health Education Foundation, **105–6**
Health Professions Educational Assistance Act, 14
Hearing impaired, 6–7. *See also* Disability concerns
Higher Education Act, 13, 14, 16, 20, 27, 35, 50, 53, 54, 61, 65, 66, 83, 90, 114, 136, 140, 144, 171, 174, 186, 203
Hispanic concerns, 121, 125. *See also* Diversity; Minority group concerns
Home and School Institute, Inc., **106–7**
Home economics, 36–37
Home study, 174
Humanities education, 128–29
Human Resources Research Organization, **107–8**

Individuals with Disabilities Act, 154, 155, 180

Individuals with Disabilities Education Act, 19

Institute for Alternative Futures, **109–10**

Institute for Educational Leadership, Inc., **110–11**

Institute of International Education, **111–12**

International education, 15, 59, 62, 65, 67–68, 86, 98–99, 101–2, 111–12, 114, 138–39, 191–92

International Reading Association, 165

Internships and experiential education, 182–83

Introspective behavior, educational groups and, xix

Iron triangle relationships, xiii

Jacob K. Javits Gifted and Talented Children and Youth Education Act, 47, 128, 171, 181

Japanese language education, 63

Jesuit education, 58

Jewish education, 71–72, 80–81

Job Training Partnership Act, 156

Joint National Committee for Languages, xvi, 21, 23, **113–14**

Journalism, student, 201–2

Junior Statesmen Foundation, **114–15**

Kettering Foundation, **117–18**

Labor concerns, 3, 4, 34, 146–47

Land-grant institutions, 157

Law and education, 51–52, 134–35, 185–86, 201–2. *See also* Civics, education and; Political science

Leadership in education, 110, 114–15, 138, 172

Liberal arts education, 30–31, 42, 50–51, 87–88, 89–90, 103–4, 128–29

Linguistics, 78, **119–20**

Linguistic Society of America, 119–20

Literacy, 195

Loans and lending issues, 16, 20, 53, 77, 83, 90, 136, 140, 157

Marketplace principles, and interest group politics, xviii

Medical education. *See* Health and medical concerns

Middle States Association of Colleges and Schools, 15

Military education, 53

Minority group concerns, 16, 18, 20, 28, 38, 54, 67, 79, 89, 135, 138, 186. *See also specific groups*

Modern Language Association, 63, 78

Mujeres Activas en Letras y Cambio Social, **121**

Music, education and, 8, 121–22, 148–49

Music Educators National Conference, **121–22**

National Alliance of Black School Educators, **123–24**

National Art Education Association, **124–25**

National Association for Chicano Studies, **125**

National Association for Core Curriculum, **125–26**

National Association for Equal Opportunity in Higher Education, **126–27**

National Association for Gifted Children, **127–28**

National Association for Humanities Education, **128–29**

National Association for the Advancement of Colored People Legal Defense and Education Fund, xvi

National Association for the Education of Young Children, **129–30**

National Association for Women in Education, **130–31**

National Association for Year-Round Education, **131–32**

National Association of Bilingual Educators, 78

National Association of Catholic School Teachers, **132–33**

National Association of College Admission Counselors, **133–34**

National Association of College and University Attorneys, 4, **134–35**

National Association of College and University Business Officers, xvi, **135–36**

National Association of Educational Buyers, Inc., **136–37**

National Association of Elementary School Principals, xvi, **137–38**

National Association of Equal Opportunities in Higher Education, xvi

National Association of Foreign Student Advisors' Association of International Educators, 4, **138–39**

National Association of Independent Colleges and Universities, xvi, **139–40**

National Association of Independent Schools, **140–41**

National Association of Partners in Education, Inc., **141–42**

National Association of Principals of Schools for Girls, **142–43**

National Association of Private, Nontraditional Schools and Colleges, **143–44**

National Association of Private Schools for Exceptional Children, xvi, **144–45**

National Association of Professional Educators, **146–47**

National Association of School Psychologists, xvi, **147–48**

National Association of Schools of Music, **148–49**

National Association of Schools of Public Affairs and Administration, **149–50**

National Association of Schools of Theatre, **150–51**

National Association of Secondary School Principals, xvii, **151–53**

National Association of State Boards of Education, xvii, **153–54**

National Association of State Directors of Special Education, xvii, **154–56**

National Association of State Directors of Vocational/Technical Education, xvii, **156–57**

National Association of State Universities and Land-Grant Colleges, xvii, 4, **157–58**

National Association of Student Financial Aid Administrators, xvii

National Association of Student Personnel Administrators, Inc., **158–59**

National Association of Teachers of Singing, 8

National Association of Trade and Technical Schools, xvii

National Catholic Business Education Association, **159**

National Catholic Education Association, **159**

National Christian Education Association, **159–60**

National Coalition for Women and Girls in Education, 130

National Coalition of the Deaf-Blind, xvii

National Committee for Citizens in Education, **160–61**

National Community Education Association, **161–62**

National Council for Accreditation of Teacher Education, **163–64**

National Council for Research on Women, 130

National Council for the Social Studies, **164**

National Council of La Raza, xvii

National Council of State Directors of Adult Education, xvii

National Council of Teachers of English, **165–66**

National Council of Teachers of Mathematics, xvii

National Council of the Churches of Christ in the U.S.A.—Education, Communication, and Discipleship Unit, **166–67**

National Council of University Research Administrators, **167**

National Council on Measurement in Education, **168**

National Earth Science Teachers Association, **168–69**

National Education Association, xvii, 4, **169–72**

National Education Report Card Act, 19, 171, 180

National Head Start Association, xvii, **172–73**

National Home Study Council, xvii, **174**
National Indian Education Association, xvii
National Learning Center, **174–75**
National Organization for Women, 194
National Parents-Teachers Association, **175–77**
National Retired Teachers Association, 17–18
National Rural Education Association, **177–78**
National School Boards Association, xvii, **178–80**
National School Health Education Coalition, xvii, **180–81**
National Science Teachers Association, **181–82**
National Security Education Act, 114
National Society for Internships and Experiential Education, **182–84**
National Student Nurses' Association, **184–85**
National Women's Law Center, **185–86**
New England Association of Schools and Colleges, Inc., **186–87**
Nonprofit organizations, xvii
Nontraditional education, 143–44
North American Council of Automotive Teachers, **187–88**
North American Professors of Christian Education, **188–89**
Northwest Association of Schools and Colleges, **189–90**
Nursing, education and, 184–85

Older Americans Act, 46
Organizational consulting, 5
Organizational will, educational groups and, xviii
Outcomes assessment, 15, 62, 96, 97, 155, 168
Overseas Education Association, xvii, **191–92**
Overseas Teachers Act, 192

Partnership for Service Learning, 56
Partnerships, educational, 111, 141–42, 156, 160, 172

Personnel, college and university, 81–82. *See also* Administration
Piggyback group, xviii
Policy, education, xiv, xv, xviii. *See also specific entries*
Political action committees, 36, 77, 172
Political correctness, 41, 202
Political science, 37, 115, 117, 149–50
Portuguese language education, 23
Prekindergarten Early Dropout Intervention Act, 35
Presidential Classroom for Young Americans, **193–94**
Principals, 142–43
Professional development, xviii
Professors, 25–26, 72, 198–99
Project on Equal Education Rights of the NOW Legal Defense and Education Fund, **194–95**
Psychiatry, education and, 198–99
Psychologists, 147–48
Public administration, education and, 149–50
Public Health Service Act, 54
Push Literacy Action Now, **195–96**

Reading Is Fundamental, xvii
Regulatory Impact on Student Excellence Act, 19, 171, 179
Religion, 11, 41–42, 179. *See also* Christian education; Jewish education
Retirees, 17
Rural education, 177

School choice. *See* Vouchers
School Science and Mathematics Association, **197–98**
Science education, 48
Sexual harassment, 28, 131
Social studies, 164
Society for Health and Human Values, **198**
Society of Professors of Child and Adolescent Psychiatry, **198–99**
Southern Association of Colleges and Schools, **199–200**
Spanish language education, 23
Special education, 154–55

Speech Communication Association, **200–201**
State colleges and universities, 19–20
Student Loan Abuse Prevention Act, 77
Student Press Law Center, **201–2**
Student Right to Know and Campus Security Act, 16
Tax issues, 11, 41, 84, 104, 145, 157, 179
Teacher Education Council of State Colleges and Universities, 20
Teachers: accreditation and, 163; Afro-American, 123–24; automotive, 187–88; Catholic school, 132; core curriculum and, 125–26; earth science, 168–69; education of, 12–13, 61–62, 81, 86, 125–26, 146–47; English, 165–66; French, 21–22; German, 22–23; graduate student, 89; Japanese, 62–63; liberal arts, 50–51; mathematics, 197–98; overseas, 191–92; Portuguese, 23–24; retired, 18; science, 48, 168–69, 181, 197–98; Spanish, 23–24; technical writing, 63–64; unions, 34–36, 169–72. *See also* Professors
Teachers of English to Speakers of Other Languages, 78
Technical writing, 63–64

Testing, 29–30, 44
Theatre, education and, 150–51
Theological schools, 64–65
Twenty-first Century Teachers Act, 19, 20, 35, 152, 170

Umbrella organizations, xiv
United Negro College Fund, xvii, **203–4**
United States Student Association, xvii
Urban Affairs Association, **204–5**
Urban education, 90–91, 204–5
U.S. English, **205**

Very Special Arts, xvii
Veterans Education and Disability Compensation Act, 174
Veterinary medicine, 53–54
Vocational education, 21, 76–77, 156–57, 187–88
Vouchers, 11, 35, 79–80, 179

Washington Information Directory, ix
Washington Representative, ix
Women's educational concerns, 26–28, 38, 51, 67, 121, 130–31, 142–43, 185–86, 194–95

Year-round education, 131–32

About the Authors

GREGORY S. BUTLER, Assistant Professor, Department of Government, New Mexico State University, has written a number of articles and text materials dealing with political philosophy and American political institutions and processes.

JAMES D. SLACK is Director of the Master of Public Administration Program and Professor of Government at New Mexico State University.